PRIMARY AND SECONDARY EDUCATION

PRIMARY AND SECONDARY EDUCATION

Dr. Anamika
Lecturer, Deptt. of Education,
Drona College of Management and Technical Education,
Dehradun

CENTRUM PRESS
NEW DELHI-110002 (INDIA)

CENTRUM PRESS
H.O.: 4360/4, Ansari Road, Daryaganj,
New Delhi-110 002 (India)
Ph.: 23278000, 23261597

B.O.: No. 1015, Ist Main Road, BSK IIIrd Stage
IIIrd Phase, IIIrd Block,
Bangalore - 560 085 (India)
Tel.: 080-41723429
Visit us at: www.centrumpress.com

Primary and Secondary Education

First Edition, 2009

PRINTED IN INDIA

Printed at Balaji Offset, Delhi

Contents

Preface

Primary education is the first stage of compulsory education. It is preceded by pre-school or nursery education and is followed by secondary education. In North America this stage of education is usually known as elementary education. In most countries, it is compulsory for children to receive primary education, though in many jurisdictions it is permissible for parents to provide it. The transition to secondary school or high school is somewhat arbitrary, but it generally occurs at about eleven or twelve years of age. Some educational systems have separate middle schools with the transition to the final stage of education taking place at around the age of fourteen. The major goals of primary education are achieving basic literacy and numeracy amongst all pupils, as well as establishing foundations in science, geography, history and other social sciences. The relative priority of various areas, and the methods used to teach them, are an area of considerable political debate.

Secondary education is the stage of education following primary school. Secondary education is generally the final stage of compulsory education. However, secondary education in some countries includes a period of compulsory and a period of non-compulsory education. The next stage of education is usually college or university. Secondary education is characterized by transition from the typically compulsory, comprehensive primary education for minors to the optional, selective tertiary, "post-secondary", or "higher" education (e.g., university, vocational school) for adults. Depending on the system, schools for this period or a part of it may be called secondary schools, high schools, gymnasia, lyceums, middle schools, colleges, vocational schools and preparatory schools, and the exact meaning of any of these varies between the systems.

Primary education is shaped according to the prevailing social and philosophical milieu and is regarded as the foundation for the entire superstructure of children's moral, spiritual, intellectual and physical development. The secondary education which serves as a bridge between primary and higher education is expected to prepare young persons between the age group 14-18 in the world of work and entry into higher education. Secondary education has its importance in the national development as it provides large skilled manpower for the economy and prepares for higher, technical and professional education. It is the stage where a proper understanding of work ethos and values of a humane and composite culture is provided to future citizens of the country.

The present book is an authentic in-depth analysis of contemporary situations, progress and challenges in the field of secondary education.. An attempt has been made to cover up most of the topics included in M.Ed. syllabus of the Indian universities.

— *Dr. Anamika*

UNIT-I

Levels of School Education

Introduction

The formal admission ceremony was known as 'Upanayana'. With the accomplishment of this ceremony the child had to leave his home for the 'ashrama' where he would receive education. It was supposed to be the rebirth of the child and was known as 'Dvijya', which means, "twice born". Sanskrit was the language of teaching. It was supposed to be the language of learned men. The academies of higher learning were known as 'Parisads'. The education system involved of three basic processes, which included 'Sravana', 'Manana' and 'Nidhyasana'.

In the 'Sravana' stage of education, students received 'shrutis' knowledge, which was passed orally from one generation to another. The second stage was 'Manana' which means that pupils had to think themselves about what they have heard. They have to make their own inferences and assimilate the lesson taught by their teacher into the life. The third stage 'Nidhyasana' means complete comprehension of truth and its use in the life.

In ancient India women were given the equal right to education and teaching. Women seers like 'Gayatri' were prominent participants in educational debates and the proceedings of the 'Parishads' (Assemblies). It was mainly the Brahmins followed by Kshatriyas that received education at the Gurukuls while the boys from the lower caste learnt their family trade from their fathers.

Few of the most important universities of India in the ancient times were Taxila, Vikramshila and Nalanda. Taxila University of 7th century BC was famous for medical studies and a galaxy of eminent teachers such as Paniṇi, the well known grammarian, Kautilya, the minister of Chandragupta Maurya, and Charaka, a medical teacher of repute.

Nalanda was the highest learning centre not just of India but also of the entire South Asia. Students from foreign countries like China, Japan, Korea used to come here for higher studies. It had around 10,000 students and teachers on its roll cards. The University had eight colleges. And one of the colleges had four-storied building. It was one of the earliest examples of residential cum learning complex.

Vikramshila University. Varanasi was famous for religious teachings. In the South, Kanchi was famous for its studies while the Vallabhi University was no less. Huan Tsang in his records mention the university to be at par with Nalanda and Vikramshila universities.

India had several great minds at work, which contributed in every aspect of life. The concept of zero, decimal and Pythagoras Theorem were all developed here.

As India progressed from ancient to medieval its education system deteriorated. Various factors were responsible for the degradation of this most efficient and most ancient education system of the world.

Present

The present educational system of India is an implantation of British rulers. Wood's Dispatch of 1854 laid the foundation of present system of education in India. Before the advent of British in India, education system was private one. With the introduction of Wood's Dispatch known as Magna Carta of Indian education, the whole scenario changed. The main purpose of it was to prepare Indian Clerks for running local administration. Under it the means of school educations were the vernacular languages while the higher education was granted in English only. British government started giving funds to indigenous schools in need of help and thus slowly some of the schools became government-aided.

Contemplating on the new system which was introduced Mahatma Gandhi expressed his anguish in following words, "I say without fear of my figures being challenged successfully, that today India is more illiterate than it was fifty or a hundred years ago, and so is Burma, because the British administrators, when they came to India, instead of taking hold of things as they were, began to root them out. They scratched the soil and began to look at the root, and left the root like that, and the beautiful tree perished.

The village schools were not good enough for the British administrator, so he came out with his program. Every school must have so much paraphernalia, building, and so forth. Well, there were no such schools at all. There are statistics left by a British administrator which show that, in places where they have carried out a survey, ancient schools have gone by the board, because there was no recognition for these schools, and the schools established after the European pattern were too expensive for the people, and therefore they could not possibly overtake the thing. I defy anybody to fulfil a program of compulsory primary education of these masses inside of a century. This very poor country of mine is ill able to sustain such an expensive method of education. Our state would revive the old village schoolmaster and dot every village with a school both for boys and girls."

Today education system in India can be divided into many stages:

Pre-Primary: It consists of children of 3-5 years of age studying in nursery, lower kindergarten and upper kindergarten. At this stage student is given knowledge about school life and is taught to read and write some basic words.

Primary: It includes the age group of children of 6-11 years studying in classes from first to fifth.

Middle: It consists of children studying in classes from sixth to eighth.

Secondary: It includes students studying in classes ninth and tenth.

Higher Secondary: Includes students studying in eleventh and twelfth classes.

Undergraduate: Here, a student goes through higher education, which is completed in college. This course may vary according to the subject pursued by the student. For medical student this stage is of four and a half years plus one year of compulsory internship, while a simple graduate degree can be attained in three years.

Postgraduate: After completing graduation a student may opt for post graduation to further add to his qualifications.

Education Governing Bodies

The Central Board of Secondary Education (CBSE): This is the main governing body of education system in India. It has control over the central education system. It conducts exam and looks after the functioning of schools accredited to central education system.

The Council of Indian School Certificate Examination (CISCE): It is a board for Anglo Indian Studies in India. It conducts two examinations 'Indian Certificate of Secondary Education' and 'Indian School Certificate'. Indian Certificate of secondary education is a k-10 examination for those Indian students who have just completed class 10th and Indian school certificate is a k-12 public examination conducted for those studying in class 12th.

The State Government Boards: Apart from CBSE and CISCE each state in India has its own State Board of education, which looks after the educational issues.

The National Open School: It is also known as National Institute of Open Schooling. It was established by the Government Of India in 1989. It is a ray of hope for those students who cannot attend formal schools.

The International School: It controls the schools, which are accredited to curriculum of international standard.

School Education—Different Levels

Elementary Education

According to the Constitution of India, elementary education is a fundamental right of children in the age group of 6-14 years. India has about 688,000 primary schools and 110,000 secondary schools. According to statistics two third of school going age children of India are enrolled in schools but the figures are deceptive as many don't attend schools regularly. At least half of all students from rural area drop out before completing school. The government has rolled out many plans to increase the percentage of elementary education. The plans such as 'Sarva Siksha Abhiyan (SSA), District Primary Education Program (DPEP), Operation Blackboard, Mid Day Meal have been successful to great extent.

Sarva Siksha Abhiyan (SSA)

The main goal of this program is that all children of 6-11 years of age should complete primary education by the year 2007 and all children of 6-14 years of age should complete eight years of schooling by 2010. This plan covers the whole country with special emphasis on girl education and education of Schedule Caste (SC) and Schedule Tribe (ST) children and children with special needs. The SSA centres are mainly opened in those areas, which do not have any school or where schools are very far off. Special girl oriented programs include:

Girl education at elementary level.

- National Program for Education of Girls at Elementary Level (NPEGEL)
- Kasturba Gandhi Balika Vidyalaya (KGBV)
- Mahila Samakhya Scheme.

Primary and Secondary Education

The Indian government lays emphasis to primary education up to the age of fourteen years. The Indian government has also banned child labour in order to ensure that the children do not enter unsafe working conditions. However, both free education and the ban on child labour are difficult to enforce due to economic disparity and social conditions. The District Primary Education Programme (DPEP) was launched in 1994 with an aim to universalize primary education in India by reforming and vitalizing the existing primary education system. 85% of the DPEP is funded by the central government and the remaining 15 percent is funded by the state. The DPEP, which has opened 160000 new schools including 84000 alternative education schools delivering alternative education to approximately 3.5 million children, is also supported by UNICEF and other international programmes. This primary education scheme has also shown a high Gross Enrolment Ratio of 93–95% for the last three years in some states. Significant improvement in staffing and enrolment of girls has also been made as a part of this scheme. The overall primary school conditions in India as a whole continued to remain lag behind internationally due to understaffing coupled with lack of developed infrastructure and sufficient financing. Education has also been made free for children up to the age of 14 or class IX.

The main components of this District Primary Education Program are:

- Construction of classrooms and new schools
- Opening of non-formal schooling centres
- Setting up early childhood education centres.
- Appointment of teachers.
- Providing education to disabled children.

Operation Blackboard

It was started in 1987-88. The aim of this program is to improve human and physical resource availability in primary schools of India. According to this program every primary school should have at least two rooms, two teachers and essential teaching aids like blackboard, chalk, duster etc.

National Bal Bhavan

The National Bal Bhavan was opened with the aim of developing overall personalities of children of all strata of society irrespective of their caste, creed, religion and gender. It supplements school education by helping children to learn in play way and natural environment.

Other important endeavours taken up by Indian government for the development of education in India includes:

- Navodaya Vidyalaya Samiti
- Kendriya Vidyalaya Sangathan
- Integrated Education for disabled children
- National Council of Educational Research and Training

Secondary Education

The National Policy on Education (NPE), 1986, has provided for environment awareness, science and technology education, and introduction of traditional elements such as Yoga into the Indian secondary school system. A significant feature of India's secondary school system is the emphasis on inclusion of the disadvantaged sections of the society Professionals from established institutes are often called to support in vocational training. Another feature of India's secondary school system is its emphasis on profession based vocational training to help students attain skills for finding a vocation of his/her choosing.

A special Integrated Education for Disabled Children (IEDC) programme was started in 1974. Another notable special programme, the Kendriya Vidyalaya project, was started for the employees of the central government of India, who are distributed throughout the country. The government started the Kendriya Vidyalaya project in 1965 to provide uniform education in institutions following the same syllabus at the same pace regardless of the location to which the employee's family has been transferred.

University Education

This massive system of higher education in India constitutes of 342 universities (211 State, 18 Central, 95 deemed universities) 13 institutes of national importance, 17,000 colleges and 887 polytechnics. University Grant Commission (UGC), a national body, coordinates and looks after the maintenance of standard of university education in India. The university education in India starts with undergraduate courses. Depending upon the nature of course pursued its duration may vary from three to five and a half years.

Academic Degree Course

This undergraduate course in India is of three years' duration. After completing this course student get a Bachelor's degree in the subject studied such as Bachelor of Arts, Bachelor of Commerce or Bachelor of Science.

Status of Primary and Secondary Education in India

Primary education is a fundamental right in India, and an important Millennium Development Goal to which India and the Bank are totally committed. The Government of India recognizes education as a critical input for the development of human capital, jobs for its people, and economic growth for the country.

It flagship elementary education program – the Sarva Shiksha Abhiyan (SSA)-or Education for All-aims to enrol all 6-14 year-olds in school by 2010. It also aims to have all these children complete eight years of schooling by that year. India has over 194 million children in 1.1 million habitations across the country, making the SSA one of the largest programs of its kind in the world.

Universal Elementary Education-A Government Priority

The government is giving unprecedented priority to universal elementary education. It is therefore putting major financial and technical resources into this program.

The Sarva Shiksha Abhiyan program is collectively supported by the World Bank, the European Commission and United Kingdom's DFID; of these the World Bank is the single largest contributor. In the first phase of support, between 2003 and 2006, the World Bank contributed $500 million of the total program cost of $3.5 billion. World Bank lending for the program is on concessional terms, with no interest and a repayment period of 35 years, with the first ten years as a "grace" period when no repayment is required. Over 7,000 NGOs are participating in the SSA.

They are helping to provide alternative education programs or "bridge courses" to bring out-of-school children into the school system. They are also involved in monitoring the quality of education, capacity-building of Village Education Committees, and many function as reference groups advising States, Districts and Blocs.

The first phase of the program focused on improving access to schools for all primary age children, particularly for the hardest-to-reach communities, with a special focus on girls, children from disadvantaged communities, and those with special needs. It also supported training for teachers, monitoring and evaluation of outcomes, strengthening of financial management systems, and dissemination campaigns to mobilize communities in favour of education.

Progress in Primary Education

Two decades of focused programs in basic education have brought about a remarkable improvement in education indicators in India:

- Out of school children, most belonging to marginalized social groups, have been reduced from 25 million in 2003 to 9.6 million in 2005-06.
- Net Enrolment Rate at primary level has risen from 68% in 1993 to 85% in 2005-06.
- Transition Rates from the primary to the upper primary level have risen from 75 percent in 2002 to 83 percent in 2006.
- The gender gap has reduced. There are now 92 girls for every 100 boys in primary school.
- The social gap has narrowed. By 2005-06, scheduled caste children made up over 18% of all primary school children, better reflecting their presence in the overall population. Children belonging to scheduled tribes made up over 9% of all primary school students.

Challenges Ahead

Primary Education: Despite these gains, the demand for education far exceeds supply at all levels, both in terms of access and quality. About 10 million primary age children remain out of school and social disparities persist. Some independent surveys have shown that half of all children in the 7-14 age group cannot read.

The key challenge ahead is to finish the "access agenda" while dramatically increasing focus on the quality of education provided. This requires more attention to classroom processes, basic reading skills in early grades, teacher quality and accountability, community or parent oversight, and better evaluation and assessment of learning outcomes.

Secondary Education

At the secondary level, both access and quality remain a challenge. Gross enrolment rates are around 40 percent. This is partly because children drop out after primary school and there is not enough emphasis on secondary education.

There are significant gaps between genders, social groups, urban and rural areas. Most secondary students are urban boys from wealthier population groups.

A significant proportion of enrolment is in private schools. Private aided and unaided schools account for 60 percent of all secondary enrolment, and their numbers are growing.

The low quality of primary education affects the quality of learning at the secondary level. In addition to this are issues of inappropriate curriculum and poor teaching practices.

Going forward: SSA II

In the second phase of the program, during the 11th Plan from 2007-12, the country estimates to spend the enormous sum of Rs.71,000 crores or US$17.75 billion on primary education.

As with SSA I; the second phase of the program will also be collectively supported by the World Bank, the European Commission and United Kingdom's DFID. The World Bank expects to provide US$500 million in December 2007 for SSA II. The Bank will still remain a small player, financing less than 10% of the total government expenditures on the program.

SSA II will include an increased focus on upper primary education. It will also focus on expanding access to secondary education and improving its quality.

World Bank Analysis and Research

The World Bank is conducting various studies in education. In elementary education, studies are evaluating the impact of:

- Incentive payments and schooling inputs on student learning
- Dissemination of education information on school governance and student outcomes
- School characteristics and student outcomes
- Instructional time on task survey.

The Bank is also engaged in conducting analytical work in early childhood education and secondary education:

- Early Childhood Development – with a focus on integrated (health/nutrition/education) approaches-this will feed into US$ 450 M Integrated Child Developmen Services Project
- Secondary Education – major analytical study related to expanding access, particularly for girls and marginalized groups.

Establishment of Primary and Secondary Schools

In India, all levels of education from primary to higher education, are overseen by the Ministry of Human Resource Development (Department of Higher Education and Department of School Education and Literacy), and heavily subsidized by the Indian government, though there is a move to make higher education partially self-financing.

There are broadly four stages of school education in India, namely primary, upper primary, secondary and higher secondary (or high school). Overall, schooling lasts 12 years, following the "10+2 pattern". However, there are considerable differences between the various states in terms of the organizational patterns within these first 10 years of schooling.

The Indian government is committed to ensuring universal elementary education (primary and upper primary) education for all children aged 6-14 years of age. Primary school includes children of ages six to eleven, organized into classes one through five.

Upper Primary and Secondary school pupils aged 11 through 15 are organised into classes six through ten, and higher secondary school students ages sixteen through seventeen are enrolled in classes eleven through twelve.

In some places there is a concept called Middle / Upper Primary schools for classes between six to eight. In such cases classes nine to twelve are classified under high school category.

In India, education is compulsory until age 14.

In India, the main types of schools are those controlled by:

- The state government boards like SSLC, in which the vast majority of Indian school-children are enrolled,
- The Central Board of Secondary Education (CBSE) board,
- The Council for the Indian School Certificate Examinations (CISCE) board,
- National Open School and
- "International schools." which is similar to the schools in the West in pattern and syllabi and are considerably more expensive than regular schools.

The presence of a number of education boards (SSLC, ICSE, CBSE, IB, IGCSE) leads to non-uniformity. ICSE and CBSE boards, are sometimes favourably considered at the time of admission, although it cannot be said with certainty that their syllabuses are harder. A large number of SSLC (State board) students therefore complain that their ICSE and CBSE counterparts are given an advantage during college admissions, which are extremely competitive and sought for. Most colleges though account for these differences during admissions. The syllabi prescribed by the various boards are accused of being archaic and some textbooks (mostly ones written for the SSC) contain many errors.

The boards are recently trying to improve quality of education by increasing percentage of practical and project marks. However, critics say even this is memorized by students (or even plagiarized). This is attributed to pressure from parents who are eager to see high scores more than overall development.

Types of Schools

Central Government Funded and Managed: The government funded central schools are called *Kendriya Vidyalaya's*.

The *Kendriya Vidyalaya's* were set up to cater to the educational needs of children of transferable Central Government employees including Defence and Para-Military personnel by providing a common programme of education.

Features:

- All KV's are affiliated to Central Board of Secondary Education (CBSE)
- All KV's are co-educational, composite schools
- The quality of teaching is kept reasonably high by an appropriate teacher-pupil ratio
- No tuition fee for boys up to Class VIII and girls up to Class XII
- No tuition fee for Scheduled castes and scheduled tribes students and children of KVS employees

Fee Structure: for boys studying at senior secondary level is INR 200 (NZ$ 7) per month.

The *Kendriya Vidyalaya Sangathan* (KVS) is the umbrella for KV schools and administers 929 schools with 911,993 students. The Minister of Human Resource Development is in-charge of the KV scheme and is the Chairman of the KVS.

Central & State Funded Schools: There are a large number of central & state government funded senior secondary schools in India, these are managed by the local Municipal Corporations.

These schools offer free education, food, uniform, etc. to students. The medium of instruction in these schools is usually the local language. They are affiliated either to the Central Board of Secondary Education (CBSE) or the State Boards. They cater to the very poor section of the society.

Private Schools: There are a large number of private schools in India, which are completely funded by private individuals, bodies, trusts, etc. These schools cater to the middle and upper class population of India.

Most private schools are affiliated to the Central Board of Secondary Education (CBSE) and the Indian School Certificate Examination (ISCE) and offer their standard exams. Recently there has been a growth of private schools offering the International Baccalaureate (IB) and A-Levels. Some of these private schools offer international qualifications only, whereas some offer it alongside the CBSE/ICSE.

Types of Private Schools

Public Schools: Usually cater to day pupils only. These schools usually offer the CBSE or ISCE curriculum. Their fee structure varies anywhere between INR 1,500 –INR 5,500 per month based on the reputation of the school. For examples of public schools are Delhi Public Scho or Modern School etc.

Private Residential Schools: They are usually fully residential schools with a very small day scholar population. These schools usually offer the ISCE curriculum, have big campuses and are typically located outside big cities. The fee structure varies anywhere between 12,000-INR 17,000 per month for fees and board. Fees will partially depend on the reputation of the school. Many of these schools are located away from the large cities in Hill Stations. For examples of residential schools, such as the Doon School or Lawrence School.

International Schools: These schools can be residential or day pupil or a mix of both and are usually located in the big cities like Delhi, Mumbai, Bangalore, etc. They usually offer either IB or A-Levels or both. Some of the main private schools who are well established in particular cities, have established separate international schools offering international qualifications to cater to expatriate Indians, or very affluent business class families who intend to send their children overseas for university education.

The fee structure varies between INR 20,000 – INR 25,000 per month, based on the reputation of the promoter. Examples of international schools, Pathways World School or Dhirubhai Ambani International School.

Overseas Education at Secondary School Level: The market for Indian students going overseas at secondary school level is very limited. This is due to a number of factors:

- Good quality private schools in India, offering high quality education
- Lower cost of education in India compared to other countries
- Preference to take Indian CBSE / ISCE qualifications for university entrance
- English used as the medium of instruction, meaning if students do go overseas for further education, they have no language difficulties
- International qualifications like A-Levels and IB are now available in India
- Concerns regarding sending children below 17 years of age overseas for education However, there are a very small number of students going overseas at secondary school level
- Parents re-locating overseas

- Students facing problems coping with the education system in India (the education system in India is extremely competitive)
- Family linkage to a particular school, especially with UK public schools
- Student exchange programmes
- Scholarship schemes.

Schools can get affiliation from popular boards only if they are owned, operated by not-for-profit organizations.

One concern common to a large segment of the urban Indian population with children is admission in a "good school". With the increase in urban population, there has been an exponential growth in the demand for educational services, and most cities still lag in supply.

Given the skewed demand-supply ratio in the education sector, one tends to wonder why the private sector has failed to exploit such a promising business opportunity. The answer may lie in the legal regime governing primary and secondary education, or what is commonly referred to as the "K-12" sector.

Education, including technical education, medical education and universities, falls under List III in the Constitution, that is, the concurrent list, and may be legislated upon by both the Union and state governments.

Typically, it is state laws that govern school education. These laws deal primarily with procedures for setting up schools, obtaining government recognition and the governance and operation of government-aided schools. Regulations pertaining to unaided private schools are usually sketchy, generally prescribing minimum pay scales for teachers, educational qualifications and the like.

Importantly, there are no uniform guidelines laid down by states on admission procedures, or with respect to the fees that may be charged by private unaided schools. Concerned parents have often protested about the ever increasing costs of education, and disputes over hikes in school fees have reached the courts.

The Supreme Court's ruling, in the case of Modern School v. Union of India and Others (All India Reporter, 2004, Supreme Court, Page 2,236) is an important ruling regarding the commercialization of education and the question of earning profits from running schools.

Relying on earlier Supreme Court rulings, the apex court held that the determination of the fee structure of unaided educational institutions was part of the right to practise any profession, and that in this respect unaided institutions may exercise autonomy.

Institutions are entitled to a reasonable surplus from operations, although the fees charged must be commensurate with the infrastructure provided, and should not result in the "commercialization" of education, or "profiteering". It was also held that the director of education (an office under the Delhi Schools Act, 1973) is authorized to regulate fees and other charges levied by private unaided schools, with a view to preventing the commercialization of education.

Given that schools are generally free to determine their fee structure, what are the hurdles that face the private sector, when it comes to investing in educational infrastructure?

The answer lies in the regulations governing recognition and affiliation of private unaided schools.

Schools catering to the middle class are not viable business ventures unless they are affiliated to a state board, the Council for the Indian School Certificate Examinations (schools generally referred to as ICSE schools), or the Central Board of Secondary Education (CBSE). Only students from schools affiliated to these boards are eligible to take exams conducted by these boards. Generally, certificates granted by these boards are considered for college admissions.

In order to apply for affiliation to the ICSE, CBSE or state boards, private unaided schools are required to be owned and operated by either a charitable trust or a society (an entity that is required to have a charitable objective). Often, state laws also require that schools be run by not-for-profit trusts or societies in order to be eligible for recognition and affiliation to the state board, making schools run by companies ineligible to be affiliated with the more popular school boards.

A trust and a society are both entities that are generally used by not-for-profit organizations to operate charitable activities, where any funds generated by such activities are reused for such charitable purpose.

Where a school is run by a charitable trust, the settlers of the trust (that is, the entrepreneur that has settled the trust and set up the school) are typically not entitled to any distribution of profits generated by the school. Similarly, with charitable societies, profits generated by the activities of the society may only be re-employed towards the charitable objective for which the society has been set up, making the sector unattractive to private investors.

UNIT-II

Primary Education

Aims and Objectives

The importance of aims and objectives of education is recognised by all the educational, professional, political, nonpolitical and religious associations, organisations and groups at various levels in their memoranda, letters and brouchures. It is said that education without clear cut aims is like a rudderless ship. The following comparisons emphasise this point fully well.

Every pilot has a route-chart and set timing of landing at predetermined destination. There is constitution or set of Principles and traditions through which a country is governed Similarly, there should be properly defined and declared principles, aims and objectives of education or the basis of which policies and programmes of education nave to be formulated to achieve the set goals wit out wasting scarce energies and resources in chasing the wild goose.

It is generally felt that our educational system has not followed the desired aims as a result that it does not produce ideal citizens in the country. It has followed, rather a narrow aim of preparing individuals for livelihood, as mentioned in one of the documents received from an organisation.

The main reason of failure of educational system is that it basically stands or, pre-independence system. The main Objective of its products was how to take degree and to earn money and to be careerist without consideration of ethical values and national spirit. On the other hand, it has also been pointed out that it is unressonable to criticise educational system alone because it is based on the other subsystems accepted by us.

The Aims and objectives of Education for All in India are as follows (MHRD, Annual Report: 1997-98):

Access

Universal enrolment of all children, including girls and persons belonging to Scheduled Castes and Scheduled Tribes; Provision of primary school for all children within one kilometre of walking distance and of facility of non-formal education; and Improvement of ratio of primary to upper primary school to at least 1:2.

Retention

Reduction of dropout rates between Classes I to V and I to VIII to 20 and 40 per cent respectively; and Improvement of school facilities by revamped Operation Blackboard, to be extended to upper primary level also.

Achievement

Achievement of minimum levels of learning by approximately all children at the primary level, and introduction of this concept at the middle stage on a large scale.

Monitoring

Local level committee, with due representation to women and teachers, to assist in the working of primary education to oversee its functioning; and Improvement of the monitoring system for universalisation of elementary education.

The Government of India has initiated a number of schemes to achieve the goals of EFA amongst which the scheme of Operation Blackboard (OB) is the most prominent one. The main objectives of OB Scheme (1987) are as follows (MHRD, Annual Report: 1993-94):

A building comprising at least two reasonably large all-weather rooms with a deep varandah and separate toilet facilities for boys and girls; At least two teachers in every school, as far as possible one of them a women; and Essential teaching-learning material including blackboards, maps, charts, toys and equipment for work experience.

The scheme is recently revised so as to:

- Provide flexibility to schools in providing teaching-learning materials relevant to their curriculum and local needs:
- To relate the scheme with micro planning wherever undertaken, so that supply of inputs is matched by demand side interventions to promote participation;
- Intensify training in the use of teaching-learning equipment's; and
- Extend the scheme to upper primary schools.

In addition, a number of externally funded projects and programmes are also currently under implementation amongst which the World Bank assisted District Primary Education Programme is the most prominent one. The programme that was launched in 1994 in 42 districts of seven states is currently under implementation in about 150 districts spread over fifteen states. The main objectives of DPEP programme are as follows:

- Emphasizing the local area planning with district plans being formulated in their own right instead of being derived from a state plan project document;
- Infusing greater rigor and professional inputs in planning and appraisal;
- More focused targeting in educationally ward districts and districts where total literacy campaign have been successful;
- More focused coverage would initially focus on primary stage (Classes I-V and its NFE equivalent) with stress on girls and for socially disadvantaged groups; and
- Emphasizing capacity building and networking of district, states and national level institutes in the fields of education management and social services to provide the resource support for the programme.

Activities—Linkage with Elementary Education

The Kasturba Gandhi Shiksha Yojana, a programme to establish residential schools for girls in all the districts which have a particularly low female literacy rate has been announced. A sum of Rs. 2500 million has been provided in this year's budget. The central government has also decided to grant financial incentives and scholarships for the girl child born in families

Since independence, the central and state governments have been expanding the provision of primary formal and non-formal education to realise the goal of Universilisation of Elementary Education (UEE). The challenge now is to sustain and deepen current reforms in education and encourage local planning and management of strategies for expanding and improving primary education.

With a view to cushioning the impact of rising costs of text books and exercise books, the government has exempted writing and printing paper supplied to all State Text Book Corporations from excise duty. It is expected that this would make school text books more affordable for students from weaker sections of society.

Removal of systemic deficiencies in the implementation of UEE and forging ahead necessitates the creation of informed public opinion and a facilitative environment akin to that of the Total Literacy Campaign. This has to be achieved through effective and sustained advocacy, massive community mobilisation and consciousness building. With this perspective, a national programme of media publicity and advocacy has been planned. The programme will target: i) teachers and all those involved in education of children; ii) students and parents of students, particularly non-literate parents; and iii) community opinion leaders, living below the poverty line.

Several central and state level initiatives have been in operation from the early 1980s. While the design of these projects vary substantially, all of them address the objectives and strategies of the National Policy on Education 1986. They pay special attention to increasing girls' enrolment, improving educational outcomes, strengthening community involvement, improving teaching and learning materials and providing in-service teacher training.

Operation Blackboard

This scheme launched in 1987, is aimed at improving the school environment and enhancing retention and learning achievement of children by providing minimum essential facilities in all primary schools. The scheme has brought about a remarkable quantitative and qualitative improvement in primary education. In all, 523,000 primary schools have been covered as originally envisaged. These schools have been provided with central assistance.

Decentralisation

Decentralised planning and management of elementary education is a goal set by the National Policy on Education, 1986. The Policy visualises direct community involvement in the form of Village Education Committees (VECs) for management of elementary education. The POA, 1992, emphasised micro planning as a process of designing a family-wise and child-wise plan of action by which every child regularly attends school or NFE centre, continues his or her education at the place suitable to him/her and completes at least eight years of schooling or its equivalent at the NFE centre.

The 73rd and 74th constitutional amendments provide for decentralisation of the activities and facilitate transfer of power and participation of the local self-government institutions or the Panchayati Raj Institutions. It has created a congenial ambience for the PRIs to play a more dynamic and proactive role. States are expected to evolve institutional arrangements both in rural and urban areas for undertaking these activities. These structures have been providing voice to women, Scheduled Castes and Tribes, minorities, parents and educational functionaries. They have also, been delegated with responsibilities with regard to location and relocation of existing primary and upper schools on the basis of micro planning and school mapping. In this regard, decentralisation of school management to grassroots level bodies is an important policy initiative.

During the 8th plan period several innovative efforts hove been made under the ongoing projects to establish decentralisation. For instance, the District Primary Education Programme has shifted the planning mechanism from the state to the district level, and Lok Jumbish has gone one step further by assigning decision making processes to a block level committee. At the village level, a VEC has the main responsibility for community mobilisation, school mapping, micro planning, renovation and construction of school buildings and improvement of pedagogical curriculum. In fact, the VECs of Shiksha Karmi schools have been activated as a result of the Lok Jumbish programme.

Since 1993-94, the scheme has been expanded to cover upper primary schools. More then 47,000 upper primary schools have been granted central assistance of Rs. 40,000 each for purchase of teaching-learning materials. Also, primary schools with enrolment exceeding 100 have been augmented with a third teacher. A Special Orientation Programme for Primary Teachers (SOPT) to facilitate optimum utilisation of materials supplied has also been launched to cover all primary school teachers in the country.

The total expenditure under the scheme from 1992-93 to 1995-96 has been Rs. 8,163 million. The outlay for 1996-97 is Rs. 2,910 million.

Offshoots of Primary Schools

National Programme of Nutritional Support to Primary Education (School Meal Programme)

This scheme was launched on 15 August, 1995 to give a boost to UEE in terms of increasing enrolment, retention and attendance in primary classes by supplementing nutritional requirements of children attending primary schools. It is an ambitious scheme that has been operationalised throughout the country in a very short period. The programme envisages provision of nutritious and wholesome cooked meal of 100 gms of food grains per school day, free of cost, to all children in classes I-V by 1997-98.

During 1995-96, 378 districts, 225,000 schools and 33.5 million children have been covered with an expenditure of Rs. 4,412 million. In 1996-97, the scheme was extended to cover 55.4 million children with an expenditure of Rs. 8,110 million. The scheme has become fully operational in 1997-98 covering nearly 110 million children in primary classes. A positive impact on school enrolment and retention has been reported.

District Primary Education Programme

The DPEP launched in November, 1994 is conceived as a beachhead for overhauling the primary education system in India. The programme aims at operationalising the strategies for achieving UEE through district specific planning and disaggregated target setting. It draws upon the accumulated national experience of several state level initiatives that were started earlier. It moves away from the schematic piecemeal approach of the earlier programmes and takes a holistic view of primary education with emphasis on decentralised management, community mobilisation and district specific planning based on contextually and research based inputs.

The basic objectives of DPEP are:

- To provide all children with access to primary education either in the formal system or through the non-formal education (NFE) programme.
- To reduce differences in enrolment, dropout rates and learning achievement among gender and social groups to less than 5%.
- To reduce overall primary dropout rates for all students to less than 10%.
- To raise average achievement levels by at least 25% over measured base line levels and ensuring achievements of basic literacy and numeracy competencies and a minimum of 40% achievement levels in other competencies by all primary school children.

The Government of India finances 85 % of the project cost as a grant to the DPEP State Implementation Societies and the concerned state government provides the rest. The central government's share is resourced by external funding. As of now, IDA has approved credit amounting to $260 million and $425 million under Phase-I and Phase-II respectively. The European Union (EU) is providing a grant of 150 million ECU. The ODA (UK) is extending a grant of $80.21 million. The grant from the Netherlands amounts to $25.8 million.

The first phase of the programme was launched in 42 districts in the states of Assam, Haryana, Karnataka, Kerala, Maharashtra, Tamil Nadu and Madhya Pradesh. In the second phase, the programme has been launched in 80 districts of Orissa, Himachal Pradesh, Andhra Pradesh, West Bengal, Uttar Pradesh and Gujarat and in Phase I States.

DPEP has been able to set up project management structures at district, state and national levels, create the environment and capacity for micro planning, take up the challenge of pedagogical innovation, create a responsive institutional base which includes both government and non-government institutions, enhance community participation and strengthen the process of catering to special focus groups such as tribals, scheduled castes, women and other marginalised sections. The first phase of the programme is under evaluation. The initial trends of impact studies are very positive. DPEP has made a decisive impact on increasing enrolment, reducing repetition rates and improving class room processes.

While the DPEP has been targeting backward districts with female literacy below the national average and where TLCs have stirred up a demand for elementary education, several state level initiatives have shown tremendous potential. These are directed at improving literacy levels in the five low literacy states of Andhra Pradesh, Bihar, Uttar Pradesh, Madhya Pradesh and Rajasthan.

Bihar Education Project

Bihar Education Project (BEP) was launched in 1991 with the express purpose of bringing about quantitative and qualitative improvement in the elementary system in Bihar. The project lays emphasis on the education of deprived sections of society, such as SCs, STs and women. Participatory planning and implementation are crucial ingredients of the project.

A midterm review highlighted certain major achievements such as: a) a strong Mahila Samakhya component; b) organisation of VECs and community involvement in programme implementation at grassroots level; and c) non-formal education through NGOs. The review suggested:

- consolidation of the programme in the existing seven districts,
- establishing strong linkages between BEP and the education system in Bihar,
- giving greater focus to the primary stage of classes I-V,
- building better linkages with the activities in other states under DPEP and other programmes,
- providing more emphasis to MLLs and teacher training, and conducting periodic base line studies.

It has now been decided to extend the project to the second phase of two years duration. The total outlay for the second phase (1996-98) is estimated to be Rs. 613 million to be shared between UNICEF, Government of India and Government of Bihar as per the existing funding formula of 3:2:1. The total project outlay for BEP is Rs. 3600 million. It is proposed to merge the project with DPEP during the next five years.

Uttar Pradesh Basic Education Programme

A project "Education for All" prepared by the Government of Uttar Pradesh was approved by The World Bank in June, 1993. The project is currently in operation in 12 districts. It is planned to expand the coverage to 15 districts under DPEP-II. It has an outlay of Rs. 7,288 million spread over seven years. International Development Agency (IDA), the soft loan window of The World Bank, would provide a credit of US$163.1 million and the state government's share would be approximately 13 per cent of the total project cost.

The progress of implementation of the project so far has been satisfactory. The construction work of schools and Block Resource Centres is being completed as per schedule. Training materials for teacher trainers on DIETs have been prepared. The first cycle of in-service teacher training was completed in October, 1995. About 40,000 teachers have been trained.

Andhra Pradesh Primary Education Project

The Andhra Pradesh Primary Education Project (APPEP), practised in the south central state of Andhra Pradesh, with a female literacy of just 34 %, adopts a two-pronged strategy of improving classroom transaction by training teachers and giving a fillip to school construction activities. The project has trained an estimated 80,000 teachers in 23 districts and more than 3,000 teaching centres have become operational. The project is assisted by the ODA with an estimated outlay of Rs. 1,000 million in the 8th Plan.

Shiksha Karmi Project

The Shiksha Karmi Project (SKP) is being implemented since 1987, with assistance from the Swedish International Development Cooperation Agency (SIDA). The project aims at universalisation and qualitative improvement of primary education in the remote and socio-economically backward villages of Rajasthan, with primary focus on girls.

Since teacher absenteeism has been found to be a major obstacle in achieving the objective of UEE, the project uses the novel approach of substituting teachers in dysfunctional schools with local youth known as Shiksha Karmis who are provided with rigorous training and supervisory support. An important feature of this innovative project is the mobilisation and participation of the community in improving the functioning of primary schools.

The project is being implemented as an externally aided scheme with reimbursement of 90 % in Phase I and 50 % in Phase II, from SIDA. The project, with an outlay of around Rs.212 million in Phase I and Rs.490 million in Phase II, places strong emphasis on vigorous and continuous in-service training.

The SKP also runs non-formal classes called Prehar Pathshalas-schools of convenient timings. For girls' education, Angan Pathshalas are being run in three blocks. The programme at present covers over 150,000 students in 1,785 schools and 3,520 Prehar Pathshalas, involving over 4,271 Shiksha Karmis.

The project is known for its open participative style and continuous experimentation to achieve its objectives. The approach, strategies and achievements of the SKP have attracted national and international recognition. The project is slated for a major expansion with SIDA assistance in the 9th Plan. The total projections for the 9th Plan are estimated to be Rs. 4260 million.

Lok Jumbish Project

Barely five years old, Lok Jumbish (LJ) has made an indelible impression in the primary education landscape of Rajasthan. The coverage of the project has extended to 75 blocks, covering a population of approximately 12 million. Significantly, it has also achieved a major breakthrough in welding together government agencies, teachers, NGOs, elected representatives and the people into an interactive group effort to promote universalisation of primary education.

The seven guiding principles of Lok Jumbish are:

- a process rather than a product approach;
- partnerships;
- decentralised functioning;
- participatory learning;
- integration with the mainstream education system;
- flexibility of management; and
- creating multiple levels of leadership committed to quality and mission mode.

Special focus has been given to environment building in all training programmes under LJ. This helps in the development of an understanding about issues involved in people's mobilisation, use of different media forms and clarity about the messages to be given to the people.

The first phase of the project was for a period of two years from 1992-94, with the expenditure shared between SIDA, Government of India and Government of Rajasthan in the ratio 3:2:1. The second phase stretches up to 1998, with the sharing modality remaining the same. The allocation for LJP is Rs.1100 million for Phases I and II and Rs.4000 million for Phase III. A Norwegian grant of Rs. 200 million is also available.

Management and Administration of Primary Schools

The education sector has become a major focus of attention amongst development partners in the last two years, driven primarily by the desire to assist India in achieving the United Nations (UN) Millennium Development Goals (MDGs) for education. The Government aims to improve national competitiveness and reduce poverty through its Medium Term Strategic Plan. It is committed to the achievement of the MDGs and the Education for All (EFA) goals, and if current efforts are sustained, these key education goals are set to be reached by 2010.

Key challenges for the Government include widening access to education without compromising quality, improving quality in a newly decentralised environment, and ensuring that the newly increased funds for education are well spent. To address this, the Ministry of Education is working through its strategic plan for 2005-2009, which has three pillars to its strategy, including (1) Improving access, (2) Increasing quality, and (3) Improving the governance and management of education. Globally, the European Commission (EC), along with a number of development partners, seeks where possible to provide support to partner governments through SWAPs and budget support. This approach is based on two key principles: one, that programmes are led by partner governments, and two, that they have the common goal of improving the efficiency and effectiveness with which internal and external resources are used. This reflects a mutual concern to improve results of government and donor spending both by focusing resources on the priorities stated in national planning documents and by improving the quality of spending.

A number of development partners are currently supporting programmes in basic education, including:

Australian Agency for International Development (Ausaid), United States Agency for International Development (USAID), Asian Development Bank (ADB), Japan International Cooperation Agency (JICA), UN Children's Fund (UNICEF) and UN Educational, Scientific and Cultural Organisation (UNESCO). Large amounts of development assistance funds are being made available to support education reform and development. There is growing interest in moving towards a SWAP among this group, which formalised inter-donor coordination in 2005 with the establishment of the Education Sector Working Group (ESWG), currently co-chaired by the EC and the Netherlands for one year. This group is taking forward the Paris Declaration on Aid Effectiveness, and is seeking to work with the Government in support of achievement of MDGs. World Bank support to basic education is moving into a new phase towards teacher quality support and district level SWAPs, joining forces with the Netherlands and the EC, meanwhile both the ADB and Ausaid have developed major programmes aimed at working towards a SWAP in Indonesia.

For development assistance through a SWAP to become effective, the Government needs to take full ownership of the process, to take a lead in donor coordination and harmonisation, and establish a platform for policy dialogue at sector level which will allow development partners to monitor developments in education and to engage productively with the Government. Alongside this, a medium term expenditure framework will allow development partners' assistance to fill financing gaps, and will give the Government much clearer information than it has at present on how development assistance is being used and can be used in the future.

Professional Developments

Professional development refers to skills and knowledge attained for both personal development and career advancement. Professional development encompasses all types of facilitated learning opportunities, ranging from college degrees to formal coursework, conferences and informal learning opportunities situated in practice. It has been described as intensive and collaborative, ideally incorporating an evaluative stage. There are a variety of approaches to professional development, including consultation, coaching, communities of practice, lesson study, monitoring, reflective supervision and technical assistance.

Classroom Management

Classroom management is a term used by teachers to describe the process of ensuring that classroom lessons run smoothly despite disruptive behavior by students. The term also implies the prevention of disruptive behavior. It is possibly the most difficult aspect of teaching for many teachers and indeed experiencing problems in this area causes some to leave teaching altogether. In 1981 the US National Educational Association reported that 36% of teachers said they would probably not go into teaching if they had to decide again. A major reason was "negative student attitudes and discipline". (Wolfgang and Glickman)

According to Moskowitz & Hayman (1976), once a teacher loses control of their classroom, it becomes increasingly more difficult for them to regain that control (Moskowitz & Hayman, 1976). Also, research from Berliner (1988) and Brophy & Good (1986) shows that the time that teacher has to take to correct misbehavior caused by poor classroom management skills results in a lower rate of academic engagement in the classroom (Berliner, 1988; Brophy & Good, 1986).

Classroom management is closely linked to issues of motivation, discipline and respect. Methodologies remain a matter of passionate debate amongst teachers; approaches vary depending on the beliefs a teacher holds regarding educational psychology. A large part of traditional classroom management involves behavior modification, although many teachers see using behavioural approaches alone as overly simplistic. Many teachers establish rules and procedures at the beginning of the school year. They also try to be consistent in enforcing these rules and procedures. Many would also argue for positive consequences when rules are followed, and negative consequences when rules are broken. There are newer perspectives on classroom management that attempt to be holistic. One example is affirmation teaching, which attempts to guide students toward success by helping them see how their effort pays off in the classroom. It relies upon creating an environment where students are successful *as a result of their own efforts...*

Management of School Building

During The Construction Period: Liaison with the local authority and the contractor:

1. Before construction activities commence on site, it is important for the school to be aware of the project communication arrangements between the local authority project manager and the contractor. Regular site meetings are likely to be held, and it may be appropriate for the school to be represented, or to be briefed on progress.
2. In many projects, day-to-day communication should be encouraged between the school co-ordinator and the contractor's site manager regarding 'housekeeping' matters which will affect the running of the school.
3. As well as having a clear understanding of the design and contract programme, the school should also be aware of what terms and conditions, if any, were included in the contract regarding the contractor's working restrictions, health and safety, security and so on. The school itself will have no authority to enforce the terms of the contract. It is therefore essential to establish a single point of contact with the local authority for all communication regarding the project.

Keeping Staff and Pupils Informed

4. The flow of information to and from school users is very important throughout the project. This is usually an element of the school co-ordinator's role.

5. Existing communication arrangements within the school such as regular departmental and whole staff meetings should be used wherever possible rather than setting up separate project meetings. However, staff should be able to raise individual issues directly with the school co-ordinator.
6. Pupils are usually kept informed about the project through school assemblies and feedback is often provided through the pupil council or through 'house structures' where these operate in secondary schools.
7. The project is also likely to feature heavily on the agenda of any School Board and PTA meetings. The HT and school co-ordinator, as well as the contractor, may well be expected to make regular progress reports at these meetings.
8. *One secondary school undergoing a major refurbishment set up a specific project users group which met monthly throughout the duration of the project. The group consisted of members representing staff, pupils, parents and others from the school community. Meetings were chaired by the HT and were attended by the local authority project manager and the contractor.*

Managing Hazards and Disruptions

9. The contractor will manage the health and safety and security aspects of the construction activities in any project. However, this in itself does not prevent the school from having to consider a number of health and safety matters or having to prepare at certain times for considerable disruption to the normal day-to-day running of the school.

Health and Safety/security

10. The school will need to monitor its health and safety management procedures throughout the project and carry out additional risk assessments where appropriate. In particular, any alterations to fire escape routes and gathering points, access arrangements and site boundaries should be clearly

identified. Arrangements should be clearly displayed in the school with signage amended as appropriate. Fire drills should be undertaken each time escape routes are changed.

11. Prior to construction commencing on site, all school users should be briefed on the health and safety arrangements for the project. Presentations to school assemblies by the contractor, often incorporating protective clothing and some basic statistics about construction site safety, are generally considered to have more impact than if these were delivered by the school management team.
12. As school holidays approach further advice should be issued to pupils regarding the hazards of building sites. Security monitoring will be provided by the contractor but in some instances it may also be appropriate to alert the local police who may patrol the site at high risk periods.
13. Where work needs to be carried out in occupied buildings, contractor's staff may require to gain access to parts of the construction site through operational parts of the school. These situations generally place greater responsibilities on the contractor's staff and school users. These responsibilities need to be understood by all.
14. It may be considered appropriate in these situations for the contractor's staff to wear agreed forms of identification and to be prepared to be challenged by staff on school premises. It may also be considered necessary to caution contractor's staff to avoid initiating contact with pupils. It has also been known for school pupils to abuse construction workers, so the conduct of school users must also be considered and managed.
15. Despite contractual agreements, breaches in health and safety procedures can still occur in these situations. For example contractor's staff may leave doors unlocked or materials and equipment unattended in circulation routes. School users should be particularly vigilant about

possible hazzards and procedures should be in place to report such incidents.

Managing Disruptions

16. A certain degree of inconvenience is unavoidable during a major construction project. The level of disruption likely to be experienced by the school will depend upon a variety of factors such as the scale and type of building operations, their proximity to the school activities, the time at which the works are carried out, and the constraints of the existing buildings and site.

17. The following examples are the most common disruptions reported by schools during construction projects:

- *Dust and dirt : Apart from being particularly uncomfortable, airborne dust and dirt can give rise to medical complaints leading to staff and pupil absences. Locating classrooms which require natural ventilation away from construction activities, and insisting on the constructing and maintaining of seals in affected areas can help to minimise the ingress of dust and dirt. In some cases, it may be appropriate to arrange additional cleaning for the school during the project.*
- *Noise : Health and Safety regulations ensure that noise levels will not be hazardous to health, but they may still be extremely distracting. Where construction works are in close proximity to the school, the contractor may be excluded from undertaking certain noisy activities during particular periods such as exams. It may also be possible for the school to request the contractor, on an informal basis, to reduce noise levels for short periods from time to time.*
- *Distractions from increased traffic, both vehicular and personnel : In order to avoid continuing distraction it may be possible to locate particularly sensitive school classes and activities away from the*

main site access and construction works. Ensure site activities are appropriately screened and avoid allowing contractor's staff access through pupil areas.

- *Frequent changes to access points and circulation routes : the need to advise school users of continuing changes in access arrangements can be disruptive and resource intensive. This should be considered when agreeing the sequence of phasing of the construction works.*
- *Planned and unplanned interruptions to water, gas, power, ICT services ; prior consultation and contingency planning with staff about the consequences of a particular service failure or disconnection will allow the school to better manage these situations when they occur.*
- *Reduced playground space, loss of playing fields and car parking : The loss of amenities during the construction process is often an unavoidable source of inconvenience to school users. However, early consultation with those affected, provides the opportunity to investigate and implement alternatives.*

Completion

Migration Management

18. In new-build projects, the actual move into the new building can present a logistical challenge for the school. Where possible, staff (and in some cases pupils) should tour the new building prior to completion. This allows users to get an initial feel for the layout of the new building, and assists staff in taking ownership of the new spaces.

19. In many cases, it has proved worthwhile to employ a specialist 'migration manager' to work with the school to co-ordinate the move. This professional service can be provided by some removal companies, or could be a separate commission to a firm of project managers.

20. It is important to be flexible in providing staffing cover to release teaching and non-teaching staff to undertake tasks associated with the move.Teaching staff are usually given one or two days of non-teaching time to manage the packing of resources and equipment, with the actual moving of materials being carried out by removal staff under the supervision of the migration manager. The unpacking and setting up of new accommodation may also take one or two non-teaching days.

21. *In one school, pupils assisted in preparing for the move. The tasks associated with the exercise, such as making inventories and the management of packing, were incorporated into a module of the Home Economics curriculum.*

22. This process may take much longer for some practical departments, which may have a significant amount of teaching material to move and store. Specialist removal arrangements may be required for particularly bulky, sensitive, hazardous or valuable items such as grand pianos, ICT equipment, toxic chemicals or trophies and art works. In these cases, detailed inventories may be required, and insurance arrangements checked as part of the planning exercise.

23. Where a major move is planned over a summer break period, it may be necessary to temporarily set up two offices at the school site to maintain a continuous communication link for the school during the change-over from one administration set-up to another.

24. The process of introducing students into a completely new building will also require significant planning. In a large secondary school, for example, it may be necessary to provide induction information at an assembly followed by an orientation tour of the building. This could be carried out in year groups on a staggered basis over the course of a whole school day.

Marking the end of the Process

25. It is important to celebrate the completion of the school project with some formal ceremony. This should not be arranged for immediately after the school has taken occupation of the new or refurbished building, as it will take some time for the staff and pupils to settle in and to optimise their use of the new accommodation. Equally, the event should not be left so late as to miss capturing the initial enthusiasm and anticipation which is associated with taking ownership of a new facility.

Post Completion

26. Once occupied, a new or substantially refurbished building may present teething problems for some time. The role of the school co-ordinator is sometimes at its most demanding during this period, and it may be necessary to continue their remit, as well as enhancing other support staffing, for up to 6 months following 'completion' of the project.

27. The school is likely to receive numerous requests from visitors wishing to view the new building for up to and beyond a year after completion. Guided tours can become a drain on staff resources, and a large number of visitors can prove a disruption to teaching and learning. In many cases, visitors may wish to take photographs of the school and this may not be appropriate in areas used by pupils. Providing information about the school building on a handout or on the school website may reduce the demand for general visits. Including a 'virtual tour' or downloadable images of the building can avoid the need for visitors to take their own photographs.

Post Occupancy Evaluation

28. Consultation with stakeholders throughout a school building project is an important part of the school estate strategy. Conducting an evaluation on how well the new school has met the needs and expectations of school users is a logical conclusion to this consultation process.

29. Recent guidance on Evaluation published under the school estate strategy [9] suggests that a post occupancy evaluation should be carried out on every major school building project about one year after completion. This type of evaluation will demonstrate the local authority's progress on improving its school estate, identify issues in the new building which can be addressed through 'fine tuning' and inform the thinking and briefing for future school projects.

Equipments

Tracking and managing routine equipment maintenance and calibration on an ongoing basis is a difficult task for organizations with a large number of vehicles or equipment. And failure to properly maintain equipment can prove costly due to reduced life, additional repair costs and equipment down time. Spreadsheet and paper-based solutions have severe limitations because they cannot be easily reviewed by management and don't provide automatic alerts when maintenance activities are required. In addition, tracking and sharing information with everyone responsible for various pieces of equipment can be a difficult process. All pupils have the right to a workplace that is suited to their needs. Schools shall have access to necessary equipment, furniture and fittings and educational resources.The Ministry may issue regulations concerning the safety of the pupils.

Library

- Provides appropriate resources (including digital resources) and information to meet the needs of the school community
- Utilises current technology to provide efficient access to and effective communication of information
- Provides opportunities and resources for teachers to integrate information skills into learning activities
- Is provided with sufficient funding to achieve the school's educational aims
- Enriches students reading experiences and develops their skills as independent learners

- Supports the teaching and learning process
- Has adequate professional and trained support staff
- Is planned and designed to be a pleasant and stimulating learning environment
- Is monitored regularly to assess its use
- Improves student literacy standards
- Models and monitors priorities based on contemporary library principles

Effective school libraries must be responsive to educational and technological change and must also contribute to students learning and general school improvement. In order to achieve this, an ongoing process of evaluation must be carried out. Evaluation is used to monitor the school's use of the library and to improve the effectiveness of information services so that student learning outcomes are improved. The outcomes of the evaluation should be distributed widely and used effectively to make changes and improvements to the information services and to inform future action.

Some key questions that can guide the evaluation:

- Do the resources meet the individual learning needs of students of all ages and abilities?
- Are the library and its resources easily accessible to the students?
- Are there sufficient resources in the library to meet the needs of the curriculum?
- Are there sufficient resources in the library to also cater for personal and leisure interests?
- Are the resources relevant and of good quality?
- How much use do the students and staff make of the library?
- How does the library affect school improvement, including student achievement?

Records and Registers

The department maintains records on students to assist in fulfilling its obligations as specified in the Education Act. Such records are essential to the process of enhancing learning, maintaining student health and welfare, educational planning, school administration and reporting to parents and students. All school records and documents remain the property of the Minister. Information about students should only be recorded if it is relevant and must be retained for the period for which it is valid and relevant to the student's education or welfare. For the retention periods for student records. All comments in a students file should be signed and dated. Notes or comments made by a departmental employee concerning and student are deemed to be an official record and must be managed accordingly, including being recorded in the pupil record folder. Where notes are made in a diary, they should be confined to a diary used exclusively for work purposes.

Records must be retained for various minimum periods, as specified in *General Disposal Schedule 15 for Administrative Records* and *General Disposal Schedule 22 for School Records*, after which they may be destroyed, or where appropriate transferred to State Records as permanent archives. Whilst some individual documents may have a short retention period, once they form part of the pupil record folder they must be retained until the entire folder can be legally disposed of. Individual official records must not be culled from the pupil record folder. Whilst the contents of the pupil record folder may differ between sites it is recommended that all records relating to a student be managed in the folder. At a minimum it is suggested the following should be placed on the folder:

- Enrolment, admission and pupil information
- Assessment records and reports
- Transfer advice
- School leaver statement / student achievement record
- Records of absences
- Leaving details (forwarding addresses / occupation etc)
- Medical and family information
- Student information card
- Work experience records
- Discipline records.

Hostel

Hostels provide budget oriented, sociable accommodation where guests can rent a bed, sometimes a bunk bed, in a dormitory and share a bathroom, lounge and sometimes a kitchen. Rooms can be mixed or single-sex, although private rooms may also be available. Hostels are generally cheaper for both the operator and the occupants; many hostels employ their long-term residents as desk clerks or housekeeping staff in exchange for free accommodation. An effort should be made to distinguish between establishments providing longer-term accommodation (often to specific classes of clientele such as nurses, students, drug addicts) where the hostels are sometimes run by Housing Associations and charities) and those offering short-term accommodation to travellers or backpackers.

Role of Local Panchayats—Functions of Primary Schools

Decentralisation and Community Involvement

With the enactment of the 73rd and 74th Amendment Act (Panchayati Raj ACT), 1992, the focus is now on democratically elected bodies at the district, sub-district, Panchayat and municipal levels. These Panchayati Raj bodies, which are to have adequate representation of women, Scheduled Castes and Scheduled Tribes, minorities, representatives of parents, educationists, and appropriate institutions, will have the responsibility of preparing development plans and implementing educational programmes besides dealing with those subjects closely related to education such as health, social welfare and women and child development.

Detailed parameters for a decentralised management of education have been worked out by a CABE committee on Decentralised Management of Education. The committee's recommendations indicate how educational structures should be set up at the district, taluk/ mandal and village levels in pursuance of the Constitutional Amendments. The recommendations of the Committee have been endorsed by the CABE in its meeting held on 15 October, 1993.

State governments have initiated the process of establishment of structures for decentralised planning and management and are in the process of drawing up appropriate legislation which provides for Panchayati Raj Committees for Education.

The breadth and scope of the Panchayati Raj Act provides an exceptionally 'enabling' framework for viable strategies and interventions that would play a commanding role in promoting universal elementary education. The responsibilities vested with the district level body, for instance, cover planning, which includes, inter alia, area development, spatial planning, institutional planning, administrative and financial control and personnel management with respect to primary, middle, secondary and higher secondary schools and educational programmes.

The district level body will also implement, supervise and monitor all educational programmes, including non-formal and adult education. Besides, it will draw upon the expertise of DIETs and other institutions for substantive curricular and pedagogic inputs into district level programmes of Elementary Education (EE), Non-formal Education (NFE) and Adult Education (AE). From the district level, the process of decentralisation percolates down to the village level.

The Panchayati Raj Act envisages the formation of Panchayats for a village or a group of villages. These panchayats will have elected representatives. Each panchayat would constitute a Village Education Committee (VEC) which would be responsible for the administration of education programmes at the village level. The major responsibility of the VECs would lie in operationalisation of micro-level planning and school mapping in the village through systematic house to house surveys and periodic discussions with parents. Ensuring participation in primary education of every child in every family would be one of the prime aims of the VECs.

UNIT-III

Curriculum and Evaluation

Principles of Curriculum Development and Programmes for Implementation

In formal education, a curriculum plural: curricula is the set of courses, and their content, offered at a school or university. As an idea, curriculum stems from the Latin word for *race course*, referring to the course of deeds and experiences through which children grow and mature in becoming adults.

Historical Conception

In *The Curriculum*, the first textbook published on the subject, in 1918, John Franklin Bobbitt said that curriculum, as an idea, has its roots in the Latin word for *race-course*, explaining the curriculum as the course of deeds and experiences through which children become the adults they should be, *for success in adult society*. Furthermore, the curriculum encompasses the entire scope of formative deed and experience occurring in and out of school, and not only experiences occurring in school; experiences that are unplanned and undirected, and experiences intentionally directed for the purposeful formation of adult members of society.

To Bobbitt, the curriculum is a social engineering arena. Per his cultural presumptions and social definitions, his curricular formulation has two notable features: (i) that scientific experts would best be qualified to and justified in designing curricula based upon their expert knowledge of what qualities are desirable in adult members of society, and which experiences would generate said qualities; and (ii) curriculum defined as the deeds-experiences the student *ought to have* to become the adult he or she *ought to become*. Hence, he defined the curriculum as an ideal, rather than as the concrete reality of the deeds and experiences that form people to who and what they are.

Contemporary views of curriculum reject these features of Bobbitt's postulates, but retain the basis of curriculum as the course of experience(s) that forms human beings in to persons. Personal formation via curricula is studied at the personal level and at the group level, i.e. cultures and societies (e.g. professional formation, academic discipline via historical experience). The formation of a group is reciprocal, with the formation of its individual participants.

Although it formally appeared in Bobbitt's definition, curriculum as a course of formative experience also pervades John Dewey's work (who disagreed with Bobbitt on important matters). Although Bobbitt's and Dewey's idealistic understanding of "curriculum" is different from current, restricted uses of the word, curriculum writers and researchers generally share it as common, substantive understanding of curriculum.

Dynamic Methods of Teaching and Innovations in Teaching Techniques with Particular Emphasis on the Teaching of Mother-tongue, Science, Mathematics and Social Skills

Current Theories about Curriculum Development

Focus on the 21st century: Wilson et al. (1991) conducted a 3-year collaborative research project to develop curricula for the 21st century. The study used a Delphi survey of 150 leaders in business, government, and education. Dominant themes included change and adaptability, global interdependence and cultural diversity, quality of life, technology, and self-actualization.

Holistic, Multidisciplinary Curricula: Several authors (Hunkins and Hammill, 1994; Relan and Kimpston, 1991) believe that curricula should be holistic, unfettered by preestablished rules, responsive to conditions of constant change and unpredictability, emergent rather than fixed, and inviting synthesis rather than fragmentation of thinking. If curricula are integrative rather than subject-focused, learners will be exposed to a holistic view of knowledge. Subject-focused curricula fail to provide learners with the intellectual skills needed in a competitive society, whereas integrated curricula allow learners to be actively involved in their own education. Integrated approaches to curriculum design have been associated with "intermingling" of disciplines such as thinking, reasoning, and problem-solving capabilities (Relan and Kimpston, 1991; Komski, 1990). Interdisciplinary curricula offer strong advantages and can best be prepared and delivered by designers working as teams (Martinello and Cook, 1994).

***Strong tie to the Workplace*:** Askov (1992) recommends a strong tie to concerns of the workplace to hold the attention of adult learners. At the same time, however, curriculum development should incorporate learning strategies and thinking processes, not merely "content" (Meyers et al., 1991).

***Focus on Outcomes*:** Curriculum design should take into account intentions and outcomes. It should encourage students to make choices and explore their consequences. (Coleman, 1991).

***Valuing of Cultural Diversity*:** Intercultural communication courses are necessary for teachers at every level. Multiculturalism and cultural diversity will have immense impact on global society, and multicultural issues should be incorporated into traditional curricula (Sessoms, 1994).

Overview of the Cyclical Curriculum Development Process

As practiced by the CTS, curriculum development and delivery is a cyclical process that involves

- Identifying learning needs
- Assessing the audience
- Understanding cultural diversity

- Developing goals and objectives
- Evaluating the learning experience
- Facilitating the learning process
- Selecting methods and aids
- Selecting and tailoring content
- Delivering the learning experience
- Developing an action plan.

The entire process is evaluation-oriented. The cycle starts with identifying training outcomes which set the framework for evaluation. It winds its way through the phases and ends after the learning experience, when performance is assessed against the expected outcomes. This assessment may point to the need for a new journey: a repetition of part or all of the cycle to make adjustments or add new materials that will make the learning experience more effective. Within the curriculum design and delivery cycle there are close, yet flexible, interrelationships among the parts. The impact of decisions made in one part usually can be seen in the activities in the following parts. Also, the cycle is designed so that the instructor/ facilitator can either move sequentially from part to part or modify the sequence to best fit audience learning needs. For example, the results of an initial needs assessment or situation analysis might indicate a lack of knowledge concerning risk and resiliency factors among various community groups. This might

become the basis of a new curriculum design and delivery effort. Even after the goals and objectives have been finalized, new research results could still be incorporated in the remainder of the process (design, development, implementation, evaluation). If the new research points to a change in the goals and objectives, they could also be revised.

Major Considerations: The following are essential conditions for successful curriculum design:

- A performance problem or learning need that can be alleviated by training or education must be identified before the learning event can be designed.

- Measurable goals and objectives must be formulated specifying the learning that will occur so that the desired outcome can be achieved.
- All learning activities must enable participants to acquire the knowledge, skills, or attitudes necessary to meet the goal and objectives.
- The learning event must be evaluated to determine whether or not the goals and objectives have been met.

Improvisation of Aids and Materials for Teaching

Essential Elements of the Curriculum Design and Delivery Cycle

Identifying Outcomes for Training: The systematic investigation of the outcomes assists the trainer in determining whether or not the issues(s) identified in the outcomes can be addressed by training. Possible outcomes include information sharing, motivation/awareness building, educational activities, action planning, environmental change, creation of alternatives to substance use, and shifts in professional practices and/or behavioural norms. First, it is necessary to collect and analyze information about the issues outlined in the outcomes. Appropriate information collection methods are chosen based on all available resources. Finally, information is collected and analyzed to show in measurable terms, if possible, the exact nature of the issues identified in the outcomes and what steps are needed to translate the outcomes into practice. Also, the analysis should include the extent to which the outcomes affect the goals and tasks of the organization/business/agency.

Understanding the Audience: It is Important to look at the intended audience in terms of age range, gender, educational background, cultural background, learning style, and on-the-job responsibilities. This information is useful in designing the content and methods to be used in learning events. Besides the individual characteristics of audiences, we develope a means of looking at the circumstances in which audiences operate to guide curriculum development efforts. This method is called situational analysis.

Developing Goals and Objectives: The goals and objectives indicate what participants would learn and be able to do as a result of the learning event. The goals should be stated so that learning objectives can be formulated in measurable terms. Along with learning objectives, long-term objectives should be developed to establish a basis for evaluation.

Valuing Cultural Diversity: Increase participants' understanding of cultural identities and how these identities affect learning and behaviour. Action plans for developing cultural competence ensure that participants will continue to expand their understanding beyond the period of formal training.

Education Policies and the Curriculum in India

India is a union comprised of twenty-five states and seven territories. The Constitution provides directives regarding the development of education throughout the country. The areas in which the respective central and state governments, have domain have been identified in the Constitution as the *central* list, *state* list and *concurrent* list. Until the late 1970s, school education had been on the *state* list, which meant that states had the final say in the management of their respective school systems. However, in 1976, education was transferred to the *concurrent* list through a constitutional amendment, the objective being to promote meaningful educational partnerships between the central and state governments. Today, the central government establishes broad education policies for school curricula development and management practices. These serve as guidelines for the states.

Evaluation of Pupil Progress

The Curriculum Development Process

The process of curriculum development in India lies between the two extremes of centralization and decentralization. From time to time, the national government formulates the National Policy on Education which includes broad guidelines regarding content and process of education at different stages. These guidelines are further elaborated by the National Council of Educational Research and Training (NCERT).

Using as its foundation the NPEs of 1968 and 1986, two curriculum initiatives have been launched by NCERT: (a) The Curriculum for the Ten-Year School—a framework (1975); and (b) The National Curriculum for Elementary and Secondary Education—a framework (1988).

The curriculum framework prepared at the central level provides a broad overview of the school curriculum including general objectives, subject-wise objectives, suggested scheme of studies, and guidelines for the transaction of the curriculum and the evaluation of pupil outcomes. These detailed curricula, syllabi and instructional materials are developed at the national level.

The NCERT has also developed the syllabi and instructional materials used in the schools run by central organizations. However, the states consider whether to *adopt* or *adapt* the NCERT syllabi and instructional materials. Thus, the NCERT curriculum framework is always *a suggestion* rather than *prescriptive* and it is not enforceable by law in the states. However, it is readily accepted by the states because of the NCERT's credibility and the participatory development approach it follows. (The NCERT curriculum framework is developed on a consensus basis; all the states and union territories are involved in the curriculum elaboration).

The National Curriculum

The following social, cultural, political, economic and educational parameters have guided the development of the national curriculum framework:

- All citizens of India should have equal access to education. The specific needs of the disadvantaged sections of the society ought to be met through the curriculum;
- Education regarding India's cultural heritage needs to be imparted to students in order to develop national identity and a spirit of togetherness;

- It is essential to impart knowledge of the citizens' duties and rights, and ideals of the Constitution of India to children;
- In view of the erosion of values, it is imperative through the curriculum to inculcate moral and social values amongst students;
- Besides national identity and unity, it is also imperative to develop international understanding through the curriculum;
- Protection of the environment and conservation of natural resources should be major objectives of school curriculum;
- In view of the increasing population of the country, it is imperative to include suitable content relating to population education in the syllabi of different subjects;
- The curriculum should aim at preparing a child for life, which means that relevant knowledge should be imparted and appropriate skills, competencies and values developed;
- Education plays a significant role in national development by increasing human resources. Therefore, the primary objective of the curriculum ought to be total development of the child's personality; All the processes of education should be child-centred, with the teacher playing the role of a facilitator during the process of learning;
- The curriculum should aim at developing students' creative potential;
- The curriculum should develop a scientific approach amongst students;
- Work should not be considered as distinct from education. Instead, work should be adopted as a medium for imparting education;
- The process of evaluation should be continuous and comprehensive;

- Media and educational technology ought to be employed to make the transactions of curriculum effective.

An important development since the National Policy on Education was formulated in 1986 has been the acceptance across the country of a common structure of education and the introduction by most states of the 10+2+3 system. There are eight years of elementary education (five years of primary school and three years of upper primary/middle schooling) and four years of secondary education (two years of general secondary and two years of higher secondary).

The education system seeks to give due recognition and importance to the social organization, traditions, customs and value systems of the various communities, particularly Scheduled Castes and Scheduled Tribes. This is supported among other ways by the development of materials and curricula in their languages. The main characteristics of the national curriculum, developed in accordance with the above-mentioned principles, are described in the following sections.

General Education

The national curriculum envisages the first ten years of school as the period of general education and that the diversified curriculum should be introduced at the end of general education (i.e. at the beginning of the senior secondary stage.) This plan provides all students with an opportunity to receive instruction in each of the curricular areas considered essential for their overall development.

Area of Internal Assessment—Patterns and Techniques of Evaluation

The national curriculum framework also envisages an undifferentiated curriculum for all children-irrespective of sex and place of residence (i.e. urban or rural).

Minimum levels of learning

The 1986 NPE recommended the establishment of minimum levels of learning (MLLs) for the various subject areas at the different school stages. In this context, a Government of India committee (under the Chairmanship of Professor R.H. Dave) elaborated the MLL curriculum concept that designates the *competencies* to be mastered by the primary level pupils in each *subject*, at *specific points in time*. For the first five years of primary schooling, the MLL covers the mother tongue, mathematics, social science and science. The MLL approach implies that the teacher's responsibility is not confined to syllabus coverage. Rather, teachers must be responsible for their pupils mastering designated competencies. This approach has necessitated on-going development of MLL-based textbooks and MLL-based evaluation. It has also introduced a higher concept of *teacher accountability*. Teachers are now held responsible for pupil competency development and not merely for teaching the prescribed syllabus—as was the previous practice.

Common-core Elements

The 1988 National Curriculum Framework (NCF) recommended compulsory core curriculum elements to be taught throughout the country. Most of these core elements are aimed at the development of national identity and a spirit of togetherness leading to national unity. The common core elements recommended in the NCF are: the history of India's freedom struggle; constitutional obligations; content essential for the development of national identity; common cultural heritage of India; democracy, secularism, socialism; gender equality; environmental conservation; removal of social barriers; the small-family norm; and development of a scientific approach. The core elements are not to be treated as separate subject areas. Rather, the content is to be interwoven into the different subject areas. Here, it should be noted that, for the first time during India's post-independence period, conscious efforts have been made to place *values* at the centre stage of curriculum.

Continuous and Comprehensive Evaluation

The NCF also considered the limitations of the existing evaluation system, which relies mostly on one-shot, end of-the-year impact evaluation. This annual examination measures skills attainment and the affective domain is generally ignored (i.e. attitudes development). To remedy this, the NCF recommended that evaluation should be treated as an integral part of the classroom teaching/learning process. Furthermore, evaluation, conducted periodically, should provide the type of feedback on student achievement that enables teachers to improve their methodology, if required.

Interactive Teaching

It is recognized that both the educational curriculum content and process must be re-oriented in order to bring about overall quality improvement. During the past few years, successful attempts have been made to re-orient the educational content to current development and demands of both society and the different disciplines. However, this initiative has not been accompanied by a corresponding change in the modes of curriculum transaction, which remains predominantly one of verbal exposition by the teacher. The expository style of teaching, involving mostly one-way communication, puts the learner in the role of a passive recipient—a mere *object* of education. This situation is not conducive to the development of creative, critical and analytical thinking by students. An interactive teaching methodology involving continuing dialogue between the teacher and pupils (discussion, investigation, problem-solving, etc.) could provide an educational environment more conducive to developing certain abstract cognitive skills.

Scheme of Studies

The 1988 National Curriculum Framework has recommended, along with the appropriate time weightage at the upper primary and secondary levels:

Languages. The NCF envisages the study of three languages at the upper primary and secondary stages: first, the mother tongue/regional language; second, Hindi or English (in the case of non-Hindi-speaking states); and third, one of the modern Indian languages (English in Hindi-speaking states; Hindi *or* English in non-Hindi-speaking states).

Mathematics. Functional mathematics are taught at the upper primary stage; arithmetic, including commercial mathematics, should be completed, to a very large extent, by the end of the upper primary stage.

Science

The upper primary science teaching objectives are to develop an understanding of the nature of scientific knowledge; and certain physical, chemical, biological principles and their relationship to the operation of scientific principles in nature, as well as in daily life.

Social Sciences

The study of social sciences at the upper primary stage is comprized of the study of history, geography, civics and contemporary issues and problems.

Arts

The aim of art education is learner sensitization to the beauty in line, colour, form, movement and sound. The upper primary programme incorporates:

(i) drawing, painting, printing, collage, clay modelling, puppet construction;

(ii) free expression artistic creation;

(iii) handling of simple musical instruments;

(iv) movement, mime, simple dance forms, community singing;

(v) simple concepts of visual and performing arts;

(vi) stories of great personalities in the field of arts, and stories connected with other countries.

Health and Physical Education

This area focuses on the holistic health of the learner and the community, thereby establishing the important place of mental and emotional, as well as physical health. The first ten years of content focuses on general promotion of healthful living as well as on major health problems of the country. In physical education, sports and games, the emphasis is given to indigenous traditional games. Furthermore, as a system which promotes the integral development of body and mind, yoga receives special attention.

Morals and Values

These areas are treated as an integral curriculum component for which all teachers are responsible.

Work Experience

The work experience incorporates purposive, manual work resulting in either goods or services useful to the community. It is an essential component at all stages of education and is to be provided through wellstructured, graded programmes. At both the upper primary and secondary stages, work experience emphasizes agricultural and technological processes to facilitate the integration of science, mathematics and technology into community life.

State-level Curriculum Implementation

The available feedback from the states indicates that, for the most part, they have revised their curricula along the lines recommended by the 1986 NPE and 1988 NCF. However, several have made adjustments that respond to specific local needs or socio-political pressures. Following are some highlights that reflect the dynamics of curriculum implementation at the state level.

Languages

All states (except Tamil Nadu) have adopted the three language formula. Although it was envisaged that only one language (mother tongue or regional language) would be taught at the primary stage, many states have taken the initiative and introduced a second and third language at this level. For example, Punjab state recently decided to introduce English, along with the regional language in class I. In the state of Sikkim, English is taught as a subject and used as the medium of instruction—beginning right from class I. The policy of using English as the medium of instruction beginning in class I is being implemented in almost all the private, unaided schools throughout the country. (The growth of these private schools has mushroomed during the past few years and this trend is likely to accelerate in the future.)

Another interesting variation encompasses classical language teaching—an area that the NCF did not address. Most of the Hindi-speaking states, and even central school organizations, have made provisions for teaching Sanskrit as a third language. In fact, to accommodate the study of Sanskrit along with other languages, some states have even made provisions for the teaching of a fourth language. (In Uttar Pradesh, Sanskrit is compulsory and taught as part of Hindi.) It would appear that Sanskrit is in demand because it is associated with ancient Indian culture and is the mother_ to many modern Indian languages.

Upper primary stage	***Time weightage (%)***
1. Three languages	32
2. Mathematics	12
3. Social science	12
4. Science	12
5. Health and physical education	10
6. Arts	10
7. Work experience	10

Other Scholastic Areas

Several states have modified the NCF science and social sciences recommendations. For example, in place of the integrated science approach, they have opted for the single-subject discipline approach. West Bengal has made provisions for the teaching of history and geography only at the upper primary stage.

Non-scholastic Areas

In India, work experience, arts, and health and physical education are generally categorized as non-scholastic areas. The curriculum framework has emphasized that these areas are essential for all around development of the child's personality. However, being non-examination subjects, these areas are not taken seriously by the teachers and students. In some states, arts has not been made a compulsory subject at the secondary stage. In the states and schools where arts is a compulsory or optional area, only the visual arts are taught. Performance arts like music and dance are taught only in a limited number of schools. In the states of Punjab, Haryana and Himachal Pradesh, arts has been clustered with home science and agriculture and the students have been given the option to choose any one of these areas.

Values Education

The NCF also envisaged that values education should permeate all aspects of school life and, therefore, should be integrated into all the curriculum areas. However, states like Haryana, Goa, Himachal Pradesh, Karnataka, Punjab, Sikkim, Tamil Nadu, Andhra Pradesh and Uttar Pradesh have all introduced moral education or moral science as independent subject areas, with distinct time allocations. Apparently, this has occurred in the light of pleas that, given the progressive weakening of the moral fabric of society, the integrated approach does not provide values education with the prominent place it deserves.

Competency-based Textbooks

After the identification of MLL (minimum levels of learning), introductory advocacy programmes were launched to promote the concept as an approach to curriculum development, teaching and learning and pupil evaluation. A number of states have since produced primary-stage competency-based textbooks in different curricular areas.

Curriculum Outcomes

The Curriculum Review: The Government of India found it necessary to appoint a National Advisory Committee (NAC) to look into frequent complaints about the *excessive burden* of the curriculum on children. The NAC submitted report findings in 1993. This report, which took note of the widespread perception regarding the heavy load of the school curriculum, also identified the roots of the problem: inability to distinguish between information and knowledge; society's competitive social ethos; the desire to catch up with developed countries; centralized curriculum development processes; non-participation of teachers in the various curriculum development processes; excessive dependence on experts; incomprehensibility of textbooks; and absence of an academic ethos in schools.

The committee further determined that the academic burden perception is tied to *incomprehension*, a problem which can be addressed (to some extent) by modifying the curriculum development goals, as well as the textbook writing process and by improving the school environment by providing the required infrastructure. Most of the NAC recommendations were accepted by the Government. All state governments were asked to initiate appropriate follow-up measures to implement the recommendations of the committee, including review of curriculum and textbooks.

Evaluation of Textbooks

The textbooks used in different states and union territories are already subject to periodic evaluation. They are reviewed from the perspective of national integration—the objective being to promote peace and harmony in the country and enable children to learn to live together with people of different religious, linguistic, ethnic and cultural groups. During these reviews any content deemed to have a secular bias or to be destructive to national unity is identified and recommended for removal. Textbooks are also continuously evaluated from the standpoint of gender, scientific temper and relevance, etc.

Improving Quality of Curriculum Transaction

NCERT, the Central Board of Secondary Education (CBSE), the State Councils of Educational Research and Training (SCERTS) and the State Boards of Secondary Education have initiated a number of projects to improve the quality of curriculum transmission in schools. To improve the quality of mathematics education, CBSE has launched the project Operation Mathematics emphasizing the re-orientation of all teachers. The CBSE has also developed source materials in the education areas of: environment, values, consumer and population. Furthermore, a network of training institutions has been established in the country to enhance teacher competencies through inservice education.

Emerging Trends in Curriculum Development

In the light of changing societal needs and aspirations, certain high demand-driven areas are likely to have an impact on the school curriculum. It appears that, among other areas, language education, values education and information technology shall be matters of serious debate in the next cycle of curriculum renewal. Art education is also scheduled for reform in the next cycle of curriculum renewal.

Language Education. The introduction of English at the primary stage is one of the demands which school systems are finding difficult to resist. Perhaps this demand is based on the assumption that the study of English can give children an edge in a highly competitive society.

Values Education. After the establishment of a National Commission for Human Rights, momentum has been gathering for incorporating this area into the school curriculum. The interim report issued by Justice Verma's Committee (on the fundamental duties of citizens) strongly recommended that fundamental duties should be incorporated at all stages of the school curriculum, as well as into different teacher-education programmes. The incorporation of human rights and citizens' fundamental duties into the curriculum can help pupils *learn to live together*, one of the four pillars of learning identified by the International Commission on Education in the Twenty-first Century.

Computer Education is expected to soon occupy a prominent space in India's school curriculum, it being recognized that, in the information age, skills in the use of the technologies are invaluable.

Teaching Strategy for Primary Schools in India

THE SUCCESSFUL experiments in Rajasthan and other states in multi-grade teaching indicate that it is a viable strategy for small schools as well as mono-grade schools. The teaching strategy now needs to be institutionalised in a systematic way.

The Multi-Grade, Multi-Level (MGML) strategy has been deemed successful in improving the quality classroom instruction world over, by providing more space for children for self-learning and group learning, along with systematic teacher guided learning. Successful experiments in Rajasthan and other states in multi-grade teaching indicate that it is a viable strategy for small schools as well as mono-grade schools.

In-house discussions and visits of the Sarva Shiksha Abhiyan functionaries to various states of India and Republic of Columbia have convinced them to implement MGML strategy for qualitative improvement in classroom instruction for all kinds of schools.

The features of a successful MGML strategy are as follows:

- Reorganisation of curriculum and syllabi into learning units or milestones of learning.

Development of material on various learning segments of each unit as follows:

- Teacher directed activity sheets;
- Group learning worksheets;
- Individual practice worksheets.
- Systematic implementation of the strategies with teachers trained in the following aspects:
- Material management;
- Time management;
- Space management;
- Use of advance organisers like daily review and preparation for the next day;
- A support system at cluster level with a lead school / model school;
- State Resource Group dedicated to MGML strategy for development of material in a phased manner for the full primary cycle;

- A core group of academicians drawn from the education department, non-government organisations (NGOs) and educators to periodically evaluate and monitor the progress;
- A pool of master trainers (MTs) who are well-versed with the MGML strategy and the content of primary grades.

Since the successful implementation of MGML solely rests on the teaching-learning material, which needs to be deliberately developed and validated with quick try-outs with a group of students before the larger use, the following activities need to be initiated sequentially.

- Formation of a resource group of 10 experts and support staff under the leadership of an individual who has done such work and placing the group at an NGO with well-defined terms of references;
- Induction training of resource group members;
- Identification of existing resources (both material and human) to set up a resource centre at an NGO;
- Formation of state level core group and organising its quarterly meetings;
- Development of material for grades I and II in workshop mode (15 experts engaged for one month);
- Try-out of the material in some select schools in a block. The schools can be of three kinds, i.e., multi-grade, mono-grade and alternative schools with self-pacing;
- Production of printed material and training of MTs;
- Systematic and closely monitored institutionalisation of MGML in cluster model schools in the first year for classes I and II;
- In the second phase, the material development for grades III to V will be done in the workshop mode (18 experts for one month);
- The field trial of the material be done in select schools of the district as before, and material be printed;

- The training of teachers of a few thousand schools for verification of the strategy before its universalisation.

Based upon these major activities, the detailed sub-activities and action plan can be worked out by the resource group to systematically implement the MGML strategy.

Evaluation

Evaluation is an important component of the teaching-learning process. It helps teachers and learners to improve teaching and learning. Evaluation is a continuous process not a periodic exercise. It helps in forming the values of judgement, educational status, or achievement of students. Evaluation in one form or the other is inevitable in teaching-learning, as in all fields of activity of education judgements need to be made. Hence, it is desirable that teachers must acquire knowledge and understanding about the various aspects of evaluation and its application in classrooms.

Since we are confined to educational evaluation, at the very beginning let us provide you, with the major elements of the Teaching-Learning Process and the role of evaluation in the teaching-learning process. This unit will provide you with the need, importance, concept and characteristics of evaluation. Evaluation, measurement and assessment are also explained, in order to clarify distinction among these terms. After going through this unit, you will be able to: describe the teaching-learning process, analyse the role of evaluation in the teaching-learning process, explain the need and importance of evaluation, define and explain the concept of evaluation, list the characteristics of evaluation, and distinguish between evaluation, assessment and measurement.

Teaching-Learning Process

The purpose of classroom teaching is to influence pupil behaviour in the desired direction. The desired direction is guided by the educational objectives formulated by the school and the teacher. The teacher first of all, must be conscious of the goals and aims of education. More specifically, the teacher must formulate instructional objectives for various lessons-id units in the systematized and rearranged syllabus in a subject of study. Secondly, the teacher should be in a position to construct effective learning experiences on the basis of student learning and the modes of effective communication channels. Finally, the teacher will determine the extent to which these objectives are being achieved.

Hence, three major elements in the education process are objectives, learning experiences and learner appraisal. Representation of Educational Process The above representation is a dynamic one and shows interaction among three major elements as she-by directional arrows. Objectives refer to one's intention of desired behaviour that letters should acquire. The term learning experiences, refers to those activities and experiences that the learners undergo in order to acquire the desired behaviours.

The teacher plays an important role in providing learning experiences. Learning experiences involve interaction of students and content with the help of a teacher. The teacher uses various teaching methods and techniques for providing learning experiences to the learner. These learning experiences lead to behavioural changes among learners. So, learning involves modification in the behaviour of a learner through learning experiences. In order that there may be an appreciable learning on the part of students, it is important that teaching must be effective.

The teacher must provide situations for close interaction of students with content by using appropriate teaching methods and techniques. Hence effective teaching leads to successful learning experiences. Besides teaching, the learning experiences can also be brought about through a number of ways such as the library, laboratory readings, radio, films, film strips, science clubs, field trips or such other learning situations in real life. Learned appraisal is concerned with ascertaining the extent to which the objectives have been met.

The representation of the educational process shows the linking of each element with each of the other. Let us explain the linkage of three major elements of educational process.

Begging with objectives, the arrow pointing to learning experiences indicates that objectives serve as a guide for the selection or creation of learning experiences.

For example, if a geometry course is aimed at developing deductive thinking abilities in learners, then experiences require work other than geometry content. This may include home assignment I to work on newspaper editorials, advertisements and also individual projects. The point is that Need, Concept and the nature of one's objectives will be an important determinant of the learning experiences Characteristics of Evaluation that constitute the operational programme.

The arrow pointing from objectives to learner appraisal indicates that the primary focus of appraisal is on gathering evidence on the extent to which the objectives of the programme have been attained. Just as objectives provide specification for establishment of learning experiences, They also furnish specifications for learner appraisal.

For example, the development of deductive thinking among students, might require in its appraisal of learning, the evidence regarding students' proficiency to apply deductive principles to the analysis of a variety of material in life situations, which may be outside the field of geometry. Now, the arrow pointing from learning experiences to learner appraisal is indicative of the fact that learning experiences, provide examples for the development of appraisal tasks.

The objectives that the students are engaged in, during the learning phase of the programme, should furnish ideas for appraisal situations. Thus, the arrow pointing from learning experiences to learner appraisal, indicates that learning experiences furnish ideas and suggestions for learner appraisal. The appraisal task may not be identical but contain an element of novelty for the learner.

The two arrows pointing from learner appraisal to objectives and to learning experiences are especially important. In the case of the former, the arrow signifies that appraisal procedures should furnish information about the extent to which the objectives are being attained. In addition, appraisal information can furnish valuable information that may result in the modification of some objectives and the elimination of others. The appraisal helps in providing a solution to the following questions: Should the objectives be modified or perhaps eliminated?-Are the objectives realistic for the particular group of learnus?-Are the necessary references available for achieving the objectives? The arrow-pointing from learner appraisal to learning experiences, is suggestive of two important notions. First, it provides information about the extent to which learning experiences appear to be working well.

Hence appraisal procedure can suggest the modification or elimination of learning experiences. A second important idea suggested by the arrow pointing from appraisal to learning experiences is that tasks, experiences and problems developed by evaluation specialist may be suggestive of new learning experiences. The incorporation of moral and imaginative appraisal materials into the learning phase of a programme has contributed significantly to the improvement of learning experiences. The last arrow, which points from learning experiences to objectives, denotes that learning activities can result in encounters involving teachers, learners and learning materials which in turn may suggest new objectives.

Role of Evaluation

Evaluation plays an enormous role in the teaching-learning process. In learning, it contributes to formulation of objectives, designing of learning experiences and assessment of learner performance. Besides this, it is very useful to bring improvement in teaching and curriculum. It provides accountability to the society, parents, and to the education system. Let us discuss its uses briefly.

- *Teaching:* Evaluation is concerned with assessing the effectiveness of teaching, teaching strategies, methods to techniques. It provides feedback to the teachers about their teaching and the learners about their learning.
- *Curriculum:* The improvement in courses curriculum, texts and teaching materials is brought about with the help of evaluation.

Evaluation in Teaching

- *Society:* Evaluation provides accountability to society in terms of the demands and Learning Process requirements of the employment market.
- *Parents:* Evaluation mainly manifests itself in a perceived need for regular reporting to parents.

In brief, evaluation is a very important requirement for the education system. It is various purposes in systems of education like quality control in education, selection entrance to a higher grade or tertiary level. It also helps one to take decisions about success in specific future activities and provides guidance to further studies and occupation. Some of the educationists view evaluation virtually synonymous with what was previously defined as learner appraisal, but evaluation has an expanded role. It plays an effective role in questioning or challenging the objectives. This does not mean that one can loosely criticise programme objectives. One should question or challenge programme objectives only after careful study of the relationship between a programme's objectives and the need for which the programme was designed.

Need and Importance of Evaluation

Evaluation is inevitable in teaching-learning process. It is as inevitable in classroom teaching as it is in all fields of activity when judgements need to be made, however simple or complex the consideration involved. All of us are well aware, that during the course of a school day, teachers, principals and other school personnel make many decisions about students and help them to make many decisions for themselves. Effective decision making process involves evaluation. For example, the division of students into various categories, or ranks within the total group, involves measurement of their achievement and interpretation of these. The need of evaluation is so intrinsic to the teaching-learning situation that even hasty consideration seems to indicate the advantages of a systematic use of planned evaluation. Evaluation helps teachers to make better evaluative judgements. All of us are aware that we carry out activities in various aspects of teaching-learning process like:

- fulfil classroom objectives
- diagnose learning difficulties of students
- determine readiness for new learning experiences
- form students' classroom groups for special activities
- assist students in their problems of adjustment
- prepare reports of pupils' progress.

In all these activities, we cannot escape making' evaluative judgements. Decisions must be made and action must be taken. The more accurately we judge our pupils, the more effective we will be in directing their learning. The understanding of the principles and procedures of evaluation is very much needed in making more intelligent decisions in directing pupils progress towards, worthwise educational goals.

Definition of Evaluation

Different authors have different notions of educational evaluation. These sometimes dissimilar views are due to the varied training and background of the writers in terms of their profession, concerned with different aspects of the education process. Perhaps the most extended definition of evaluation has been supplied by C.E.Beeby (1977). who described evaluation as "the systematic collection and interpretation of evidence leading as a part of process do a judgement of value with a view to action."

In this definition, there are the following four key elements:

i) systematic collection of evidence

ii) its interpretation

iii) judgement of value.

Let us discuss the importance of each element in defining evaluation. The first element 'systematic collection' implies that whatever information is gathered, should be acquired in a systematic and planned way with some degree of precision. The second element in Beeby's definition, 'interpretation of evidence' is a critical aspect of the evaluation process. The mere collection of evidence does not by itself constitute evaluation work.

The information gathered for the evaluation of an educational programme must be carefully interpreted. Sometimes, uninterpreted evidence is often presented to indicate the presence (or absence) of quality in an educational venture. For example, high dropout rates are frequently cited as indications of failure of educational programmes, However, these are indicators of failure in only some cases, not all. There may be good reasons for dropout of educational programmes like certain personal problems of finding good jobs. These reasons in no way reflect on the programme.

In some cases, dropping out of an educational programme may indicate that the programme has been successful. For example, in a two year programme in computers, it was observed that almost two-third of each entering class filed to complete the two year programme. On closer examination it was found that mast of the dropouts after one year were offered good jobs by companies. The supervisors of companies felt that the one year of training was not only more than adequate for entry and second level positions but provided the foundation for further advancement. Under such circumstances, the dropout rate before programme completion was no indication of a programme failure or deficiency.

The third element of Beeby's definition, judgement of value takes evaluation far beyond the level of mere description of what is happening in an educational enterprise, but requires judgements about the worth of an educational endeavour. Thus, evaluation not only involves gathering and interpreting information about how well an educational programme is succeeding in reaching its goals but judgements about the goals themselves: It involves questions about how well a programme is helping to meet larger educational goals.

The lady element of Beeby's definition, "with a view to action", introduces the distinction between an undertaking that results in a judgement of value with no specific reference to action (conclusion-oriented) and one that is deliberately undertaken for the sake of future action (decision-oriented). Educational evaluation is clearly decision-oriented and is undertaken with the intention that some action will take place as a result. It is intended to lead to better Policies and practices in education.

Characteristics of Good Evaluation

Having defined evaluation, 'let us turn own attention to the basic features that should characterise a 'good' evaluation. Evaluation should, ideally, be valid, reliable, practicable, fair and useful. Let us now discuss these one by one. Validity A valid evaluation is one which actually tests what is sets out to test i.e., one which actually measures the behaviour described by the objective(s), under scrutiny. Obviously, no one would deliberately construct an evaluation item to test irrelevant material but very often non-I valid test items are in fact used e.g. questions that are intended to test all of factual material but which actually test the candidate's powers of reasoning, or questions which assume a level of pre-knowledge that the candidates do not necessarily possess.

We see that validity related problems are common weakness of many of the widely used test items. For example, a simple science question given to school children ('Name the products of the combustion of carbon in an adequate supply of oxygen') produces a much higher number of correct answers when the world combustion is replaced 9 'burning'. This shows that the original question has problems of validity because it is to some extent, testing language and vocabulary skills other than the basic science involved.

Evaluation in Teaching: Practicability Learning Process Evaluation procedure should be realistic, practical and efficient in tern of their cost, time taken and ease of application. It may be an ideal procedure of evaluation but may not be put into practice. This is not to be encouraged. For example, in practical examination of students, it may be convenient to assign different experiments instead of assigning one experiment to all students. By doing this, the problem of having various self apparatus for conducting one experiment can be avoided, but this may not be practicab!e. Fairness Evaluation must be fair to all students. This can be possible by accurate reflecting of range of expected behaviours as desired by the course objectives. To keep fairness in evaluation, it is also desired that students should know exactly how they are to be evaluated. This means that students should be provided information about evaluation such as nature of the materials on which they are to be examined (i.e., Context and Objectives), the form and structure of the examination, length of the examination and the value (in terms of marks) of each component of the course.

A Evaluation should also be use for students. Feedback from evaluation must be made available to the students and help them to prove their current strengths and weaknesses. By knowing their strength and weakness, students can think of further improvement. Evaluation should suggest all the needful requirements for their improvement. The requirements may be in tern of improvement in the content to be taught, teaching methods and style of learning. Hence, evaluation is very useful in diagnosing weakness and remedying them

Evaluation, Assessment and Measurement

Evaluation, particularly educational evaluation, is a series of activities that are designed to measure the effectiveness of the teaching-learning system as a whole. We are already familiar with the fact that the teaching-learning process involves interaction of three major elements i.e., objectives, learning experiences and learner appraisal. Evaluation takes care of all the interactive aspects of three major elements i.e., the whole teaching-learning system. It can be put in the following simple form as suggested by Mary Thorpe (1980).

"Evaluation is the collection, analysis and interpretation of information about any aspect of Need, Concept and a programme of education, as part of a recognised process of judging its effectiveness, its characteristics of Evaluation efficiency and any other outcomes it may have." The above definition offers the following:

i) Evaluation is not just another word for assessment. The quality of our learners' learning may well be one of the outcomes we need to evaluate. But many other factors may be equally worth looking at.

ii) 'Any other outcomes' reminds us that evaluation should be capable of picking up the unexpected e.g. unwanted side effects or interesting new possibilities.

iii) 'By recognised process', it means that evaluation needs to be systematic, planned and openly discussed. It is not just keeping records or writing a final report.

iv) It is a public commitment to purposeful enquiry.

As we have already discussed, evaluation according to Beeby's definition is "the systematic collection and interpretation of evidence leading as a part of process to a judgement of value with a view to action." (Beeby, 1977).

Assessment

By assessment, we mean the processes and instruments that are designed to measure the learner's achievement, when learners are engaged in an instructional programme of one sort or another.

It is concerned with ascertaining the extent to which the objectives of the programme have been met. The term assessment is often used interchangeably with the terms evaluation and measurement.

However, assessment has a narrower meaning than evaluation but a broader meaning than measurement. In its derivation, the word assess means "to sit beside" or "to assist the judge". It, therefore, seems appropriate in evaluation studies to limit the term assessment to the process of gathering the data and fashioning them into an interpretable form; judgement can then be made on the basis of this assessment.

Let us take an example of testing of school children by Secondary Board. Tests are administered in reading, writing, science and other academic areas. Based on the information provided by the Secondary Board, educators, citizens and political leaders then make judgements about the effectiveness of the education system. Assessment the, as we define it, precedes the final decision making stage in evaluation e.g., the decision to continue, or terminate an educational programme.

Measurement

It is mainly concerned with collection or gathering of data e.g. students' scores in an examination. It is an act or process of measuring physical properties of objects such as length and mass. Similarly, in behavioural sciences, it is concerned with measurement of psychological characteristics such as neuroticism, and attitudes towards various phenomena. The measurement involves assigning a score on a given task performed by the learner e.g., 33/50 i.e., thirty three out of fifty.

Thus, we find that evaluation involves assessment and measurement. It is a wider and more inclusive term than assessment and measurement. It can be represented as: Learning Process Hence evaluation process is quite comprehensive and it is very much desired for elective teaching and learning. Let us complain the need and use of some of terms commonly used in the context of evaluation in our schools. This term is used in schools to find out the growth of students in terms of their scholastic achievement. The examinations are conducted at different stages throughout the year. Let us briefly discuss them.

Periodic Tests: These are used to assess the scholastic achievement of children are providing instruction for a specified period. The period may be one or two months. Some schools also call these periodic tests, Monthly tests. The purpose of these tests is two fold; a) to provide feedback to children and teachers about the achievement of children. b) to help children to improving their weaknesses, These test have formative failure of evaluation and are administered periodically.

Half-yearly Examination: This type of examination is conducted after completion of half of the session. It assess the scholastic aspect of the child. It also takes in to account the achievement of children in the periodic test. Its purpose is also two-fold i.e. assessing the performance and improving upon the weakness of the child. Half-yearly examination does not nicali end of a part of the syllabus, not to be tested again.

Test: It provides a situation or a series of situations to students to find out their performance in terms of scores. The scores are known as marks. The tool used to test the performance is ill lerlus of a set of questions called, Question Paper. These tests are also called achievement tests as they concentrate mainly on the achievement of the child. Assessment of non-scholastic its acts of students.

Rating Scale: To assess the social or land personal qualities of students like regularity, discipline, the habit of cleanliness, interests and attitude etc., the teacher uses a rating scale. The rating may be done on a different number of points e.g., three points or five points depending upon the requirement of the teacher. Criteria for rating every activity maybe prepared in a three or five or any other point scale and separate proforma may be evolved for each activity. Marks obtained by each student on the basis of the criteria may be entered in the column provided for them. These marks may be added and the average calculated.

UNIT-IV

Problems of Primary Education and its Remedies

Problems of Wastage and Stagnation

Inspite of the substantial accomplishments since Independence, India has the dubious distinction of having the largest number of illiterates and out-of-school children in the world-30 per cent of the world's adult illiterates and 21.87 per cent of out-of-school children. About 19 to 24 million children in the age group 6-14 are out of school of whom about 60 per cent are girls; about 121.3 million are adult illiterates in the age group 15-35 of whom 62 per cent are women. Given the demographic pressure the numbers are likely to increase further.

The benefits of investing in basic education, both for its intrinsic value in enhancing human capabilities, as well for its instrumental worth in contributing to social development and economic growth, greater efficiency and better functioning of democratic institutions are well established. Of equal significance is the ability of education to empower women and men to acquire greater control over the circumstances that dominate their lives.

It is now recognised that fertility regulation cannot be a matter of mere promotion of contraception but has to strongly promote the socio-economic factors which strongly influence fertility behaviour such as female literacy and education. The low level of social indicators such as fertility rates, Infant Mortality Rate (IMR), sex ratio are related to the failure to achieve Universalisation of Elementary Education (UEE). If the East Asian experience has any relevance the criticality of UEE for the economic reform process cannot be over emphasised.

It is evident from the above that UEE has strong regional and gender dimensions. The Indian experience encompasses the entire Third World experience. At one end we have states such as Kerala which has achieved universal literacy as well as UEE in terms of school participation-though not in terms of learning achievement-with social indicators as good as the best among the Third World, if not the Scandinavian countries. On the other extreme we have states like UP, Bihar, Orissa and MP with indicators as worse as Sub Saharan Africa. To the extent that gender disparity is pronounced UEE is the problem of the girl child.

Teacher competence, motivation and performance are areas which require greater attention. These are crucial inputs in UEE. Whatever policies may be laid down, in the ultimate analysis, these have to be interpreted and implemented by teachers, as much through their personal example as through teaching-learning process. Except in a few places where the ethos of Panchayati Raj system has been internalised the school remains rather isolated from the local community.

Experience in India and elsewhere has established that universal participation cannot be delinked from the operations of quality and relevance of education and from learning achievement. The challenge before the nation is to enhance universal participation and universal achievement of certain minimum levels of learning. In terms of numbers alone this is the greatest challenge that human society had ever faced-more so if one were to adhere to the goal set up in the National Policy on Education, 1986 of universalising elementary education before the commencement of the twenty-first century.

Shortfalls

Inadequate Access: Notwithstanding massive expansion of elementary schools, studies have indicated that a large number of children in the age group of 6-14 years are still out of school. According to the available information, the estimated number of out of school children is 6.3 crore. The majority of out of school children aria girls and children belonging to SCs and STs in rural areas;. The Sixth All India Educational Survey (1993) has shown that there are still 11574 school less rural habitations in the country. 8th Five Year Plan had envisaged that the ratio of upper primary schools to primary schools will be improved from the existing 1:4 to 1:2. However, there has been marginal improvement and the ratio was 1:3.45 in 1995-96.

Low Participation and High Drop-out Rates: In order to improve retention, it was targeted that drop out rates will be reduced to 20% in case of primary classes and 40% in case of upper primary classes. However, this does not seem to be happening. The drop out rates are still high at 36.3% for primary school children and 52.7% for upper primary classes in 1994-95. Various reasons for children dropping out from schools are given. These include socioeconomic and cultural factors, lack of access to schools, uninspiring school environment etc. The 42nd round of National Sample Survey (1986-87) provides reason-wise analysis of distribution of drop-outs as shown in Table below:-

Table: Percentage Distribution of Drop-outs by Reason for Discontinuance

Reason for Discontinuance	Rural		Urban	
	Male	Female	Male	Female
Not interested in education/further study	26.6	33.3	23.6	28.5
Participated in household economic activities	26.8	9.4	22.8	6.7
Other economic reasons	20.6	15.0	24.2	15.4
Domestic chores	2.0	14.3	2.2	15.9
Failure	18.4	16.7	21.3	18.8
Others	5.6	11.5	6.0	14.7
All	100.0	100.0	100.0	100.0

While no systematic study to analyse reasons; of high drop outs has been done in the recent past, it is believed that the above analysis of the 42nd ROUND of National Survey is still valid. The achievements in regard to drop out rates reinforce this view. More rigorous efforts are required to be made with community participation to remedy causes such as "not interested in education/further study".

Unsatisfactory Levels of Learning: Studies have shown that the levels of learner achievement are far from satisfactory The most recent series of studies in this regard were undertaken under the DPEP These studies have selected educationally backward districts only and hence the results ought riot to be, generalised for the whole country However, the studies conducted in all the DPEP States have pointed to the poor academic performance of children.

What is surprising is that even educationally advanced States experience poor performance of children at primary levels. Therefore, low learner achievement of primary school children is emerging as an issue almost uniformly applicable to all regions of the country.

Various school related factors contributing to the low levels of achievement of primary school children have been identified. These factors include school facilities, teacher competency and internal management of schools. During the 8th Plan, schemes were initiated to address issues pertaining to school facilities and teacher competency The introduction of OB scheme addresses the former set of issues, while the scheme of establishment of DIETs addresses the latter set of issues.

However, little effort has been made to improve the internal efficiency and functioning of the schools. Local level organisational arrangements like Village Education Committees, Parent Teacher Association and the local bodies may be in a posit on to play an important role to make the schools functional. Such school based arrangements to support school management and quality improvement programmes needs to be created, operationalised and strengthened during the IX Plan.

Gender, Caste and Regional Disparities: Caste and regional disparities in elementary education are conspicuous. Gender disparities are clearly indicated in expansion of primary and upper Primary school facilities. The GER for girls in Classes I-V in 1995-96 was 93.3% as against 114.5% for boys. More significantly, this ratio did not fall below 75% for boys in any State, whereas for girls it varied from about 50% upwards. For classes VI-VIII, the GER was 79.5% for boys and 54.9% in case of girls. The difference in rural areas is even more conspicuous. No doubt, as a result of the affirmative policies of the Government, the enrolment of SCs/STs is now more or less in proportion to their respective shares in the population at the primary level. However, the drop outs in these groups, though declining over the years, are significantly large. Gender disparities are very conspicuous among SCs and STs also.

According to the available information, 75% of the estimated out of school children are believed to be in educationally backward States namely, Andhra Pradesh, Assam, Bihar, J&K, Madhya Pradesh, Orissa, Rajasthan, Uttar Pradesh, West Bengal and Arunachal Pradesh. Enrolment ratios are lower and drop out rates are higher both at primary and upper primary levels in all these States, except West Bengal as indicated in Table below:-

Enrolment Ratio and Drop-out Rates of Educationally Backward States

Sl. No.	Name of the State	Enrolment ratio (in 1995-96)			Drop out rates (in 1993-94)		
		Boys	**Girls**	**Total**	**Boys**	**Girls**	**Total**
1.	Andhra Pradesh						
	Primary	99.6	83.9	94.9	42.5	41.8	42.2
	Upper Primary	57.3	41.8	49.7	59.9	66.5	62.8
2.	Assam						
	Primary	133.4	124.0	128.0	38.6	39.6	39.1
	Upper Primary	91.6	65.9	79.1	63.8	71.8	67.6
3.	Bihar						
	Primary	93.0	55.4	75.1	61.9	66.2	63.4
	Upper Primary	47.5	21.9	35.3	76.7	82.7	78.7

Some of Important Observations

The Indian education system is facing serious challenges especially at the elementary education level. These include universal access to an infrastructure of comparable quality, improving retention, efficiency and effectiveness of the schools. While in the recent years, there has been a considerable emphasis on decentralised management and involvement of community in micro planning; the outcome is quite mixed one. This is partly due to the inadequate planning and lack of managerial and professional competencies at various levels. At the national level, broad perspective on various sub-sectors is developed.

The management, professional and financial support is provided to the state governments and the districts for implementation of various reform programs in the form of centrally sponsored schemes. Among other things, their successful implementation is contingent upon the availability of timely, comprehensive and up-to-date educational statistics on key performance indicators.

The review of official educational statistics reveals serious gaps in terms of coverage, quality of data, comprehensiveness and their availability in the desired form at the appropriate time.

For example, the educational statistics published by the MHRD do not include complete information on the number of children attending various types of institutions and program funded by the government. These include Non-Formal Education Centres, Alternative Schools and other such facilities. Similarly, a large number of unrecognised schools have come up in various parts of the country and no data is available on their number and enrolment. Similar concerns prevail for the database on educational financing, institutional infrastructure, mobility and estimation of unit costs. The published educational statistics released by the MHRD do not even recognise these limitations. Therefore, the planning and management of education at the national and state level suffers from many limitations and inadequacies and does not fully reflect the ground level reality.

Weak monitoring and evaluation systems are also the consequence of lop sided approach to planning and management of education. The norm based educational planning thus faces an uncertain future.

Past few years have also witnessed a significant expansion of the alternative modes of education including the proliferation of unrecognised schools even at the primary stage. Between 1986 and 1993, the enrolment in private aided schools (primary classes) increased at a compound growth rate of 9.5% per annum. The corresponding increase in government/local body schools was merely 1.4% per annum. As a result, the share of enrolment of private unaided schools in primary classes increased from 5.1% in 1986 and 8.6% in 1993. The pyramid of coverage of private education is narrow at the bottom and wide at the apex. Due to the lack of serious policy imperatives, the elementary education system shows the signs of a dual system-one set of schools meant for the poor and those who are unable to pay for quality education, the other catering to the requirements for quality education involving high user costs. The former is especially government supported and the latter is in the form of private initiatives. Despite the positive impact of private schools, the government policy for their regulation/control is not clearly spelt out.

Historically, successive phases of regulation and deregulation of private sector were attempted with mixed outcomes. Recently conducted achievements studies reinforce the perpetuation of differential access to quality schooling and persistence of gender and social gaps in the levels of achievement.

Focus on equity and social justice is important for developing country like India, where nearly 40% of its population still continues to live below the poverty line. The proportion of poor living in some educationally backward states is even higher than the national average. The real challenge to the success of educational reforms lies in these areas. The vicious circle of underdevelopment comprises of lack of access to basic services like health, nutrition, education and employment. Where and how to break this vicious cycle is an issue for the development planners. A new path for the development trajectory has to be chartered.

The recent evidence from NSSO and other studies demonstrates that a large proportion of children are attending private unrecognised primary schools. This proportion is highest in Haryana (18.7%) and is followed by Punjab (15.5%), Uttar Pradesh (10%) and Bihar (9.2%). The all India average share of children enrolled in unrecognised schools at primary stage was 4.8% as compared to 2.6% for upper primary classes. The rural urban differentials were striking in almost all the states. At the national level, some decline in Class I enrolment was observed in the last 3-5 years. This could be due to the shift of children from formal to non-formal or to other modes of education including unrecognised schools. It is paradoxical that the states with high proportion of children attending unrecognised schools are from both the economically advanced regions of Punjab and Haryana as well as from the economically poor regions of Uttar Pradesh and Bihar. Some states like Maharashtra have exercised strict controls on the functioning of unrecognized institutions.

Persons in 5-24 years age group belonging to relatively poor families have high proportion of non-attendance and low participation as compared to those belonging to the top 20% fractile group. The children belonging to high-income families stay longer in the educational system whereas the children from low income brackets dropout early. Therefore, the chances are that few children belonging to poor families would be enrolled and those enrolled are likely to exit early as compared to the children belonging to the upper strata of the society.

For the purpose of the present study, a special survey of the unrecognized primary schools was conducted in four districts of Haryana to investigate their enrolment profile, teacher characteristics and availability of infrastructure and other facilities. The survey covered 878 unrecognised schools in 13 blocks of the selected districts. The fieldwork was conducted with the help of BRC and CRC coordinators during early 1999. Data for the recognised schools in the same blocks was obtained from DISE. There were 1242 recognised schools in the sample study area.

The unrecognised schools are smaller in size but have a lower PTR and perhaps a lower per unit institutional cost as compared to the government schools. This is possible due to the recruitment of large number of teachers at very low wages. Many teachers were even unqualified and untrained. In terms of the availability of infrastructure facilities, the unrecognised schools are better as far as student classroom ratio, availability of drinking water and toilet facilities is concerned. The private schools were found to be ill equipped as far as the availability of library book, reference book, charts teaching-learning materials were concerned. There is no system of periodic teacher training for the teachers working in these schools.

Although primary education is free in all government and local body schools, not many parents opt to send their children to the schools. The NSS data showed that only 54.1% of children attending primary classes received free education in Haryana. The proportion of children receiving free education was lowest in the urban areas (13.6%). Unrecognised schools charge fee ranging from Rs. 30 per month to Rs. 60 per month. A few schools charged exorbitant fee, ranging from Rs. 1500-2500 per month. The other household costs were also substantial even for the poor people.

A shift away from the government schools is discernible as the intake at Grade I has shown declining trends in the recent years. This can happen only due to two reasons. First, due to decline in the birth rate and secondly as a consequence of the structural shift in enrolment share of various modes of education. The latter is likely to be the major factor contributing to the decline of Grade I enrolment in the recent years. Considerable duplication/overlapping in enrolment among the government, NFE and the private unrecognised schools was also identified. It was not possible to estimate the proportion of overlapping enrolment from the school records. A household survey would be required to estimate the fictitious/duplicate and overlapping enrolment.

It is estimated that in the study area, the number of unrecognised schools is doubling every five years. If the trend continues, the number of unrecognized schools would be roughly 1.5-2.5 times the number of government/local body primary schools. The rapid increase in the demand for private education is the result of a number of factors. While quality can be defined in different ways, at the primary stage it is related to achievement in the public examination. The most important among these are the demand for quality education, dissatisfaction with the performance of government schools and the ability of the parents to pay for the cost of quality education, especially when the average household income tends to rise. Some teachers mentioned that many parents do not want to tell others that their children study in government schools.

The household expenditure on primary education based on the NSS survey was also analysed. A negative association was observed between the poverty ratio and the average per student expenditure at primary stage. Wide variations in per student expenditure were observed between rural and urban areas. The study did not collect any data on the levels of achievements and learning outcomes of the learners in unrecognised schools. However, with few exceptions, the achievement studies conducted under DPEP show that the achievement levels of learners from private schools are generally higher than those from the government schools. In terms of attendance and school functioning, both the teachers and the students regularly attend the unrecognised schools. The attendance rates in unrecognised schools were much higher as compared to the government schools.

The study has many implications for the policy towards the role of private sectors in the development of elementary education. So far, the government has controlled the entry/exist points for this sector and other options remain unexplored particularly with a view to develop partnership and not to promote the perpetuation of a dual system. This calls for a perceptible change in the attitude and policy towards private education. While it is recognised that commercialisation of education should be discouraged, but at the same time, these institutions should be able to generate some surplus which can be further invested to provide support to the deserving learners. It is also important that the role of private sector should be seen as a supplementary to that of the government and not as a substitute. There are many options for the involvement of private sector, especially if the focus shift to performance and output related indicators. Quality assurance is an important dimension of primary education and is significant not only for the private but also for the government schools. The dividing line should not be drawn on the basis of school management but related to the school performance, efficiency and effectiveness. The recent initiative in the form of SSA of the central government must be based on the above considerations, otherwise institutional reforms will not be able to achieve much. If the real school choice is to be provided to be parents/ learners, it must be a choice that can be exercised effectively.

Single Teacher Schools—Improper Infrastructure—Financial Problems of the Students—Rural Class Teaching

The destiny of India is now being shaped in her classrooms—Education Commission, 1964-66

This is how the Education Commission described the role of education in social and economic transformation of India. While the development planners rightly recognized that expansion of educational facilities has to be accompanied with significant improvements in quality and relevance of education at all levels, the outcome is quite disappointing. At the international level, the development experience in social sectors shows that a literate society has enormous gains over an illiterate society and no illiterate society has ever been able to modernize and progress. We are now transiting to a knowledge society where the quality and relevance of education would play a crucial role in economic development. Poor quality of teaching learning and systemic level inefficiencies affect the learners as well the society in may ways. The long-term implications include lower productivity levels of the perspective workforce, resistance to modernization and perpetuation of inefficient production systems where cost benefit ratio adversely affect the economic sustainability of production processes.

Concerns for Quality of Education

As far as the provision of access and coverage is concerned, India today boasts of its educational system being the second largest in the world. It consists of nearly 610 thousand primary and 185 thousand upper primary schools, about a quarter million nonformal education centres, about 1.87 million teachers and 110 million students study in primary classes in the recognized schools (1997-98).

As per 1991 Census estimates there were about 115.6 million children in primary school going age group in the country. The latest educational statistics indicate a GER of 89.7 percent for primary classes (81.2 percent being for girls and 97.7 percent for boys). The number of students in primary classes in India is larger than the total population of the neighbouring Bangladesh. No doubt, the system can claim it to be one of the largest, but it can not make similar claims for efficiency, quality and achievement of learners?

Various five years plans incorporated programs and strategies based on periodic assessment of the progress of education by the Ministry of Education, Commissions and Committees appointed by the central and state governments. The National Policy on Education (NPE), 1986 and the revised NPE, 1992, reiterated the urgency to address the quality concerns in schools education on priority basis. Quality can not improve by itself.

It requires reforms in teacher training; improvements in the facilities and infrastructure in schools; teachers' motivation; and a change in the style of teaching to make it attractive to the students. However, in actual practice, there has always been a trade-off between quality and quantity, in favour of the latter. This not only affected the internal efficiency of the educational system but also resulted in a situation where only a few graduates of the school and higher education system could attain the expected skills and competencies. The labour market policies and predominance of public sector employment opportunities did not put enough pressure on the educational systems to change as the degree was more important than the acquired knowledge and skills. The gap between the planned and the realized goals of education continues be so large that even the basis of educational planning and underlying assumptions can be easily challenged.

The basic educational planning models have gone off the trajectory both at the central as well in the states. Bringing it back on the tracks remains a serious challenge for the development planners. The interstate and intra-state variations in school facilities, quality of teachers and learning outcome are large and so are social and economic conditions of the areas where the primary schools operate. While indicators to measure the access, retention and internal efficiency of the educational system in terms of participation rate, accessibility, repetition rates, promotion rates, dropout rates and input-output ratio have been developed, but little information is available about the learners' achievement of cognitive and non-cognitive competencies. Under the no detention policy, followed by most of the states, a child is not even tested on the learning outcomes for many years after entering the school. The no detention policy prohibits the use of examinations in first few years of schooling. The proposed system of continuous and comprehensive evaluation is yet to be implemented on sustainable basis. Reforms in the quality of education have not received serious attention of many states.

Defining Quality of Education

Assessment may be defined as 'any method used to understand the current knowledge that a student possesses. The idea of current knowledge implies that what a student knows is always changing and that we can make judgment about student achievement through comparison over a period of time. Good assessment techniques provide accurate estimates of student performance and enables teachers and decision-makers to make appropriate decisions. The current debate about the determinants of student achievement, specifically the contributing effect of teacher variables, has its origin primarily in the findings of the Coleman Report (1966). In developing countries, the examination results are often used as a proxy for the quality of education. However, such a method is fraught with great problems, as the examination system is limited in scope and coverage as far as learning is concerned. The research has established that acquiring both cognitive and non-cognitive competencies are necessary for a child's overall development. However, most of the research in learning achievement has focused on the assessment of cognitive skills acquired by the students. An equally reliable measure of quality of education is whether pupils are learning effectively, improving their knowledge, skills and abilities; widening their experience and growing socially and morally or not. Ability to work with others, readiness to accept responsibility and to work for public good are highly praised characteristics among school leavers. But assessment tools do not test for such skills.

While there is no consensus among educationists regarding the definition of the quality in education but there are several ways of measuring quality in education. In the context of school effectiveness, the concept of quality is linked to the efficiency of teaching learning processes. Quality is a relative concept and not something that is absolute. One useful approach could be to select a range of educational indicators that are explicit and measurable representing various facets of quality.

The quality of education and its determinants remain a topic of interest since the beginning of formal education. It is possible to develop indicators to measure learning along important dimensions, closely related to the curriculum, both in standardized assessment instruments and in alternative for ms of assessment. Non standardized assessment refers to the traditional form of assessment by teachers on regular basis through classroom interaction, questions, assignment of homework and other such techniques. The results of such assessment may be accurate or faulty, depending upon the teachers' skill as a judge of various indicators and their applicability in a given situation. Standardized tests have prove d useful in comparing, generalizing and indicating levels of attainment based on pre-defined standards. It is assumed that levels of learners' achievement are assessed at best through standardized achievement tests. Since the beginning of sixties, the measurement of students' academic performance on regular basis has been an ongoing effort in the advanced countries. Based on these results policy level interventions are made so that the deficiencies in learners achievement can be overcome. In India, the large scale achievement studies were conducted only in the recent years for primary education. The methods and tools for assessing learning outcome at other levels of education are yet to be put in place. The country is yet to evolve a policy for periodic collection and analysis of learners achievement data and using it for monitoring the quality of education at various levels. Considerable research is needed to improve the achievement testing methodology, achievement tests and tools of analysis. The analysis and feedback from achievement studies must be used for curriculum reforms and for restructuring of teacher training contents and methodology of training. In the last few years, international organizations like the World Bank, UNICEF, UNESCO and UNDP have produced valuable studies on educational assessment and measurement. The Fourth Survey on Research in Education in India (Buch, 1991) identified many studies, essentially at the M.Phil. and Ph.D. level, addressed to the achievement of primary school children. These researches are more of conceptual nature and their use in policy planning was practically nil.

Shukla (1994) conducted another study on about 66,000 students to find out the level of attainment of primary school children in 25 states/UTs. Among other things, the study showed different patterns of educational attainment in different states. Pupil's achievement was related to the education of the father and the facility for learning and educational environment at home. Considerable research evidence is available on the factors affecting the learning outcomes. While a study by Heyneman and Loxley (1982) showed that 90 percent of variance in students science achievement is explained by school and teacher variables and only a small proportion by home related factors, the study by Kingdon (1998) shows that home background and school influence are both important to students achievement in India.

Jangira (1994), while synthesizing the results of Baseline Assessment Studies of the DPEP states found that student's performance in reading and arithmetic was low. There was a marked difference in achievement levels among states and between schools. In a study conducted in Karnataka, covering 2,598 class IV learners and 442 teachers, it was observed that the learning achievements are not significantly different between rural and urban schools. However, a significant difference was observed among the schools belonging to different management agencies (Aggarwal, 1995a). Similar studies were also conducted in many states as a part of the DPEP baseline learners' studies. The findings of the study on Kerala covering 3,089 class IV learners and 502 teachers suggests that the type of management of the school is not an influencing factor in learning achievement. The study found that the level of school infrastructure and variations in the availability of teaching-learning materials is not clearly related to learning achievement (Varghese, 1994).

Learners Achievement and Quality of Education

The interest among developing and developed countries to compare information and experience about achievement in terms of both the standards which are prescribed and the standards that are actually achieved by the learners is indicated by the growing number of countries participating in the cross-national comparative studies on learning achievement. At the international level, the International Evaluation Agency (IEA) has developed achievement tests which are administered across the participating countries and used for establishment and comparison of learning outcome of children of specified age groups in developed and developing countries. The OECD has a long tradition of assessing achievement level in various countries and providing comparative statistics.

In addition to the international studies, many countries have also adopted a unique approach for assessing learning outcomes at various levels on regular basis. In France, for example, the focus of external assessment is to provide information on the attainment of individual pupils so that teachers can respond effectively to specific weaknesses or strengths as revealed through assessment studies. In United States, assessment studies have been conducted for a long time and have been used for national assessment and international comparison of learning outcome of American pupils with other developed countries. In England and Wales, all students are assessed at the end of ages 7, 11 and 14.

The information on achievement of pupils is made available to the schools and public. It is considered essential that the public has the right to know about the performance of schools and be able to make comparative judgements between schools. In Ontario, Canada, all grade 3 pupils (8-9 year olds) are assessed on various literacy and numeracy tasks in a comprehensive testing programme. The programme is designed to set benchmarks for achievement at this level. In Australia, some states such as Victoria and New South Wales, test all students of a similar age. The information on performance of pupils is made available to the pupils and schools and not to the public. New South Wales conducted state-wide tests in literacy and numeracy at years 3 and 5 for many years. The common element of all these tests has been to help teachers improve their programmes. From Target to Action, published by the Department of education (UK) provides examples how schools have used the assessment results to monitor the effectiveness of their teaching learning strategies and to set targets for improving their students achievement.

Review of Empirical Research on Achievement

The review of empirical research on learners' assessment shows that there are two distinct phases. The period up to 1990 is characterised as the first phase and the researches and empirical studies undertaken after 1990 fall into the other category. A main characteristic of the empirical studies in the first phase was that these were mainly academic in nature and the administrators did not use their findings for policy reforms.

The present paper examines the studies undertaken after 1990. There was a significant departure during nineties as far as assessment and measurement of learners' achievement is concerned. Earlier studies were confined to small samples and each followed a different sampling design and achievement tests. Therefore the findings were not strictly comparable. Moreover, most of the studies were cross-sectional in nature and at no point of time temporal comparisons were made. Temporal analysis is necessary to understand the dynamics of policy formulation and educational reforms in teaching learning processes. In early nineties, a major initiative to achieve universal primary education came in the form of District Primary Education Programme (DPEP) which has now emerged as a major vehicle for bringing about a qualitative change in primary education. The DPEP model has also been replicated on a large scale through many innovative projects.

Learning Achievement Levels in Delhi

Recently, a study on learning achievement for primary schools in Delhi was conducted by the author. The study covered all types of primary schools/sections in Delhi and was based on a sample of 169 schools. Besides other aspects, the achievement levels in language and mathematics were assessed through competency based tests developed by the NCERT. The overall mean score based on Class I competencies was 80.2 percent for Language and 78.2 percent for Mathematics. The mean score for English and Hindi medium schools was statistically different in mathematics. The mean score for the SC children was 8-10 percent points lower than those of the children belonging to general category. The differences in mean achievement scores due to gender were reflected both in language and mathematics. However, the girls scored much lower in mathematics as compared to the boys. The achievement scores based on class IV competencies were very low as compared to class I mean achievement scores. The gap was large in mathematics as compared to language. The mean score in mathematics for Hindi medium schools was 40.46 percent as compared to 56.5 percent for the mean score in language. The gap between mean score in mathematics and language is considerable and statistically significant. In view of the low achievement scores, the underachievers are large in number. About 50 percent of learners in Hindi medium schools failed to obtain more than 40 percent score in mathematics.

The corresponding share of learners in language was 23 percent. The differences in achievement become more pronounced as one examines disaggregated scores for gender, caste, management and related attributes. Children with pre-primary education in Hindi medium schools achieved 8-10 percentage points more than those who did not have pre-primary education. This corroborates the impression that SC children are deficient in learning outcomes.

Significant differences (15-18 percentage points) in the mean achievement score were also observed between different types of management. The schools managed by MCD reported the lowest mean scores. More than 20 percent children were reportedly scored less than 20 percent in MCD schools. The poor performance of MCD schools is thus a cause of concern. The large differences in the achievement scores between class I and Class IV points to a gap in the quality of teaching learning and classroom interaction processes. While Class I achievement score is based on oral test, the class IV scores were based on the written test. Even within the class IV tests, the performance was poorest in mathematics as compared to language.

It appears that children could understand and express orally but have difficulties in written communication. This has significant bearing on the teaching of language and expression in the form of written text. The achievement levels of children studying in English medium schools were analyzed separately. The mean score was 47.8 percent in mathematics as compared to 49.7 percent for language.

About 38 percent of children failed to score more than 40 percent in mathematics and 24 percent failed to cross this threshold in language. Therefore, the general impression that all is well with English medium schools is not correct. While it is true that their performance is far better than the government schools, but the extent of underachievement is also very high. Within the language, the underachievement is more serious in reading comprehension. This is a clear reflection on the poor quality of classroom teaching learning processes. Based on the detailed analysis presented above, the following issues were identified as far as provision of primary education in Delhi is concerned:

- Inadequate/absence of access to a comparable quality of education.
- Overcrowding in the existing government schools.
- Mismatches between demand and supply of schooling facilities.
- Dilapidated condition of class rooms, particularly those running in rented buildings. Repairs oriented buildings can not be undertaken under Rent Control Act.
- Lack of sanitation and water facilities in old school buildings.
- Excessive reliance on centrally sponsored schemes has also created its own problems. The states seldom initiate programs of educational development at their own initiatives and wait for central government initiatives.
- The educational planning for UEE in the urban context requires special emphasis.

The traditional methods of removing supply side constraints would not succeed in achieving UEE objectives.

Assessment of Learners Achievement in DPEP Districts

The large-scale studies for the DPEP project were conducted in 46 districts covering eight states in 1993/94. Some unique features of achievement studies conducted under DPEP were:

- A common national framework for the design and data collection of baseline and mid-term studies in all districts.
- Use of nationally developed standardised achievement tests in all the states.

- The period of data collection was same for baseline and mid-term assessment studies for all the 42 districts belonging to phase I of the project.
- Provided inputs for the curriculum revision, preparation of new textbooks, teachers' guides and supplementary teaching learning materials.
- Provided inputs for the restructuring of teacher training curriculum as well as the training methodologies.
- The studies brought about an awareness about research based interventions.

Achievement tests were conducted for assessing the levels of learner's achievement of students at the end of Class I and the penultimate class of primary education cycle in mathematics and language based on Class I and Class IIII/IV curriculum. Class II tests were oral in nature. The tests developed by the NCERT for the Primary Education Curriculum Renewal Project were used for DPEP achievement studies. Class IV/V standardised tests were developed by the TSG/NCERT. A total of 24,504 students of class IV/V, 23,056 students of class II and 5,114 teachers were covered under the baseline studies for the phase I districts. The period of reference was 1993-94 academic session. The study suffered from one limitation that it was confined to government schools only. Thus it was not possible to compare the differences in achievement level between children from the private and public schools. Such an analysis is necessary in the present context when the demand for private schooling is increasing exponentially even in smaller rural habitations. The results of the learning assessment studies conducted under DPEP were quite revealing. Letter and word reading are basic skills which require 100 percent mastery for developing further skills. But surprisingly, none of the districts even achieved 80 percent in either of the tests. Like students teachers also found it difficult to handle mathematics questions. A mathematics test conducted on 42 teachers showed that most of them could not even correctly do a question on LCM while 64 percent could not give a correct title to a paragraph in the language comprehension test (NCERT, 1992). The studies also identified that supervision was the weakest link in educational administration. Two third of teachers reported that they did not receive any type of assistance or help from their head teachers and the same proportion mentioned that there was no supervision by the Block education Officers. In Karnataka study, it was found that a significantly large number of teachers were themselves first generation learners. Many teachers covered under the survey were not even properly qualified and did not attend any in-service programme during the five years preceding the survey (Aggarwal, 1995a).

Trends in Learning Achievement

The second round of studies was conducted as a part of the mid-term assessment (MAS) for the 42 phase-I districts. While the MAS used tests different from the one used at the time of BAS, an effort was made to compare the results of the 1993/94 and 1997/98 studies. The MAS data covered 66,831 students, 6,221 teachers and 2068 schools spread over 42 districts belonging to phase I of the DPEP. The important findings of MAS were:

- A comparison of learners' mean score in language (class I competencies) for the BAS and the readministered test under MAS had revealed a mixed picture. In 28 of 42 districts the gains were positive and ranged between 0-36 percent. However, for the remaining 14 districts, the mean score in language was lower by 0-18 percent. In the case of mathematics, 33 out of 42 districts showed positive gains and the remaining nine districts showed a significant decline in mean scores.
- A similar analysis for class III competencies showed that 13 districts out of a total of 15 districts showed positive gains in language test. The decline in the remaining two districts was not significant. The mathematics results indicated that mean score for 11 out of 15 districts showed significant gains.
- The analysis of data for Class IV competencies indicated that the mean scores in language for 18 out of 27 districts showed gains, of them 15 showed statistically significant gains. The decline was more pronounced in

some districts of Madhya Pradesh. Similar trends were observed in the case of mean scores for mathematics.

- The analysis also confirms the general trend that the performance of students in Class I both in language and mathematics was better than their counterparts in class III and IV. This is a matter which has to be seriously examined. This confirms the decline in educational standards as the students move from lower to the higher classes. It also signifies the issues related with the transition from oral to written mode of evaluation. Are the students well prepared for this transition?
- The DPEP goal of reducing the difference in mean achievement score between boys and girls have been accomplished in 40 out of 42 districts in language and 31 out of 42 districts in mathematics. However, similar objectives for the SC/ST population are yet to be achieved.
- The study confirms a moderate effect of teacher training on mean achievement scores. Students' achievement stands positively related to the availability of competency based teaching learning materials.

Inter-district Variations in Mean Achievement Scores: Class I

Perhaps a striking finding of the achievement studies was the large differences in average achievement score between the best performing and the worst performing districts. The mean percentage score in language varied from 44.5 percent for Rewa district in Madhya Pradesh to 85.5 percent for Belgaum district in Karnataka. The minimum and maximum achievement score in mathematics also followed a similar pattern i.e. it varied between 36.5 percent for Guna district to 87.5 percent for the Belgaum district. Thus the mean score for the best district was roughly twice that of the districts having the minimum score.

There was a positive association between the mean percentage score in language and mathematics. The correlation between the two being 0.73. Thus the districts with high achievement level in mathematics also depict high achievement level in language. Therefore, sustained efforts will be required in improving competencies in both the subjects in low performing districts.

Many districts belonging to Madhya Pradesh fall in the category of low achievement districts both in language as well as in mathematics. It is important to note that many of these districts are characterized by high degree of deprivation. The share of SC and ST population in some of these districts is very large. For example, the districts with the second lowest mean score in language had more than 60 percent of its population classified as SC and ST.

Inter-district Variations in Mean Achievement Scores: Class III/IV

The dispersion with regards to achievement scores was similar to that of Grade I competencies. The achievement score in language varies from 30.9 percent for Satna to 67.6 for Raiśen district. Similarly, the mathematics mean score varies from 20.6 for Sehore to 61.3 percent for Dhubri districts. For 32 out of a total of 42 districts, the average score in mathematics was lower than that of language.

How does one explain such a lower performance in mathematics as compared to language? The mean score in language and mathematics are consistently lower in Class III/IV than the corresponding mean score in Class I. Why should the scores decline as pupils move to higher classes?

This is particularly intriguing, as the phenomenon is true for both the subjects. One possible reason could be that class II tests were oral and classes III/IV were written. To what extent the difference could be attributed to the transition from oral to written form of examination?

There were many districts, which performed poorly as far as mathematics was concerned (table 1). One in every three districts has an average score of less than 30 percent in mathematics.

Table 1: Classification of districts by levels of achievement, MAS-1997

Range	Language		Mathematics	
	Class I	Class III/IV	Class I	Class III/IV
Below 30	0	0	0	13
30-40	0	17	2	18
40-50	2	17	2	5
50-60	15	8	14	4
60-70	15	0	10	2
70-80	8	0	11	0
>80	2	0	3	0
Total	**42**	**42**	**42**	**42**

Source: NCERT, 1998.

Achievement Scores: Gender Dimension

It is generally believed that girls are more deprived than the boys. This is well reflected in the historically obtained patterns of educational attainment and levels of literacy. Data has also suggested that the DPEP districts have registered higher growth rate of enrolment for girls as compared to boys. The analysis of enrolment and retention data for the DPEP districts has shown that most of the districts, the Index of Gender Equity was more than 95, thus showing the near absence of gender related inequities (Aggarwal, 1998a). Is this also true of learning achievement?

The analysis shows that differences in achievement of boys and girls were not very striking. The distribution of districts into various classes for mean achievement scores for class III/ IV between boys and girls is shown in Table 2. While the overall levels of achievement continue to be low both for the boys and girls, the differences in achievement patterns were not very significant excepting for a few districts. The average score was lower for mathematics than for language.

Table 2: Classification of districts by level of achievement, MAS 1997-Class III/IV

Range	**Language**				**Mathematics**			
	Boys	**Girls**	**Urban**	**Rural**	**Boys**	**Girls**	**Urban**	**Rural**
Below 30	0	2	1	0	15	16	14	16
30-40	16	16	14	18	14	14	14	16
40-50	19	16	16	16	7	6	9	5
50-60	7	8	10	6	4	5	3	3
60-70	0	0	1	2	2	1	2	2
70-80	0	0	0	0	0	0	0	0
>80	0	0	0	0	0	0	0	0
Total	42	42	42	42	42	42	42	42

The rural urban differences in achievement scores were more striking as compared to gender disparities. In the case of language, the rural students seem to be performing better than the boys. It is the other way round for mathematics. This phenomenon needs to be examined in detail. The performance of the rural children in mathematics was very low as 32 out of the 42 districts had mean score of less than 40 percent-an exceptionally low performance of the pupils with rural background. Thus, the position with respect to teaching of mathematics is very unsatisfactory in class III/IV. These findings have serious implications for the planning and management of DPEP for the next few years. Will DPEP be able to prepare a framework for the universalisation of primary education in a manner that all children not only attain the objectives of DPEP but also able to cross the threshold by which 80 percent of the competencies are attained by 80 percent of the students.

Extent of Under Achievement in Various Classes

A detailed analysis of the underachievement patterns is attempted in this section. The cutoff for the underachievers can be defined in many ways. For the purpose of this study, it is considered that any child who scores less than 40 percent should be considered as underachiever and the children who attain more than 80 percent should be considered as high achievers.

Mean Achievement for DPEP-I Districts: Mathematics

Although this findings is not based on the same set of students who are observed over a period of time, yet the sample is large enough and cross-section data reflects the likely trends which would have been obtained over a period of time. The extent of underachievement (less than 40 percent) in language varies from 21.8 percent in class I to 36.2 percent in class III and 66.3 percent in class IV. Thus, nearly two third children of class V should not have been there as their competency levels were too low in language. By pushing them to higher grades, the underachievement is rewarded.

The extent of underachievement in mathematics is much higher than that of language. It is estimated that 19.8 percent of class I students fall within the category of underachievers as compared to 59 percent for class III and 72.2 percent for class IV. Translated in absolute numbers, this implies that 14,371 class IV learners out of a total of 19,894 got 40 percent or fewer score in mathematics. More than half (52. 1 percent) pupils could not score more than 30 percent. How does one reconcile such poor levels of performance where nearly three fourth children fail to acquire even 40 percent score, what to talk of 80 percent score for all the children. Let us consider the high achievers, especially in class III/IV.

In language, 1.9 and 0.3 percent children were able to achieve mastery level (more than 80 percent). In mathematics, 2.3 and 1 percent of children were able to achieve mastery level competencies in classes III and IV. How to attain the intended target of achievement of 80 percent for 80 percent of students? The NCERT studies have not examined the correlates of learning. While the data was collected on these aspects, the analysis and findings have not been released. The NCERT study does mention that the schools having competency based instructional materials faired well as compared to others. Similarly, it has been pointed out that parents' educational qualification is positively related to their achievement score. Despite significant efforts, all is not well with the educational system. It is not only that many children do not have access to proper schooling facilities, but the internal efficiency of the educational system is also very low. This is reflected in high proportion of children leaving the school system without completing the primary cycle of education and low achievement among those who continue to stay in the system.

Free and Compulsory Primary Education—Staff Pattern and Content of Teacher Training of Primary School Teachers—In-service Programmes for Professional Growth

The concern for quality of education has been voiced from time to time in India. The National Policy on Education (NPE), 1986 and the revised NPE, 1992, again highlighted the urgency to address the quality concerns on priority basis. Quality can not improve by itself. It requires multi-pronged and strategic reforms in teacher training; improvements in the facilities and infrastructure in schools; teachers' motivation; and a change in the style of teaching to make it attractive to the students. The policy also recommended that a system of continuous and comprehensive evaluation would be established. Besides the state level schemes to improve access and quality of education, a number of Centrally.

Sponsored Schemes and externally funded projects, undertaken in the recent years, are experimenting with various models of bringing about increased coverage, retention and improvement in quality. It is demonstrated by many researches that a solid foundation in mathematics and language is necessary for primary school children to navigate the information in technological age. Students with strong grasp in mathematics have an advantage in academics as well as in the job markets. In the recent years, a number of new approaches have been developed to assess the achievement levels. In India, some of these methods have yet to be tried to establish their applicability. In the simplest of the terms, it may be mentioned that assessment should be viewed as a tool for improving educational standards, provide information to educators to determine which practice has resulted in desired outcomes and to what extent. The study has raised many issues that have serious implication for quality improvement in primary education. Some of these issues are discussed below.

a) There is a clear evidence to suggest that achievement levels tend to decline as the children move along the educational hierarchy. This is true of both the English and mathematics test. This shows that schools are not able to cope with the teaching learning load as the pupils' progress through various grades.

b) The temporal comparison of learners' performance has shown some gains in the first few years of DPEP. While this a welcome outcome and confirms the broader direction of reforms, it also raised many questions about the negative/decline in achievement level in certain other districts. While the contextuality of the district is an important parameter of planning, the implementation processes should also be reviewed to isolate the factors, which have facilitated/impeded the trends in learning outcome.

c) The students from privately managed schools perform better as compared to the students from government and aided schools, although the evidence is limited. It is also clear that despite better performance, even the private schools are far away from achieving the goals set up by the MLLs.

d) There are no mechanisms for assessing the achievement levels for children studying through non-formal and alternative schools. Since these systems are more of informal and flexible, it is important to establish their credentials through effective monitoring and evaluation.

e) The overall scores of class V learners based on class IV competencies are low for both mathematics and language. The low achievement in mathematics is indeed a matter of concern. The long term effect of low achievement in mathematics is revealed by the secondary and senior secondary examination results where most of the children fail in mathematics and the overall result stays around 50 percent. It is therefore important to evaluate the mathematics curriculum and related instructional materials.

f) The teachers are at the centre stage of the educational system. There is no system to identify teacher training needs. The teacher training packages do consult the teachers but once finalised, their content is same for all the teachers. Is it possible to identify the level of competencies attained by teachers in language and mathematics so that a proper module on their capacity building is developed.

g) Upgrade curriculum periodically, integrate technology and high quality instructional materials and to help students in learning the applications of mathematics in real life. Teachers should be encouraged to develop and use locally relevant instructional materials.

h) Underachievement, even if it defined at 40 percent level, is very high in classes III and IV. The extent of underachievement among class V learners was 66 percent in language and 72 percent in mathematics. Those achieving mastery level competencies constituted a small fraction of the total students. The prescribed norms are that 80 percent children should be able to learn 80 percent competencies. Thus, there are miles to go before the target of MLLs can be achieved.

i) The class II tests were oral in nature and class III/IV were written. The sudden drop in the level of mean achievement scores also points to another phenomenon i.e. the transition from oral to written mode of examination. Are the students well prepared for this transition. Perhaps at no point of time, the students are taught about this transition. This aspects need to be examined by the pedagogists.

j) A national testing agency or a research cell in the national/state institutions should be established to undertake continuous and comprehensive analysis of learners' achievement at primary and upper primary stage. The cell should assists the state governments to meet the challenging mathematics standards at primary stage, work closely with teachers unions and other NGOs for upgrading the skills of teachers on continuous basis. Educational administrators needs assessment information that will help them remove barriers to learning by telling schools to decide on what works well and what does not. Enable teachers to identify students learning needs early, before the problem becomes too big. The school administrators should also ensure that the dialogue between the schools and children is better informed; giving parents a better picture of the progress of their children and the effectiveness of the schools.

k) In the Indian context, there is no mechanism for the training of head teachers of primary and upper primary schools in school leadership. In most countries, such training is a part of the capacity building exercise. Review of the professional development strategies for the teachers and head teachers stressing both subject matter expertise and pedagogical mastery is thus necessary.

l) As more and more data becomes on students achievement, it needs to be organized systematically so that the researchers and can have access to these database for testing of various types of alternative hypotheses. In conclusion, it is pertinent to note that the assessment studies undertaken in the recent years have brought to focus many issues which require immediate attention. These efforts will go a long way in developing local specific strategies and help the system to develop an integrated model of UEE, where the focus is not only on removing supply side constrains by providing more teachers, facilities, instructional materials etc., but also in identifying the critical inputs that optimise the learning outcomes in a given situation.

SSA, DPEP, ABL in Tamil Nadu

Education for All

Trend and out reach at Tamil Nadu in India The world convention on to Meet fundamental Learning requirements was adopted by the World Conference on Education for All at Jomtien, Thailand, in March 1990. The meeting design comprehensive review of policies concerning basic education. The Education for All (EFA) 2000 appraisal is a major global attempt that aims to enable the participating countries to

(i) Construct a comprehensive picture of their progress towards their own Education for All goals since the 1990 Jomtien Conference,

(ii) Identify priorities and promising strategies for overcoming obstacles and accelerating progress, and

(iii) Revise national plans of action accordingly. EFA indicators which are grouped according to the following six 'Intention Magnitude':-

1. Expansion of early childhood care and development;
2. Universal access to and completion of primary education;
3. Improvement in learning achievement;
4. Reduction of adult illiteracy rate;
5. Expansion of provision of basic education and training in essential skills required by Youth and adults; and

6. Increased acquisition by individuals and families of the knowledge, skills and values organized for better living.

For this purpose a National Assessment Group was constituted in the Department of Education, Ministry of Human Resource Development consisting of senior officials of the Department concerned with EFA and representatives of specialized national institutions, like NCERT, NIEPA and NCTE. During its deliberations, the Group felt that the Indian exercise should be carried out in a larger perspective which takes into account the following important developments:

The wide range of programmes initiated for achieving Universalisation of Elementary Education after formulation of National Policy of Education, 1986; The massive effort made in the form of literacy campaigns to reach education to the masses; and Enormous amount of activities in the field of primary education witnessed in the country on an unprecedented scale in the 1990s through projects and programmes specifically focused on EFA.

The EFA 2000 exercise is, therefore, seen not merely as a stock taking exercise but also as an effort to review and fine-tune strategies and programmes of basic education.

It is with this dual perspective in view that it has been planned:

(1) to make the exercise quite comprehensive covering every dimension of basic education;
(2) to get the various component areas reviewed by independent experts from across the country; and
(3) to evolve a plan of action for the next phase, probably the final phase, of the national effort to reach the goal of EFA.

India's EFA Assessment 2000 Country Report draws upon the following three documents:

i. Report of progress made with respect to the 18 EFA Indicators as identified in the General and Technical Guidelines given by the EFA Forum Secretariat;

ii. The State of the Art Review (Synthesis) on Learning Achievements; and

iii. The State of the Art Review on Learning Conditions.

The Department of Education in the Ministry of Human Resource Development has taken the initiative to commission twenty-four sub-sectoral studies on various aspects of EFA in India which seek to capture the varied experiences that have emerged from the projects, programmes and schemes undertaken during the last decade. The findings of these studies are proposed to be disseminated widely in India and abroad with a view to enrich the EFA 2000 Assessment exercise and provide useful inputs for policy makers, planners and administrators who are working towards achieving the goals of EFA.

Education for All – Frame Work

The goal of EFA in India are to be viewed in relation to the stage of education development that obtained on 1990 ¾ the year of world declaration on EFA. By then, fairly large expansion of in all parts of the country. Other sectors of education like adult education Non – formal education had also developed fairly well. Therefore, the main challenges in education in 1990s related to EFA have been the following: Access to basic education for the unreached segments and uncovered habitations.

Qualitative improvement in content and processes of education; to make them more responsive to learning needs of individuals-children, youth and adults, families, community and development in different sectors of social and economic life. Consolidation and newer orientation wherever required in different areas of education through innovative programmes and changed role of educational personnel. Community participation in education; making education a people's movement. Evolving effective and efficient management structures in education.

All goals and targets of EFA to be fulfilled in 1990's have to be assessed in terms of the nature of the programmes, the degree to which they have led to achievement of the goals of EFA, and the promise they hold for making the processes and supportive structure sustainable. Thus, when EFA programmes were implemented in 1990's, a new framework for development of basic education in the country was emerging which had the following broad features.

Holistic Approach

The holistic approach adopted for planning and implementation of EFA programmes is characterized by:

- A holistic view of basic education with grater linkages and integration between pre – school, primary education, non – formal education and adult education;
- Relating programmes of education with national concerns such as nutrition and health care, environment, small family norm and life skills education.
- Collaboration of different departments and sectors of development with primary education.

Education Grantee Scheme

The EGS centres in Tamil Nadu deserves special mention as an important new initiative in the 1990s the remarkable success of EGS drawn the attention of planners and policy maker. The EGS centres covered 6-11 age groups who did not battened school. The key factors on which EGS hinges are community demand and government guarantee. By projecting community demand as a start-up point, EGS addresses the issue of enrolment and retention. The EGS is seen as successful mode of reaching the unreached or 'Hard to reach'.

Education Grantee Scheme in Tamil Nadu (2004-2005)

Activities: Administration arrangement: The coordinator have appointed. Capacity building All the staff/ teachers have completed the strategy planning work shop.

Equivalence strategy The special effort is being taken to enrol the school drop out children. Duration The short duration of the programme is 60-75 days.

School hours Two to three hours Number of children per class 25 – 40 is high and low is 10-20 Teacher qualifications, Training and honorarium As per the government norm Academic support and supervision The separate supervisors for every eight to ten schools Teaching – Learning Materials The material prepared separately Collaboration with NGOs Many EGS centres running by NGOs.

Universalisation of Elementary Education (UEE)

In accordance with the constitutional commitment to ensure free and compulsory education for all children up to the age of 14 years, provision of universal elementary education has been a salient feature of national policy since independence. This resolve has been spelt out emphatically in the National Policy since independence (NPE), 1986 and the Programme of Action (POA) 1992. A number of schemes and programmes were launched in pursuance of the emphasis embodied in the NPE and the POA. These included the scheme of Operation Blackboard (OB); Non Formal Education (NFE); Teacher Education (TE); Mahila Samakhya (MS); State specific Basic Education Projects like the Andhra Pradesh Primary Education Project (APPEP); Bihar Education Project (BEP), Lok Jumbish (LJP) in Rajasthan; National Programme of Nutritional Support to Primary Education (MDM); District Primary Education Programme (DPEP).

Why Elementary Education Social justice and equity are by themselves a strong argument for providing basic education for all. It is an established fact that basic education improves the level of human well – being especially with regard to life expectancy, infant mortality, nutritional status of children, etc. Studies have shown that universal basic education significantly contributes to economic growth.

Constitutional, Legal and National Statements for UEE The Constitutional, legal, and national policies and statements have time and again upheld the cause of universal elementary education. Constitutional mandate 1950 – "The state shall Endeavour to provide, within a period of ten years from the commencement of this Constitution, for free and compulsory education to all children until they complete the age of 14 years."

National Policy of Education 1986 – "It shall be ensured that free and compulsory education of satisfactory quality is provided to all children up to 14 years of age before we enter the twenty first century." Unnikrishnan judgment 1993 – "Every child/citizen of this country has a right to free education till he completes the age of fourteen years."

Education Ministers" resolve 1998 – "Universal elementary education should be pursued in the mission mode. It emphasized the need to pursue a holistic and convergent approach towards UEE."

National Committee's Report on UEE in the mission mode 1999 – UEE should be pursued in a mission mode with a holistic and convergent approach with emphasis on preparation of District Elementary Education Plans for UEE. It supported the fundamental right to education and desired quick action towards operationalization of the mission mode towards UEE.

The Scenario so Far Consequent to several efforts, India has made enormous progress in terms of increase in institution, teachers, and students in elementary education. The number of schools in the country increased four fold – from 2, 31, 000 in 1950-51 to 9, 30,000 in 1988-99, while enrolment in the primary cycle jumped by about six times from 19.2 million to 110 million. At the upper Primary stage, the increase of enrolment during the period was 13 times, while enrolment of girls recorded a huge rise of 32 times. The Gross Enrolment Ratio (GER) at the Primary stage has exceeded 100 percent. Access to schools is no longer a major problem. At the primary stage, 94 percent of the country's rural population has schooling facilities within one kilometre and at the upper primary stage it is 84 percent. The country has made impressive achievement in the elementary education sector. But the flip side is that out of the 200 million children in the age group of 6-14 years, 59 million children are not attending school. Of this, 35 million are girls and 24 million are boys. There are problems relations to drop – out rate, low levels of learning achievement and low participation of girls, tribal and other disadvantaged groups. There are still at least one lakh habitations in the country without schooling facility within a kilometre. Coupled with it are various systemic issues like inadequate school infrastructure, poorly functioning schools, high teacher absenteeism, large number of teacher vacancies, poor quality of education and inadequate funds.

In short, the country is yet to achieve the elusive goal of Universalisation of Elementary education (UEE), which means 100 percent enrolment and retention of children with schooling facilities in all habitations. It is to fill this gap that the government has launched the Sarva Shiksha Abhiyan.

Sarva Shiksha Abhiyan (SSA) The Sarva Shiksha Abhiyan is a historic stride towards achieving the long cherished goal of Universalisation of Elementary Education (UEE) through a time bound integrated approach, in partnership with States. SSA, which promises to change the face of the elementary education sector of the country, aims to provide useful and quality elementary Education to all children in the 6-14 age groups by 2010. The SSA is an effort to recognize the need for improving the performance of the school system and to provide community owned quality elementary education in the mission mode. It also envisages bridging of gender and social gaps.

Sarva Shiksha Abhiyan (SSA)

All children in school, Education Guarantee Centre, Alternative School, 'Back to School' camp by 2003; All children complete five years of primary schooling by 2007; All children complete eight years of schooling by 2010; Focus on elementary education of satisfactory quality with emphasis on education for life; Bridge all gender and social category gaps at primary stage by 2007 and at Elementary education level by 2010; Universal retention by 2010.

Structure for Implementation: The Central and State governments will together implement the SA in partnership with the local governments and the community. To signify the national priority for elementary education, a National Sarva

Shiksha Abhiyan Mission is being established with the Prime Minister as the Chairperson and the Union Minister of Human Resource Development as the Vice Chairperson. States have been requested to establish State level Implementation Society for UEE under the Chairmanship of Chief Minister Education Minister. This has already been done in many States.

The Sarva Shiksha Abhiyan will not disturb existing structures in States and districts but would only try to bring convergence in all these efforts. Efforts will be made to ensure that there is functional decentralization down to the school level in order to improve community participation. Besides recognizing PRIs / Tribal Councils in Scheduled Areas, including the Gram Sabha, the States would be encouraged to enlarge the accountability framework by involving NGOs, teacher, activists, women's organizations etc.

Coverage and Period

The SSA will cover the entire expanse of the country before March 2002 and the duration of the Programme in every district will depend upon the District Elementary Education Plan (DPEP) Prepared by it as per its specific needs. However, the upper limit for the programme period has been fixed as ten years, i.e., up to 2010.

Strategies Central to SSA Programme

Institutional Reforms:

- As part of the SSA, institutional reforms in the States will be carried out. The state will have to make an objective assessment of their prevalent education system including educational administration, achievement levels in schools, financial issues, decentralization and community ownership, review of state Education Act, rationalization of teacher deployment and recruitment of teachers, monitoring and evaluation, education of girls, SC/ST and disadvantaged groups, policy regarding private schools and ECCE. Many States have already affected institutional reforms to improve the delivery system for elementary education. Sustainable Financing

- The Sarva Shiksha Abhiyan is based on the premise that financing of elementary education interventions has to sustainable. This calls for a long – term perspective on financial partnership between the Central and the State governments. Community ownership.
- The programme calls for community ownership of school based interventions through effective decentralisation. This will be augmented by involvement of women's groups, VEC members and members of Panchayati Raj institutions. Institutional capacity building.
- The SSA conceives a major capacity building role for national and state level institution like NIEPA/NCERT/ NCTE/SCERT/SIEMAT. Improvement in quality requires a sustainable support system of resource persons. Improving mainstream educational administration.
- The Programme will have a community based monitoring system. The Educational Management Information System (EMSI) will correlate school level data with community based information from micro planning and surveys. Besides this, every school will have a notice board showing all the grants received by the school and other details. Habitation as a unit of planning.
- The SSA works on a community based approach to planning with habitation as a unit of planning. Habitation plans will be the basis for formulating district plans. Accountability to community.
- SSA envisages cooperation between teachers, parents and PRIs, as well as accountability and transparency.
- Education of girls – Education of girls, especially those belonging to the scheduled castes and scheduled tribes, will be one of the principal concerns in Sarva Shiksha Abhiyan.
- Focus on special groups – There will be a focus on the education participation of children form SC/ST, religious

and linguistic minorities, disadvantaged groups and the disabled children.

- Pre Project phase – SSA will commence throughout the country with a well planned pre project phase that provides for a large number of interventions for capacity development to improve the delivery and monitoring system.
- Thrust on quality – SSA lays a special thrust on making education at elementary level useful and relevant for children by improving the curriculum, child centred activities and effective teaching methods.
- Role of teachers – SSA recognizes the critical role of teachers and advocates a focus on their development needs. Setting up of BRC/CRC, recruitment of qualified teachers, opportunities for teacher development through participation in curriculum related material development, focus on classroom process and exposure visits for teachers are all designed to develop the human resource among teachers.
- District Elementary Education Plans – As per the SSA framework, each district will prepare a District Elementary Education Plan reflection all the investments being made in the education sector, with a holistic and convergent approach.

Components of SSA The components of Sarva Shiksha Abhiyan includes appointment of teachers, teacher training, qualitative improvement of elementary education, provision of teaching learning materials, establishment of Block and Cluster Resource Centres for academic support, construction of Classrooms and school buildings, establishment of education guarantee centres, integrated education of the disabled and distance education.

Non-government Organization

Non – government organizations, commonly referred to as voluntary agencies in India, also participate in EFA programmes. For instance, a large number of voluntary agencies are implementing non – formal education programmes to meet the educational needs of out of school children.

Many of them focus on socially and economically back ward areas and marginalized sections of the society and on education of girls. The current decade has seen the emergence of a number of EFA programmes supported by international agencies. These include support multi – lateral agencies including UN bodies, the World Bank and the ADB.

Five UN agencies have supported the development of a joint initiative with the government of India and state governments on community based primary education. Assistance from UN agencies and bilateral dononars is in the form of grants, while the World Bank provides concessional loan assistance through IDA.

Matching contributions in cash and kind are provided by central and state governments for such projects. The last three five year plans have witnessed significant shift in the expenditure of the department of education in the central government towards primary and adult education and away from tertiary education.

That the central government is paying serious attention towards achievement of the goal of EFA is brought out by these actions of government.

Project Management and Institutional Structures & Staffing

The Programme is implemented through various Project Management and Institutional Structures viz.,

Village Education Committees (VECs)/ Parent Teacher Associations (PTAs), Cluster Resource Centres (CRCs), Block Resource Centres (BRCs), District Project Offices (DPOs) and State Project Office (SPO).

The Table that follows furnishes Districtwise number of VECs/PTAs, CRCs, BRCs in the State.

The Districtwise number of VECs/PTAs, CRCs and BRCs are given in the Table that follows.

DPOs with VECs/PTAs, CRCs & BRCs

S.N.	*Districts*	*VECs*	*CRCs*	*BRCs*	*Urban BRCs*
1	Chennai	758	110	0	10
2	Coimbatore	2069	199	19	3
3	Cuddalore	1592	172	13	1
4	Dharmapuri	1242	100	8	0
5	Dindigul	1562	163	14	2
6	Erode	1893	142	20	0
7	Kancheepuram	1563	172	13	0
8	Kanyakumari	802	89	9	0
9	Karur	836	75	8	0
10	Krishnagiri	1540	121	10	0
11	Madurai	1450	165	13	2
12	Nagapattinam	1161	100	11	0
13	Namakkal	1056	83	15	0
14	Perambalur	993	107	10	0
15	Pudukkottai	1585	145	13	0
16	Ramanathapuram	1291	124	11	0
17	Salem	1736	174	20	1
18	Sivagangai	1179	109	12	0
19	Thanjavur	1601	165	14	1
20	The Nilgiris	569	45	4	0
21	Theni	730	80	8	0
22	Thiruchirappalli	1566	183	14	2
23	Thirunelveli	2144	192	19	2
24	Thiruvallur	1552	133	14	0
25	Thiruvannamalai	1996	167	18	0
26	Thiruvarur	1008	95	10	0
27	Thoothukkudi	1535	108	12	1
28	Vellore	2432	202	20	2
29	Villupuram	2297	234	22	0
30	Virudhunagar	1375	134	11	0
	Tamil Nadu	43113	4088	385	27

Source: DISE 2005

Village Education Committees (VECs) / Parent Teacher Associations (PTAs)

There are 43,113 VECs/PTAs functioning in schools in all the Districts. VECs function in Primary and Middle Schools and PTAs are in place in high and Higher Secondary Schools. The Panchayat President is the Chairperson in rural areas and Ward Members/Councillors hold the position in Municipal and Corporation limits.

The Headmaster of the school is the member-secretary. VECs are represented by a wide spectrum of the community with 20 members. The members include PTA president, Self Help Group members, Parents, Ward Member or Elected Representatives, ECCE/ICDS organizer, NGOs, Village Administrative Officer, Health Worker, Women ward member, SC ward member, parents of the disabled children and youth club members.

All grants to schools such as school grant, teacher grant, TLE grant, Maintenance grant are routed through VEC. Funds for civil construction works – two classroom buildings, three classroom buildings, CRC buildings, toilets and water facilities – are also routed through VEC as these constructions are undertaken by the community. All funds are directly sent to VEC by District Project Office (DPO) through Cheques to facilitate quick flow of funds. VEC meetings are conducted once/twice a month in all schools which enable the members to discuss problems and issues concerning school improvement and formulate local-specific interventions.

VECs maintain Village Education Registers (VERs) in all schools, which provide reliable information about 0-5 years children, school-age children (6-14 years), out-of-school children (Dropouts and never enrolled), disabled children with various categories of disability. The Village Education Registers are updated during April, May every year for initiating the follow-up measures. The Headmaster and teachers of the school undertake this exercise involving the VEC members.

Cluster Resource Centres (CRCs)

In all the Districts, 4,088 CRCs function as teacher

empowerment centres. The CRCs have been constituted by clubbing 10-12 schools with 40-60 teachers. Each centre has a Co-ordinator and an Assistant Co-ordinator who are the senior most headmasters in the cluster. The CRC meetings are convened once in a month. Teachers share their experiences and successful innovative practices/techniques in the meetings.

Block Resource Centres (BRCs)

In Tamil Nadu, 385 BRCs in the Community Developmental Blocks function in 29 Districts. In Chennai, 10 CRCs in the Corporation Zones play the roles of BRCs. However, the programme implementation in the 17 urban Blocks in other Districts is being undertaken by the nearby BRCs. In each BRC, one supervisor in the cadre of high school headmaster, one Post Graduate Assistant and ten/twenty teacher educators in the cadre of high school teachers (B.Ed., grade teachers) are working.

District Project Offices (DPOs)

In Tamil Nadu, 30 District Project Offices are in place with one DPC in the cadre of Chief Educational Officer, one Additional DPC in the cadre of District Elementary Educational Officer (both of them ex-officio personnel) and one ADPC in the cadre of Higher secondary school headmaster.

One Teacher Training Officer, Media and Documentation Officer/Women Development Officer, one Statistical Officer, one/two Civil Consultant(s), One Junior Programmer, Two/ Three Data Entry Operator(s) have also been appointed for implementation of the programme. One Accounts and Audit Manager (Tally) has also been appointed. Civil Engineers have also been engaged.

State Project Office

The State Project Office has technical, academic, administrative and accounts staff to guide the District offices in the implementation of the programme. The following Tables furnish the staffing status in both SPO and DPOs in the State.

State Project Directorate

Staffing Status

S. N.	Category	Posts Sanctioned	Staff in position
1	State Project Director	1	1
2	Joint Directors (Deputation from School Education Department)	5	5
3	Secretary to SPD (Deputy Director) (Deputation from School Education Department)	1	0
4	Finance and Accounts Officer (Under Secretary-Finance)	1	1
5	Programmer (Deputation from Statistics Department)	1	1
6	Co-ordinators (Hr. Sec. School HMs)	5	5
7	Deputy Co-ordinators (P.G.Assistants)	4	4
8	Assistant Co-ordinators (B.T. Assistants)	7	7
	Ministerial Staff		
9	Superintendent	4	4
10	Assistant	7	7
11	Typist	3	3
12	Steno-Typist	3	3
13	Driver	3	3
14	OA	5	5
	Others		
15	Consultant *	11	11
16	Staff on Consolidated Pay *	25	25
Total		85	85

* Manpower procurement will be made based on requirement in the areas concerned.

District Project Office

Staffing Status

S. N.	Category	Posts Sanctioned Per District	30 Districts	Posts Filled
1	DPC/CEO Ex-officio	1	30	30
2	Additional DPC / DEEO Ex-officio	1	30	30
3	Assistant District Programme Co-ordinator	1	30	30
4	Training officer/Media Documentation Officer or Women Development Officer	2	60	60
5	Accountant/Finance and Accounts Officer	1	30	30
6	Statistical Officer	1	30	30
7	Superintendent	1	30	30
8	Assistant	2	60	60
9	Assistant Executive Engineer	1	30	30
10	Programmer	1	30	30
11	Data Entry Operator	4	120	120
12	Academic Consultant	2	60	60
13	Civil Consultant	4	120	120
14	Office Assistant	1	30	30
15	Audit and Accounts Manager (Tally)	1	30	30
	Total	24	720	720

The State Project Office coordinates with the State Government and the Central Government by sending periodical status reports and financial reports. It is also responsible for financial and quality audit of the programme. The State Project Director conducts periodical review meetings at the State and District levels to assess the progress of the scheme and to give necessary instructions for the proper implementation of the scheme.

Achievements under SSA

The implementation of SSA in Tamil Nadu has resulted in the introduction of new strategies and innovative experiences in the realm of Elementary Education. It has also brought in a new perspective on *special focus groups-Girls*, Children with Special Needs and SC/ST children. The role of educational research, teacher education and training has enhanced and improved the quality of education over the past four years. Most importantly, the elementary school has become enjoyable to the learners and relevant to the community as a result of the inputs given under SSA Mission. New technology like EDUSAT focuses on indigenous efforts that contribute effectively in upgrading quality of teaching learning processes. The consistent progress in every component of SSA has been significant and conspicuous and it can very well impact the future course of positive outcomes in the State's relentless journey towards achieving UEE and beyond.

District Primary Education Program (DPEP) Cells

The DPEP is a centrally sponsored scheme for holistic development of primary education covering class I to V. The three major objectives of the DPEP are to (i) reduce drop-out rate to less than 10%, (ii) reduce disparities among gender and social groups in the areas of enrolment, learning achievement etc. to less than 5% and (iii) improve the level of learning achievement compared to the base-line surveys.

Prior to the launch of SSA, DPEP covered 273 districts in 18 states and focused on hard-core low female literacy districts. No further expansion of DPEP is envisaged after the launch of SSA. The project has already been closed in 26 districts of Madhya Pradesh and Chhattisgarh. DPEP is now operational in 129 districts of nine states-Andhra Pradesh, Bihar, Gujarat, Orissa, Uttar Pradesh, West Bengal, Rajasthan, Jharkhand and Uttaranchal. The project is gradually being merged with the SSA.

District Primary Education Programme in Tamil Nadu

District Primary Education Programme-DPEP-is one of the many programmes implemented in Tamil Nadu with the objective of imparting quality primary education so as to attain 100% literacy by eradicating drop-out from the school in the middle.

Programmes

The phase I Districts viz. Dharmapuri, Thiruvannamalai, Cuddalore and Villupuram were selected for the implementation of DPEP at a cost of Rs.168.97 crores for a period of 7 years from 1994-95 based on the criterion that female literacy rate of these districts was below the national average. Under phase II Districts, Pudukkottai District where total literacy campaign has been successful, Perambalur District with a low female literacy rate and Ramanathapuram District which is backward in socio-economic conditions in the State have been selected for implementation of DPEP for a period of 6 years from 1997-98 at a cost of Rs.92.44 crores. The total project cost is shared by the Government of India and State Government in the ratio of 85:15.

Objectives

As per the objectives of this programme, out of 1814 class rooms buildings 1351 have been completed. To provide access to schooling in remote areas, 406 new schools have been opened during the last few years. During 2001-2002, about 70 schools have been proposed to be opened. 1764 posts of teachers have been created for the newly opened as well as for the existing schools. As a result, the average teacher-pupil ratio has been lowered from 1:41 to 1:39. To serve the cause of dropped-out and non-enrolled children and those who are unable to attend full time schools, 1014 alternative schooling centres are functioning. These centres have an enrolment of nearly 26629 children. On completion of the studies in these centres, children are admitted in formal schools in standard III, IV or V depending on their achievement levels. Steps are being taken to open some more alternative schooling centres.

Special Features of the Plan

Community participation is very essential for the development of schools.

Village level committee is formed in schools to make appeal to the community for enrolling all eligible school age children and to retain them without any drop out in the middle.

To ensure 100% enrolment of pupils awareness campaigns and enrolment melas are conducted to create awareness among the public. By these activities, all the eligible school age children particularly scheduled caste and scheduled tribe students will have the benefit of education up to Std. V.

Quality Improvement

Grants for improving the infrastructure facilities and to attend the repair works at the rate of Rs.2000/- per year for every primary and middle schools (except aided schools) and grant for preparing teaching learning materials for teachers working in all primary schools at the rate of Rs.500/- per teacher per year are released.

In-service training is given to teachers for imparting quality education. Training for the teachers of English was given by block resource centres. Village level committee members were oriented at the cluster resource centres.

Integrated Education for the Disabled To serve the cause of disabled children, Integrated Education Programme is implemented in 21 blocks of 8 Districts with the assistance of non-government Organisations. Out of 14549 disabled children identified, 13552 of them have been admitted in formal schools. This scheme is to be extended to 21 more blocks during 2001-2002.

Special Coaching Classes

Special coaching classes are being conducted to enhance the achievement level of Adi Dravidar and Tribal Welfare girls of Standards III, IV and V in 2411 centres after school hours. About 59277 girls are being benefited by the scheme.

Budget and Expenditure

The allocation for the various project activities is as follows:

Quality improvement-70%

Civil Works-24%

Management-6%

In phase I, out of the total grant of Rs. 124.74 crores received, a sum of Rs.117.08 crores (94%) has been spent. In phase II, out of the total grants of Rs.54.03 crores received, a sum of Rs.43.83 crores (81%) has been spent. The total budget of Rs.84.11 crores prepared by participatory process involving the community, teachers, village level committee members and DPEP Officials for the year 2001-2002 has been sent for the approval of Government of India.

Role of DIETs in Primary Teacher Training Courses

District Institute of Education and Training (D.I.E.T) is a support system for national and state level educational agencies such as NCERT, NIEPA and DTERT. "It had been envisaged that the DIET's would work for pre-service and in-service courses of elementary school teachers and for continued education of the personnel working in the non-formal and adult education programme".

Role of DIET

Tiruvallur district has one District Institute of Education and Training (DIET) at Tirur, one private AIDED Teacher Training Institute (TTI) at Madhavaram and 13 UNAIDED Teacher Training Institute (TTI) at various places in the district.

DIET at Tirur has one Principal, 7 Senior Lecturers, 10 Lecturers and one Junior Lecturer at present. There are seven branches in the DIET, which have internal linkages in their performances.

- Pre-service Teacher Education
- In-service

- District Resource unit
- Planning and Management
- Educational Technology
- Work Experience
- Curriculum Material Development and Evaluation.

DIET's have been established by upgrading the pre-service teacher training institutions.

They have been visualised as an academic and intellectual body at the District level to offer all support required to improve the standard of elementary education. DIET's mission could be briefly stated in the following terms:

- Achievement of universalisation of elementary Education
- Adult Education and functional literacy
- Excellence in the institutes own work.
- A model for other educational institutions in the District.

DIET's three main functions:

1. Better Training
2. Resource Support
3. Action Research.

As far as the training is concerned the aim of the DIET is to follow "pragmatic approach" in every area. The Primary and Elementary school children are now a day exposed to various kinds of environments. To cater to the needs of such children, the teacher must be well equipped in the pedagogy. The teacher has to be trained in the modern academic knowledge, skill and development and standards of the heart.

The orientation process, which now covers only the competencies, should be changed to the Psychological approach. Education of present day is only child-centred approach. So reforms in the training programmes must be brought out. The reforms should make Education a joyful, innovative and satisfying activity, rather than a system of rote and cheerless, authoritarian Instruction.

The DIET should make a survey of committed teachers in the District and each DIET should have a model school under its control. These teachers should consult the DIET faculty every week subject wise and implement the recommendations in the model school's T-L process.

The training programmes should be autonomous, that is, the DIET should have its own timetable for such programmes.

So far the following personnel had been trained in the DIET:

- Elementary school teachers. (Pre and In-service)
- Heads of schools, school complexes and educational officers at the block level.
- Instructors and supervisors of adult education.
- Members of District Education Council, members of VEC, social leaders and youths and volunteers who are involved in educational programmes.
- Block resource teachers and supervisors.

As far the resource support is concerned all branches of the DIET should work together under the guidance of the Principal. Now evaluation tools are non-existent. This area must be given importance. Extension activities and interaction with the field must be taken. DIET should be a resource centre for instructors and teachers. It has to provide TLMs and evaluation tools.

Major Areas of Research in Teacher Education

Action research is not obtaining generalizable scientific knowledge about educational problems but on obtaining knowledge concerning a specific local problem. Action research, being a scientific method of solving immediate problems in the schools set up, could emerge from any of the following areas:

- Classroom Situation
- Methods of teaching
- Questioning Climate
- Students discipline

- Late coming
- Not doing home assignments
- Poor attendance
- Lack of co-operation of students and Parents.
- Lack of physical amen tics in Schools.
- Text-books
- MLLS
- Lack of teachers' handbooks
- Mismatch of age and content.
- Gaps in information given.
- Guidance to teachers
- Arrangement of content, Coverage of the subject area.
- Achievement tests
- Diagnostic tests
- Planning
- Training
- Framing time table
- Self-Growth
- Desirable altitudes.
- Motivation
- Leadership.

The problems of action research could emerge from academic, social, curricular, administrative, evaluation and professional areas as above.

Activity Based Learning

A silent revolution in primary education, which began in Tamil Nadu (pop. 62 million) in 2003 when Activity Based Learning (ABL) was experimentally introduced on a modest scale, is making waves in this southern state. Since then, 37,486 corporation, panchayat, government and aided schools have implemented this pedagogy transforming the way 6 million primary school children are taught and learn in classrooms across the state.

ABL is a flexible, child-centric pedagogy which allows children to study at their own pace and employs child-friendly teaching aids to encourage self-learning. The result of a UNICEF supported initiative designed and tested by the well-known Rishi Valley School, Chittoor, Andhra Pradesh in the 1990s, ABL has proved very effective in attracting out-of-school children into classrooms. Which is probably why it is being supported by the Sarva Shiksha Abhiyan ('Education For All') wing of the state government.

Under the system, the curriculum is supported by self-learning materials comprising attractive study cards for all subjects. Classrooms are not age-specific and students of classes I-III sit together in one classroom, organised into mixed age groups but with every child studying independently and teachers acting as facilitators.

Though successful in improving learning outcomes in primary classrooms, this novel pedagogy has run into rough weather two years after it was introduced in all state-run schools. In July, primary school teachers' associations staged protests demanding withdrawal of the ABL system on the ground that there are flaws in the pedagogy. This has prompted some anxious parents to take their children out of government schools and enrol them in private institutions. Dismayed by these teacher agitations, the Tamil Nadu state government's school education department appointed a committee comprising V. Vasantha Devi, former vice-chancellor of the Manonmaniam Sundaranar University, senior educationist S.S. Rajagopalan and R. Jayakumar, physicist at the Lawrence Livermore National Laboratory, University of California, to conduct an independent review of ABL. The committee, which submitted its report in August this year, visited ten corporation and some suburban schools where the pedagogy has been operational for over three years.

The committee's report commends the ABL system for breaking traditional hierarchies within classrooms and recommends its continuation, while making several useful suggestions for improvement. It opines that ABL can work successfully only if class strength does not exceed 30. Moreover it says the pedagogy is less to blame than unavailability of learning materials; lack of teacher emphasis on group work; static rather than dynamic learning materials and that often activity cards have not been field tested before being introduced. The report suggests that teachers re-visit the fundamental concepts of ABL.

The committee's findings have shocked SSA administrators who believe that the ABL system is working smoothly in all schools. "There are some factual errors in the committee's report. ABL has improved the quality of education by addressing diversity in classrooms and motivating students to learn. According to M.P. Vijayakumar, chief architect of the ABL system, and former state project director of SSA It's a model that other states can usefully emulate".

While acknowledging the novelty and promise of ABL, independent educationists and education NGOs also accept that the pedagogy needs to be tweaked. Activity-based learning is an excellent concept and a great improvement on traditional rote learning. Therefore it's important to sustain it until it takes root. But this requires political will as well as the cooperation of teachers, parents, civil society organisations and educationists.

Quite clearly, these teething troubles need to be addressed without questioning the proven superiority of ABL pedagogy. By actively involving children in the learning process and making lessons enjoyable, ABL has not only improved learning outcomes but also stemmed the flow of school drop-outs. Most importantly teachers, slave to chalk-n-talk and rote memorisation conventions, need to welcome this and other pedagogies which reduce their workload while stimulating genuine learning in their classrooms.

UNIT-VI

Secondary Education

Aims and Objectives

The importance of aims and objectives of education is recognised by all the educational, professional, political, nonpolitical and religious associations, organisations and groups at various levels in their memoranda, letters and brouchures. It is said that education without clear cut aims is like a rudderless ship. The following comparisons emphasise this point fully well.

Every pilot has a route-chart and set timing of landing at predetermined destination. There is constitution or set of Principles and traditions through which a country is governed Similarly, there should be properly defined and declared principles, aims and objectives of education or the basis of which policies and programmes of education nave to be formulated to achieve the set goals wit out wasting scarce energies and resources in chasing the wild goose.

It is generally felt that our educational system has not followed the desired aims as a result that it does not produce ideal citizens in the country. It has followed, rather a narrow aim of preparing individuals for livelihood, as mentioned in one of the documents received from an organisation.

The main reason of failure of educational system is that it basically stands or, pre-independence system. The main Objective of its products was how to take degree and to earn money and to be careerist without consideration of ethical values and national spirit.

On the other hand, it has also been pointed out that it is unressonable to criticise educational system alone because it is based on the other subsystems accepted by us.

On the one hand we are developing and cultivating the British given economy, judicial system and system of administration and parliament, and on the other we are decrying and Criticising the education system which merely fulfils the needs of the British systems that we are propagating.

As pointed out in a memorandum of an association, "the main defect of the old education policy is that it had completely ignored the Indian culture and the interest of the masses of India and have left them economically too backward and socially too fragmented to articulate their miseries...."

The aims and objectives of education, suggested in the documents, include individual as well as social aims, with emphasis of social transformation aiming at reconstructing society to make it modernised, productive, predicative, and value oriented nation committed to its constitutional obligations.

Individual Development

Development of an individual-physically, mentally and spiritually is well known aim of education. Objectives related to this aim of individual development have been expressed in various ways in the memoranda:

- Developing physical and mental faculties
- Acquiring the capacities of understanding, appreciation and expression through word and act, are the fundamental aims of education
- Aim of education should be to make children self-confident and self dependent, and to make them strong physically and mentally
- Education is meant to develop every child's character, personality and culture and as much knowledge as the child can assimilate not merely memorize.

The best expression of complete development of an individual and the harmonious development of personality, however, is found in the following paragraph. The policy should be directed to the aim of enlightenment of head and heart; illumination of consciousness for allround development of individual personality. Education should enable a human being to attain the greatest possible harmony, internal and external, spiritual and material, for the fullest possible development of human potentialities and capacities.

Social and National Development

Social, aim of education in equally important because an individual lives in society and has his obligations towards his nation. There is a realisation that, "The present education system does riot yield required results mainly because it is divorced from the real social content and social goals".

It has, therefore, been suggested that education should be able, to discharge its natural functions and must correspond to its structure, goals and content in the interest of national development and social progress. It has also been suggested in this connection that students from young age should be made aware of the social responsibility cast on them.

At the same time, there are certain constitutional commitments, which are intimately related to this aim.. We as the citizens of the republic, are constitutionally Committed to democracy, social justice, equality of opportunity, secularisum and above all to a welfare state. It has, therefore, been suggested that, "Educational policy and educational programme should clearly reflect these commitments".

The objectives of developing a sense of national identity, unity and patriotism are advocated by many associations. It is pointed out that the national objectives of planning and programmes and development with special emphasis on popular participation and the national problems that we face in different fields should be taught at relevant stages.

Individual and social aims of education area not contrary to one another. In fact they are complementary to one another. The following view strikes a balance between individual and social aims of education.

The purpose of education should be the development of the fullest possible capacities and potentialities physical and spiritual of a 'total man'. It should make a man capable of earning his livelihood reasonably well to enjoy a happy and secure life while making effective contributions to the society and national effort of making India strong# advanced and prosperous.

Social Transformation

Education should not merely equip an individual to adjust with society to its customs and conventions, but it should enable him to bring desirable changes in the society. It has been, therefore, suggested that, "Every educational institution from secondary school to university college should be developed to become an agency of change...."

However, it is essential that we should be quite clear about the purpose of change. It is, therefore, natural to ask the, question, "Reform and change to achieve what"? What type of society we aim at and what type of citizens we wish to produce? The following ideas give an indication of the kind of changes education is expected to bring about.

Modernisation: Modernisation of society in terms of scientific and technological advancement is a view which seems to be quite popular. It is though that education should enable us to move with times and attain excellence in, science and technology. To quote an expression of this kind.

Scientific and technological advances are, gaining momentum and conscious efforts are made to incorporate them into the development sectors. This calls for modernisation of education in order to make it in conformity with the modern times and to keep pace, with the advances in the world.

Modernisation, however, is not interpreted and equated with westernisation. In fact, lot of emphasis is given to 'Indianness' while talking about modernisation. One of the suggestions explicitly points out that, hour education should integrate and unite the people of India, modernise society while preserving what is authentically Indian in our cultural and spiritual heritage". The following suggestion beautifully reconciles the twin objectives of modern technical sophistication and the ancient spirituality.

> *"New education policy of India should be built on the foundation of ancient spirituality and modern culture and technical sophistication. It should develop scientific temper and spirit of enquiry in the students".*

Productivity: Some documents have insisted on linking education with productivity and thus making individuals as productive citizens to build a productive society. One of the suggestions, in a memorandum, for example, says. "It should bring about a social transformation, and enhance greater efficiency and productivity in all sectors: agricultural, industrial and service". It is in this context that Mahatma Gandhi's system of basic education is still considered as a basically sound system and a suggestion has been made that with necessary modification elements of basic education may form part of education not only at the primary stage but at all stages in our national system of education. These elements are:

1. Productive activity in education.
2. Correlation of the curriculum with productive activity and physical and social environment.
3. Intimate contact between the school and the local community.

Community Participation: In a democracy education without community participation is barren. This aim of education is, therefore voiced by a number of groups and organisations. The change that is envisaged on this front is that of Integrating education with community in all respects. To quote a suggestion in this regard:

> *The education system in all its branches and sectors should get itself involved in activities related to problems of local Community life and shall thus endeavour through the desirable community participation community involvement in the educational field to bring all education of its rightful place in community life.*

Acquisition of Values

Moral, cultural and spiritual values in education have been given immense importance in the Memoranda documents. One of the expressions emphatically point out that, "certain basic values as respect for others, responsibility, solidarity, creativity and integrity must be fostered in our children".

It is interesting that a number of specific values have been suggested in the documents. The values which are considered important are mentioned below:

> *Emphasis should be given in cultivating good qualities like cooperation, good will, forgiveness, tolerance, honesty, patience etc. in order to encourage universal brotherhood and to prepare students worthy citizens of the country.*

Values of optimism and secularism, and service to the poor should be stressed on the young minds.

Summing up

It is worth reproducing what a document mentions about the aims of education:

The aim of education is two-fold (i) Development of the individual in society and (ii) Consequent development of the society. The aim of education in relation to individual may be spelt out as follows:

i) to produce full human personality with courage, conviction, vitality, sensitivity and intelligence so that men and women may life in harmony with the universe;
ii) to bring out the fullest potential of child and prepare him for life and its varied situations so that he becomes a cultured and responsible citizen dedicated in the service of community.

In relation to the society, the aim of education is to create:

i) a sane and learning society where made of material production will be such that no section of the society remains unemployed. In the Indian context such a made of production will be necessarily based on a decentralised economy utilising all available manpower;

ii) a society where the conditions of work and general environment will offer psychic satisfactions and effective motivations to its members.

iii) a society reconciling technological and scientific advancement with general well-being and security of its members, enhancing joy of life and eliminating all forms of exploitation.

The broad objective of education should, therefore, be to look beyond the existing society and to develop men and women amenable to the advent of a sane and healthier society of tomorrow.

While summing up, it may be pointed out that various dimensions individual and social development, social transformation, value-acquisition etc. have been well identified in the memoranda documents. The following words briefly summarise the various dimensions which are considered important indeed for marching into the 21st century:

> *We are of the opinion that Indian education should aim at producing men and women of knowledge, character and cultural values and trained skills to achieve excellence in their career and life. Let us make it clear that we wish to prepare youth to march into the 21st century on the ideals of truth and non-violence as shown to us by our great leaders.*

Secondary education serves as a bridge between elementary and higher education and prepares young persons between the age group of 14-18 for entry into higher education or work situations. The population of children in this age group has been estimated to be 88.5 million as per Census, 2001. Enrolment figures show that only 31 million of these children were attending schools in 2001-02, which means that two-third of the population remained out of school. The expansion of secondary education raises issues related to the number of private or public schools. There are 138 thousand secondary schools, 58% of which are run by the private sector and the rest by government and local bodies. The share of private schools in secondary education has been rising steadily.

The share of private unaided schools increased from 15.17% in 1993-94 to 23.56% in 2001-02, while the share of government sector schools declined by 5 percentage points and government-aided private sector school by 4 percentage points. The increase in private unaided school reflects the willingness of the parents to pay for education, as their perception is that the education in private sector is superior. One factor underlying this perception is the fact that private schools involve much more extensive education in English which is widely perceived as improving job opportunities. There are regional variations in accessibility to secondary schools and urban areas are apparently better served than rural areas.

The Secondary School Tradition of Our Country

India is the site of one of the most ancient civilizations in the world. About the 2nd millennium BC the Aryans entered the land and came into conflict with the local, dark-skinned people they called the *dasyu* ("servants"). They defeated them, spread far and wide in the country, established large-scale settlements, and founded powerful kingdoms. In the course of time, a section of the intellectuals, the Brahmans, became priests and men of learning; another group, nobles and soldiers, became the Kshatriya; the agricultural and trading class was called the Vaishya; and finally the *dasyu* were absorbed as the Sudra, or domestic servants. Such was the origin of the division of the Hindus into four varnas, or "classes." By about 500 BC the classes became hardened into castes.

Religion was the mainspring of all activities in ancient India. It was of an all-absorbing interest and embraced not only prayer and worship but philosophy, morality, law, and government as well. Religion saturated educational ideals, too, and the study of Vedic literature was indispensable to higher castes. The stages of instruction were very well defined. During the first period, the child received elementary education at home. The beginning of secondary education and formal schooling was marked by a ritual known as the *upanayana*, or thread ceremony, which was restricted to boys only and was more or less compulsory for boys of the three higher castes. The Brahman boys had this ceremony at the age of eight, the Kshatriya boys at the age of 11, and the Vaishya boys at the age of 12 years. The boy would leave his father's house and enter his preceptor's *ashrama*, or home, situated amid sylvan surroundings. The *acarya* would treat him as his own child, give him free education, and not charge anything for his boarding and lodging. The pupil had to tend the sacrificial fires, do the household work of his preceptor, and look after his cattle.

The study at this stage consisted of the recitation of the Vedic mantras, or "hymns," and the auxiliary sciences—phonetics, the rules for the performance of the sacrifices, grammar, astronomy, prosody, and etymology. The character of education, however, differed according to the needs of the caste. For a child of the priestly class, there was a definite syllabus of studies. The *trayi-vidya*, or the knowledge of the three Vedas, the most ancient of Hindu scriptures, was obligatory for him. During the whole course at school, as at college, the student had to observe *brahmacharya*—that is, wearing a simple dress, living on plain food, using a hard bed, and leading a celibate life.

The period of studentship normally extended to 12 years. For those who wanted to continue their studies, there was no age limit. After finishing their education at an *ashrama*, or forest school, they would join a higher centre of learning or a university presided over by a *kulapati* (a founder of a school of thought). Advanced students would also improve their knowledge by taking part in philosophical discussions at a *parisad*, or "academy." Education was not denied to women, but normally girls were instructed at home.

The method of instruction differed according to the nature of the subject. The first duty of the student was to memorize the particular Veda of his school, with special emphasis placed on correct pronunciation. In the study of such literary subjects as law, logic, rituals, and prosody, comprehension played a very important role. A third method was the use of parables, which were employed in the personal spiritual teaching relating to the Upanishads, or conclusion of the Vedas. In higher learning, such as in the teaching of *dharmashastra* ("righteousness science"), the most popular and useful method was catechism—the pupil asking questions and the teacher discoursing at length on the topics referred to him. Memorization, however, played the greatest role.

The Introduction of Buddhist Influences

By about the end of the 6th century BC, the Vedic rituals and sacrifices had gradually developed into a highly elaborate cult that profited the priests but antagonized an increasing section of the people. Education became generally confined to the Brahmans, and the *upanayana* was being gradually discarded by the non-Brahmans. The formalism and exclusiveness of the Brahmanic system was largely responsible for the rise of two new religious orders, Buddhism and Jainism. Neither of them recognized the authority of the Vedas, and both challenged the exclusive claims of the Brahmans to priesthood. They taught through the common language of the people and gave education to all, irrespective of caste, creed, or sex. Buddhism also introduced the monastic system of education. Monasteries attached to Buddhist temples served the double purpose of imparting education and of training persons for priesthood. A monastery, however, educated only those who were its members. It did not admit day scholars and thus did not cater to the needs of the entire population.

Meanwhile, significant developments were taking place in the political field that had repercussions on education. The establishment of the imperialistic Nanda dynasty in about 413 BC and then of the even stronger Mauryas some 40 years later shook the very foundations of the Vedic structure of life, culture, and polity. The Brahmans in large numbers gave up their ancient occupation of teaching in their forest retreats and took to all sorts of occupations; the Kshatriya also abandoned their ancient calling as warriors; and the Sudra in their turn rose from their servile occupations. These forces produced revolutionary changes in education. Schools were established in growing towns, and even day scholars were admitted. Studies were chosen freely and not according to caste. Taxila had already acquired an international reputation in the 6th century BC as a centre of advanced studies and now improved upon it. It did not possess any college or university in the modern sense of the term, but it was a great centre of learning with a number of famous teachers, each having a school of his own.

In the 3rd century BC Buddhism received a great impetus under India's most celebrated ruler, Ashoka. After his death, Buddhism evoked resistance, and a counter reformation in Hinduism began in the country. About the 1st century ad there was also a widespread lay movement among both Buddhists and Hindus. As a result of these events, Buddhist monasteries began to undertake secular as well as religious education, and there began a large growth of popular elementary education along with secondary and higher learning.

Classical India

The 500 years from the 4th century ad to the close of the 8th, under the Guptas and Harsha and their successors, is a remarkable period in Indian history. It was the age of the universities of Nalanda and Valabhi and of the rise of Indian sciences, mathematics, and astronomy. The university at Nalanda housed a population of several thousand teachers and students, who were maintained out of the revenues from more than 100 villages. Because of its fame, Nalanda attracted students from abroad, but the admission test was so strict that only two or three out of 10 attained admission. More than 1,500 teachers discussed over 100 different dissertations every day.

These were the main developments in education prior to the Muslim invasions, beginning in the 10th century. Nearly every village had its schoolmaster, who was supported from local contributions. The Hindu schools of learning, known as *pathasalas* in western India and *tols* in Bengal, were conducted by Brahman *acaryas* at their residence. Each imparted instruction in an advanced branch of learning and had a student enrolment of not more than 30. Larger or smaller establishments, specially endowed by rajas and other donors for the promotion of learning, also grew in number. The usual centres of learning were either some king's capital, such as Kannauj, Dhar, Mithila, or Ujjayini, or a holy place, such as Varanasi, Ayodhya, Kanchi, or Nasik.

In addition to Buddhist *viharas* (monasteries), there sprang up Hindu *mathas* (monks' residences) and temple colleges in different parts of the country. There were also *agrahara* villages, which were given in charity to the colonies of learned Brahmans in order to enable them to discharge their scriptural duties, including teaching. Girls were usually educated at home, and vocational education was imparted through a system of apprenticeship.

Indian Influences on Asia

An account of Indian education during the ancient period would be incomplete without a discussion of the influence of Indian culture on Sri Lanka and Central and Southeast Asia. It was achieved partly through cultural or trade relations and partly through political influence. Khotan in Central Asia had a famous Buddhist *vihara* as early as in the 1st century ad. A number of Indian scholars lived there, and many Chinese pilgrims, instead of going to India, stayed there. Indian pandits (scholars) were also invited to China and Tibet, and many Chinese and Tibetan monks studied in Buddhist *viharas* in India.

The process of Indianization was at its highest in Southeast Asia. Beginning in the 2nd century ad, Hindu rulers reigned in Indochina and in the numerous islands of the East Indian archipelago, from Sumatra to New Guinea, for a period of 1,500 years. These regions were peopled by primitive races, who adopted the civilization of their masters. A greater India was thus established by a general fusion of cultures. Some of the inscriptions of these countries, written in flawless Sanskrit, show the influence of Indian culture. There are references to Indian philosophical ideas, legends, and myths and to Indian astronomical systems and measurements. Hinduism continued to wield its influence on these lands so long as the Hindus ruled in India. This influence ceased by the 15th century ad.

The Government of India and Education

The nature and content of the National Educational Policy as well as the manner and success of its implementation obviously depends on the role of the Government of India in education. In this introductory chapter, therefore, we shall briefly discuss the role of the Government of India in education as it has evolved over the years, its present status and future prospects.

The Role of the Government of India in Education (1833-1870)

The East India Company was made to accept responsibility for the education of the Indian people in 1813.1 But a Government of India did not then exist; the authority of the Governors of the three Presidencies of Bengal, Bombay and Madras was supreme and subject only to the control of the Court of Directors of the Company in England. Between 1813 and 1833, therefore, education was an exclusive responsibility of the Provincial Governments. This situation however changed completely in 1833 when the Charter Act of that year created the office of the Governor-General of India and vested in him the sole authority to govern all the Company's possessions in India. This was basically a political decision taken with the object of creating a powerful and supreme agency within the country itself to strengthen the administration of the existing territories as well as to facilitate the conquest of new ones. But it made education, like every other subject, an exclusive responsibility, of the Government of India in which all revenues were vested and which alone could authorize appropriations therefrom. At one stroke, the Provincial Governments thus lost all their authority over education and became merely the agents of the Government of India to administer it on its behalf. They could not create a single post, however low, nor sanction a rupee of expenditure, nor make any change in policies, however small,

1. Charter Act of 1813, Section 43.
2. In the modern parlance, this is equivalent to saying that 'education' ceased to be an exclusively State subject

and became an exclusively Central subject without the approval of the Government of India. This system of a total centralization of authority continued till 1870. It would have been almost unworkable but for the fact that, In actual practice, the Government of India allowed a good deal of freedom to the Provincial Governments to adjust educational policies to their local needs and respected their proposals and advice.

During this period, there were two main occasions when the Government of India issued orders which, in substance, were tantamount to the enunciation of a National Policy on Education although this expression was not then used. The first refers to the orders issued by Lord William Bentinck, on the basis of a Minute recorded by Macaulay, that the objective of modern education in India ought to be the promotion of European literature and science among the people of India and that English should be the medium of education.' The second was the Educational Despatch dated 19th July 1854 issued by the Court of Directors it is a long document of 100 paragraphs which laid down the broad principles and programmes for educational development in India. It confirmed the orders issued earlier by Lord Bentinck and, among other things, authorized (1) the establishments of universities at Bombay, Calcutta and Madras, (2) the creation of Education Departments in the Provinces, (3) the establishment of a graded network of schools and colleges in all parts of the country, (4) the provision of grants-in aid to private schools, (both missionary and Indian), (5) training of teachers, (6) encouragement to the education of women and (7) employment of educated Indians in government service. This policy statement continued to govern all educational developments in India till 1882.

The Role of the Government of India in Education (1870-1921)

In 1870, Lord Mayo initiated a system of decentralization and delegation of authority. The centralized administration introduced in 1833 had served its purpose,: the whole of India had been conquered, the so-called Sepoy Mutiny quelled, and the British rule fully consolidated in all parts of the country. On the other hand, the weaknesses of the system which led to delays and wastefulness in expenditure and created an irresponsible attitude in the Provincial Governments came to the surface and began to gall. A move for decentralization was, therefore, inevitable, and it came none too soon.

Under the orders issued by Lord Mayo, the Provincial Governments were made responsible for all expenditure on certain services (including education) and were given, for that purpose, a fixed grant-in-aid and certain sources of revenue. This system continued to be in force up to 1876-77 when a system of 'shared revenues' was introduced. Under this system, certain revenues were designated as exclusively 'Central', certain others were designated as exclusively 'Provincial' and the remaining were designated as 'Divided' and their receipts were shared between the Central and Provincial Governments according to an agreed contract which remained in force for a period of five years at a time.

Thus the quinquennial contracts were revised in 1882-8 3, 1886 87, 1891-92 and 1896-97. In 1904, they were declared to be quasi-permanent i.e. not to be changed except in a grave emergency, and in 19) 2, they were declared to be permanent. It will thus be seen that, under these financial arrangements, the entire expenditure on education was to be borne by the Provincial Governments within the resources allocated to them. A delegation of administrative powers naturally followed this transfer of financial responsibility. It may be said, therefore, that between 1870 and 1921, most of the administrative and financial authority over education was gradually transferred to the Provincial Governments; and the Government of India merely retained a theoretical right of the control and general supervision as a sequel to its ultimate responsibility to the British Parliament.

It must be made clear however that, when necessary, the Government of India did not hesitate to intervene, to review educational progress, and to issue such directives to Provincial Governments as it felt to be necessary. The first such occasion to intervene arose when there was an insistent demand that the progress of education in India since the Educational Despatch of 1854 should be reviewed. The Government of India, therefore, appointed the first Commission on Education in India, viz. the Indian Education Commission (1882) and on the submission of its report, issued orders laying down a new National Policy on Education. Its main features were: (1) emphasis on the spread of primary education and education among girls, scheduled castes and scheduled tribes; (2) full encouragement to Indian private enterprise in secondary and higher education; and (3) creation of local bodies at the District and Tahsil levels (with considerable participation of the Indian people) and their association with the administration of primary education. These policies continued to be in force till the end of the nineteenth century.

The second occasion for a strong and sustained intervention arose when Lord Curzon became the Governor General of India. He was of the view that Indian education had grown too fast at the secondary and university stages, that its administration had become flabby because of undue freedom given to Indian private enterprise, that standards had deteriorated and that the uncontrolled expansion of secondary and higher education was leading to indiscipline and disaffection against Government.

He was, therefore, of the view that the Government of India should no longer be a 'king log' and that a policy of intensive central interest in education must be enunciated and sustained. He created the office of the Director-General of Public Instruction in India under the Central Government (1897). He also convened a Conference of the Directors of Public Instruction in the Provinces at Simla (1900), appointed the Indian Universities Commission (1902), passed the Indian Universities Act (1904) in the Central Legislature, and issued the Government Resolution on Educational Policy in 1904. He also initiated a system of large Central grants to the Provinces for educational development and these continued to be in vogue for several years afterwards. An Indian Education Service (IES) was also created in 1897 and its officers held all key posts in the Education

Departments. A second Government of India Resolution on Educational Policy was also passed in 1913. The two Resolutions of 1904 and 1913 may also be described as National Policies on Education and form a continuing sequence with the orders of Lord Bentinck, the Educational Despatch of 1854, and the Resolution of the Government [of India on the Recommendations of the Indian Education Commission (1884).

It may be incidentally mentioned that the Government of India started a practice of compiling and publishing quinquennial reviews to the progress of education in India from 1882. Such reviews were published for 1886 87, 1891-92, 1996-97, 1901.02, 1902-07, 1907-12, 1912-17, and 1921-22.

The Role of the Government of India in Education (1921 47)

This period of active Central control and financial support of education came to an end in 1921 when, under the Government of India Act, 1919, education in the Provinces was transferred to the control of Indian Ministers responsible to legislatures with an elected majority. As a corollary to this basic decision, the role of the Government of India (which continued to be responsible to the British Parliament) in education had to be limited to the minimum. Under the Government of India Act, 1919, therefore, the responsibilities of Government were divided into Central and Provincial lists in the first instance and then the latter were divided into reserved and transferred. Because of various conflicting proposals made on the subject, education was treated as partly all-India, partly reserved, partly transferred with limitations and partly transferred without limitations. The following powers were reserved to the Government of India.

1. The Banares Hindu University and such other new universities as may be declared to be all-India by the Governor-General-in Council.
2. College for Indian chiefs and educational institutions maintained by the Governor-General-in-Council for the benefit of members of His Majesty's Forces or other public servants, or their children.

3. The authority to legislate on the following subjects was reserved for the central legislature, mainly with a view to enabling the Government of India to take suitable action on the report of the Calcutta University Commission.
   (a) Questions regarding the establishment, constitution and functions of new universities;
   (b) Questions affecting the jurisdiction of-any university outside its province; and
   (c) Questions regarding the Calcutta University and the reorganisation of secondary education in Bengal (for a period of five Nears only after the introduction of the Reforms). (None of these powers were ever exercised in practice).

Except for the above matters reserved for the Government of India the whole of the education wag transferred to the control of Indian Ministers with one exception, viz. education of Anglo-Indians find Europeans was reserved. There were also some restrictions on the control which the Ministers could exercise in certain matters (e.g. the IES).

It was also decided to stop all further recruitment to the IES so that the 'service would fade out within a few years. Needless to say the system of Central grants which had made such a useful contribution to educational development also disappeared.

The Role of the Government of India in Education: A Comprehensive View

So far, we have discussed the Constitutional Role of the Government of India in education. It must be pointed out however that the constitutional role of the Government of India in education is only one aspect of its actual role which must be examined in its totality.

The other aspects of this role which modify the constitutional position very substantially are : (1) public opinion, (2) financial relations, (3) political situation, and (4) administrative arrangements. It is only an integrated view of all these aspects that can give real insights into the nature of the problem and enable us to devise practicable reforms.

Public Opinion: What is the public view of the Centre-State relations in education and how does the public except education to be administered? It is obvious that, in a truly democratic set up, the administration of education which concerns every individual intimately must be highly decentralized. The general practice in this regard is that school education or at least elementary education which has to be provided for every child, should be controlled by the local community. This, for instance, is the tradition in U.S.A. where the people are extremely alert on educational issues and where the principle of local control of school education is strongly rooted in the historical traditions of the country. In a situation of this type, the State itself has a minor role in school education and the Federal Government, even less. The position regarding secondary and higher education, however is rather different. Secondary education is usually under local control if it is provided on a universal basis. Otherwise, it is generally provided by a larger community or the State; and higher education, except in a few big cities, is generally managed by the State or by the State and the Federal Government in some kind of partnership. On the basis of this broad general practice, it should ordinarily be expected that in India elementary education should be administered at the local community level, secondary education at the district or State level, and higher education at the State level or at the State and national levels.

Unfortunately, the historical traditions in our country have been different so that local control of education at the community or district level has failed to develop adequately. It is true that we did have a tradition of some local control of education because, in the pre-British days, schools were established and controlled by the local communities rather than by the Princes who, at best, extended their patronage to a few learned scholars or schools of higher learning. But these schools, more often than not, were enterprises of individuals or of small interested groups within the community rather than of the community as a whole. Even this limited tradition also died out when

Government accepted responsibility for providing education. In the old British Indian Provinces, an attempt was made to associate local bodies at the community and district level with the provision of elementary education. This tradition has survived but has neither become vital or dynamic. In the Princely States, on the other hand, no such effort was ever made. In the post-independence period also the local control of education was not encouraged except for the Panchayati Raj experiment which has been tried earnestly only in a few areas. Consequently, the present position is that the vast masses of the people who are mostly illiterate have no interest in education as now imparted in the formal system and the tradition of local control in education is also mostly non-existent.

Public interest in education in India is mainly confined to the educated and elite groups who are the principal beneficiaries of the formal educational system and who mostly belong to the top 30 per cent of the income groups. Their main interest is in secondary and higher education where, apart from other things, their own private enterprise provides the bulk of the educational institutions. Moreover, it is the children of this elite which form about 70 per cent of the enrolment in secondary education and about go per cent of the enrolment in higher education. The basic issues that interest this elite are, therefore, the location and opening of new secondary schools, colleges and universities, their curricula and grants, in-aid and the expansion of elementary education (which provides them with a large number of fairly well-paid jobs).

As these, issues are mostly decided at the State level, the concept of education as essentially a State responsibility gets the strongest-public support. The view, gets further strengthened from the fact that, the State is probably the most convenient level from which a basic social service like education can be administered. The sap e view also finds still further support in the State levy leadership whose image and power-base largely depends upon the control of educational institutions, teachers and students. It is these supports which made education a Stale subject under the Constitution and which also continue to legitimize the position. In fact, one may even assert that education as a State responsibility is at present so well entrenched in the public mind (or in the mind of the elites that rule the country) that it is extremely difficult, if not actually impassible, to alter this situation.

One need not necessarily quarrel with this view and may agree that education may basically remain a State responsibility. But one cannot also accept a State absolutism in education and an over-concentration of authority at the State level. The power of the state, in education has therefore to be limited to a considerable extent in the larger interests of education itself. This is generally attempted in three ways.

(a) The first is administrative decentralisation where authority over education, and especially over school education, is transferred to the local community at the municipal, village, Tahsil or District levels. As pointed out earlier, this trend is weak in the country, partly because the earlier tradition of local control or popular involvement in education has almost died out, partly because such decentralisation can be most effective in elementary and adult education which continue to be our neglected sectors, and partly because the local leadership at the village, Tahsil or District level is still weak in comparison with that at the Stale level and cannot assert itself. Consequently, the unfortunate public view that the State and Central levels are the only two that really matter in education, gains undue currency and strength. This trend also finds support in the general attitudes of linguistic and other minorities and weaker sections like Scheduled Castes and Tribes who find that the local levels (whether village, block, Tahsil or District) are generally oppressive and that their oppressiveness increases as one goes down to lower levels so that their hopes of justice and fair treatment lie mainly at the State and national levels.

(b) The second is academic decentralisation, i.e. to free the educational process from bureaucratic control by respecting university autonomy which the universities should, in their turn, share with their departments and affiliated colleges), by enabling the schools to prepare their own curricula and to hold their own examinations, and in short by so delegating authority to educational institutions and their teachers that the teaching-learning process becomes free, joyful and independent of State control. Unfortunately these concepts have not gained strength either within the teaching profession or among the general public. On the other hand, the contrary trends have gained an upper hand and the academic control of the State over education, schools and teachers has increased, rather than decreased, since 1947.

(c) While we have thus been unable to check State absolutism in education either through decentralisation to local bodies or through academic decentralization, we have had a somewhat better success to control State authority in education through centralization, i.e. by giving a larger voice to the Central Government in educational matters. One powerful group that supports this demand is that of the national bureaucracy which can be transferred to any part of the country and the large trade and industrial interests that have also acquired a national character. These groups are generally in favour of a national system of education with common curricula and text books in all parts of the country-a situation which can be created only if the Central Government can have an over-riding voice in education. The university and research, system which can be best planned on a national basis also supports the same trend. Further support comes from another important group, viz., teachers, who would like to fight for uniform scales of pay and emoluments in all parts of the country and who realize that they can become a tremendous force if organized on a national basis. They are, therefore, in favour of an increasing role in education for the Centre and against any devolution of authority to the local bodies. A large section of the, intellectual elite also recognizes the need for a national policy in education from the point of view of national integration and takes the stand that while the "diversity" implied in the State control of education is both necessary and desirable, it is equally important to provide the 'unity' in this diversity through á national educational policy. It, must also be pointed out that the national leadership that grew in the freedom struggle initiated a large and intensive debate on education at the national level and that this tradition still continues unabated. Consequently, education has become, throughout the last hundred years or so, a great national concern although it remains State subject in administration. The public support for the role of the Government of India in education arises essentially from these social and political groups and from these national concerns which cannot be ignored, although not all of them are healthy and desirable, To the extent they succeed, there will be a curb on the State authority in education and a legitimate basis for the formulation and implementation of a national policy on education.

It will thus be evident 'that, while education will continue to be essentially a State responsibility (irrespective of the fact whether it does or does not continue to be in the concurrent list in the Constitution), it is equally essential to curb the trend towards State absolutism, not only by giving a more significant role to the Centre, but also by strengthening local control in education and promoting academic decentralization. Steps will have to be taken to educate public opinion on these lines in the years ahead.

Financial Relations: The Centre-State relations in financial support of education are obviously very important. Where the Centre can give large grant-in aid for educational development, it always gets considerable control over it and is in a strong position to implement national policies on education, irrespective of any constitutional provisions on the subject. Prior to 1870, the Government of India did exercise almost complete control over education because it sanctioned all the funds needed for it. This authority decreased in actual practice between 1870 and 1902 when, under the system of financial devolution initiated in that year, the entire responsibility for financing education was gradually transferred to the Provincial Governments. Lord Curzon initiated a system of specific-purpose Central grants for educational development which continued even after he left. They therefore enabled the Central Government to play a major role in expanding and improving education between 1902 and 1921. When these were legally terminated by the provisions of the Government of India Act, 191'), the Central authority to influence the development of education also declined. It may also be stated that no such specific-purpose Central grants were sanctioned for education between 1921 and 1947.

After the attainment of independence, the desire of the Government of India to expand and improve education led to the formulation of national decisions on several important issues and to the revival of Central grants to help their speedy implementation. For instance, the creation of the University Grants Commission in 1956 was partly meant to provide additional and specific-purpose grants to State Governments for the development of higher education. Similar grants were provided for engineering education under the advice of the All India Council of Technical Education. The Indian Council of Agricultural Research has provided special grants for the development of agricultural universities and agricultural education, research and training; and the Central Ministry of Health and the Indian Council of Medical Research have provided similar assistance respectively for medical education and research.

In addition to these, efforts were made to give specific-purpose grants for educational development through successive five-year plans. The education chapter of each Five Year Plan is essentially a statement of a national policy on education and of the programmes intended to implement it. A system, therefore, arose under which all schemes included in the Plans were divided into three categories: (1) Central i.e. those which were to be implemented by the Central Government and funds for which were also provided in the Central Sector; (2) Centrally-

Sponsored i.e. those which were to be implemented by the State Governments, but funds for which were provided at the Centre and were later made available to the State Governments for specific approved schemes; and (3) State i.e. those which were to be implemented by the State Governments and funds for which were also provided in the State plans. In the first and the second plans, the number of Central and Centrally-sponsored schemes was large and there were special Central grants even for State schemes. From the third plan onwards, these policies have greatly changed, mainly because of the pressure from the States, in two directions: (1) the number of centrally-sponsored schemes is being continually reduced, and (2) central plan assistance is given, not for individual State schemes of educational development and not even for all education taken together, but for the State plan as a whole, subject to only one condition, viz., the allocation for elementary education is earmarked. It is not however easy in practice to enforce this earmarking rigidly; and the net effect of all these changes is that the capacity of the Government of India to enforce its 'advice' on the State Governments through the indirect method of centrally-sponsored schemes or specific purpose grants has been greatly reduced.

The Education Commission (1964-66) recommended the enlargement of the Central sector in education and the revival of the Centrally-sponsored grants on a large scale to implement national policies in education. But this recommendation has not yet been accepted by the Government of India. On the other hand, the recommendations of the Seventh Finance Commission have adopted a hew approach altogether. The policy adopted by the first six Commissions was to transfer only such resources to the States as would enable them to cover the deficit in their budgets at the end of the plan period so that the State Governments bad to depend very largely on the Centre for financing their developmental plans. The Seventh Finance Commission has changed this policy and transferred substantial resources to the States so that they have larger autonomy to finance their development plans. This has changed the situation substantially. In the first place, the Centre now has more limited resources to expand the Central Sector. The proposal of the Commission to expand the Centrally sponsored sector has also run into hot weather. The State Governments have been pleading, since 1966, to abolish all the Centrally sponsored schemes. They are succeeding continuously and now the Centrally-sponsored schemes, especially in education, have been reduced to the minimum and they appear to be on their way out. One is not sure therefore what financial levers, if any the Centre may continue to have to influence State educational policies if these levers disappear, it will not make much difference whether education remains in the concurrent list or is retransferred to the State list.

Political Aspects: The political aspects of the problem also need some attention. It is obvious that the chances of enunciating and implementing a strong national policy are greater when the same political party is in power at the Centre and in the States (or when the different political parties in power agree on a programme of national significance).

This, for instance is the situation in the USSR where, inspite of a very large constitutional delegation of authority over education to the States, a uniform national system of education has been created and maintained by the Communist Party. In India also, national policies in education have depended for their success, not so much on Constitutional provisions as on the strength of the Congress party and the capacity of the national leadership to assert itself. Between 1921 and 1947, the Congress continually reiterated the view that India should have a national system of education which, necessarily implied the enunciation and implementation of a national policy on education. The idea also worked politically to some extent so long as the Congress remained in power at the Centre and in all States, say, between 1947 and 1967. The State Governments were then generally of the view, that a national policy in education was desirable and were more amenable to advice from the Centre, But differences began to surface when non-Congress governments were formed in some States such as Kerala or Tamil Nadu, The language problem in particular proved to be extremely difficult. Even within the Congress, unanimity of views was very difficult to be reached, while non-Congress governments like the DMK took up openly hostile stances. Differences also began to gain momentum between those who pleaded for a strong Centre and those who desired to have greater autonomy for the States. The recent elections have defeated the Congress as a national patty while the Janata Party has a long way to go to get a national status-In this state of political fragmentation, the chances of enunciating and implementing a strong national policy in education are' somewhat dubious, even if education continues to be in the concurrent list and although it is now theoretically open to the Government of India to pass an Act of Parliament embodying the national policy on education.

Administrative Aspects: Administrative arrangements play an important role in posting a national policy on education. If there is a basic decision to have a national policy on education, steps, are usually taken to create an effective administrative machinery to implement it. On the other band, if there is an effective administrative machinery, it does help, in its turn, to enunciate and implement a national policy on education.

Over the last 120 years or so, however, policy and administration have not always moved in unison.

(a) In 1855, steps were taken to create Education Departments in the Provinces which had no legal authority over education while, in the Government of India which had all the authority over education, there was no adequate machinery to look after this subject which was consequently dealt with partly in the Home Department and partly in the Political Department (in so far as education in the princely states was concerned). Between 1833 and 1870, therefore, the authority over education was largely exercised by the Provincial Government inspite of the fact that all authority was centralized and vested in the Government of India.

(b) On the other hand, there was a deliberate policy, between 1870 and 1921, to delegate increasing authority over education to Provincial Governments. But there was a good deal of administrative centralisation simultaneously. For instance, the Indian Education Service (IES) was created in 1897; and as stated already, Lord Curzon created the office of the Director General of Public Instruction at the Centre. A separate Department of Education was created in 1910 and the Bureau of Education was established in 1915. These measures, combined with the introduction of Central grants for education gave a considerable lever to the Government of India to enunciate and implement a national policy on Education.

(c) Between 1921 and 1947, however, there was a constitutional divorce between the Government of India and education; and, at the same time, the IES was abolished, the educational services were fully provincialised, and even a separate Department of Education and the Bureau of Education were abolished as a measure of economy in 1923. Consequently, the Central machinery to enunciate and implement a national educational policy became the weakest in modern history.

(d) Between 1947 and 1978, the constitutional authority of the Centre in education has been increased; and side by side, a separate Ministry of Education has been created at the Centre, strengthened from time to time and, more often than not, placed under a Minister of the. Cabinet rank. This has strengthened the administrative basis for a national policy on education. But the demand to create an Indian Education Service has not yet been conceded, inspite of the recommendation of the Education Commission (1964-66).

Administrative measures can also buttress the 'advisory' role of the Centre. For instance, the Central Advisory Board of Education was created in 1921 from this point of view, but it was abolished in 1923 as a measure of economy. It was, however, revived in 1935 and has continued to function ever since. Sporadic attempts continue to be made to strengthen its role; and their success has varied from time to time, depending mainly on the personality of the Union Education Minister and the willingness of the Government of India to back tip the 'advice' of the Board with financial support.

It has, in practice, made a fairly significant contribution to the evolution of national policies on Education. While its comparative weakness as an institutional mechanism for the formulation and implementation of national policies in education is recognised, it has not yet been possible to find a better alternative solution to the problem.

Yet another administrative step taken is to create and strengthen national institutions which could educate public opinion, give guidance to State level personnel and provide advanced level training facilities. It is from this point of view that Central institutions like the National Council of Educational Research and Training (NCERT), the National Staff College of Educational Planners and Administrators, the Central Institute of English and Foreign Languages, the Central Institute of Hindi, Central Hindi Directorate (including the Commission on Scientific and Technical Terminology), the Central Institute of Indian Languages, and the Central Sanskrit Organization were created. This programme has yielded some good results but we are far from realizing, the full potential of this strategy.

General Conclusions

What are the main conclusions that can be drawn from this brief review of the role of the Government of India in education? To begin with, it becomes clear that the enunciation and implementation of a national policy on education depends essentially on the role of the Government of India in education in all its aspects. The conditions most favourable for the purpose are:

(a) existence of a strong public opinion in favour of such a role; There is hardly any other instrument available for the purpose. Instruments like ad hoc conferences of State Education Ministers, Education Secretaries, or Directors of Education and even establishment of national bodies like the National Board of Basic Education have been tried and found to be even more ineffective.

(b) adequate Constitutional authority over education being vested in the Government of India;

(c) existence of specific purpose central grants for education which can underpin central 'advice' to State Governments;

(d) institutional devices that can enable the Centre to influence the State Education Departments through guidance and training; and

(e) existence of strong national political parties which can indirectly influence the State Governments to take common decisions inspite of their autonomy under the Constitution.

Our review has however shown that these basic conditions have varied materially from time to, time.

(1) Between 1833 when the Charter Act of that year created a unitary form of the Government of India and 1870 when Lord Mayo introduced his system of decentralisation of educational administration, education was a Central subject and a central responsibility. It was therefore easy to enunciate and implement a national policy on education. This was done, but the central authorities of this period also allowed a good deal of variation and flexibility to suit local conditions so that, inspite of a hard core of central unity, a diversified and varied system of education developed in the country.

(2) Between 1870 and 1921, the Government of India continued to have constitutional authority and responsibility for education which still made it possible for the Centre to enunciate and implement a national policy in education. But, except for the intervention of Lord Ripon on the advice of the Indian Education Commission (1884) and the Curzonian interlude (1897-1905). The general trend was to delegate more

authority to the Provincial Governments. The culmination of this policy was reached under the Government of India Act (1919) which practically divorced Central Government from education and made education almost a total responsibility of the State Governments. This position was further strengthened by the Government of India Act, 1935. Even the Constitution adopted in 1950 accepted this basic position with some modifications.

(3) Between 1950 and 1979, efforts have been made to alter this situation and to reduce the absolute authority of the State Governments in two ways. On the one hand, an effort was made to decentralize greater administrative authority to agencies at District, Tehsil, Block or village levels and to decentralize greater academic authority to educational institutions and teachers. By and large, these efforts remained weak and did not have any effective success. On the other hand, efforts were also made to give a more effective voice to the Centre in educational matters. These succeeded better. Education has now been made a concurrent subject; the planning process centralises considerable authority in the Centre; and national agencies like the Central Advisory Board of Education, the UGC., All India Council for Technical Education or National Council of Educational Research and Training also add materially to the authority of the Centre and its effectiveness in implementing national educational policies.

However, the reduction in the specific-purpose central, grants to education and the fragmentation of political life have weakened the Central authority to deal effectively with national educational issues. Public opinion continues to be divided seriously over the problem. Those who believe in greater autonomy for the States resist all attempts to give a greater authority to the Centre in educational Matters and, as pointed out earlier, would even reduce the existing authority of the Centre in education and abolish the Ministry of Education. On the other hand, there are several academics who would continue to retain education as a concurrent subject, have an Education Act passed by Parliament, create an IES, multiply and strengthen Central educational agencies and provide large specific-purpose central grants for education.

A third group of intellectuals who stand for the middle path recognizes the need of a stimulating and dynamic leadership provided by the Centre but is not in favour of vesting it with any coercive authority.

It would also like to curb State absolutism in education through decentralization of authority to local bodies and by large academic decentralization. The Central role in education has thus been one of the most controversial subjects and is continuously debated upon since 1947, and end of the controversy is not yet in sight.

It is obvious that both the formulation and implementation of a national policy on education will largely depend upon the concensus reached on these basic issues and on the manner in which the constitutional role of the Government of India in education is or is not supported by public opinion and political, financial and administrative mechanisms.

Commissions on Secondary Education—Functioning of Secondary Schools in Our Country

Appointment of the Commission

The Secondary Education Commission appointed by the Government of India in terms of their Resolution No. F. 9-5/52-B-1, dated 23rd September 1952, (Appendix 1), having completed its labours, presents the following Report based on its deliberations.

The Government of India, their communique quoted above, referred to the recommendation of the Central Advisory Board of Education made at its 14th meeting held in January 1948, that a Commission be appointed to examine the prevailing system of Secondary Education in the country and suggest measures for its re-organization and improvement. The Board reiterated its recommendation in January 1951. The Government of India had also other considerations in mind when appointing this Commission, such as the desirability of changing over from the prevailing system of secondary education which is unilateral and predominantly academic in nature to one which will cater at the secondary stage for different aptitudes and interests. The Commission appointed by the Government of India consisted of the following:

1. DR. A. LAKSHMANSWAMI MUDALIAR
   Vice-Chancellor, Madras University, (Chairman)
2. PRINCIPAL JOHN CHRISTIE
   Jesus College, Oxford
3. DR. KENNETH RAST WILLIAMS
   Associate Director, Southern Regional Education Board, Atlanta (U.S.A.)
4. MRS. HANSA MEHTA
   Vice-Chancellor, Baroda University
5. SHRI J. A. TARAPOREWALA Director of Technical Education Government of Bombay
6. DR. K. L. SHRIMALI
   Principal, Vidya Bhavan Teachers' Training College, Udaipur
7. SHRI M. T. Vyas
   Bombay
8. SHRI K. G. SAIYDAIN
   Joint Secretary to the Government of India Ministry of Education (Ex-officio Member)
9. PRINCIPAL A. N. BASU
   Central Institute of Education
   Delhi (Member-Secretary)

   Dr. S. M. S. Chari, Education Officer, Ministry of Education acted,as Assistant Secretary to the Commission.

Terms of Reference

Under the terms of reference, the Commission was asked

"(a) to enquire into and report on the present position of Secondary Education in India in all its aspects; and

(b) suggest measures for its reorganization and improvement with particular reference to-

(i) the aims, organization and content of Secondary Education;

(ii) its relationship to Primary, Basic and Higher Education;

(iii) the inter-relation of Secondary Schools of different types; and

(iv) other allied problems.

so that a sound and reasonably uniform system of Secondary Education suited to our needs and resources may be provided for the whole country."

Inauguration of the Commission

The Commission was inaugurated by the Hon'ble Minister of Edu-cation, Maulana Abul Kalam Azad, on the 6th October, 1952 in New Delhi. It immediately proceeded to consider its programme of work. Prior to the first meeting of the Commission, the Chairman and the Member-Secretary discussed the issue of a suitable questionnaire. They had the advice of some headmasters and others interested in education and, keeping in view the main functions which the Commission had to discharge sent out a detailed questionnaire, a copy of which is given in Appendix II. The questionnaire was sent to a large number of educationists, administrators and leaders of public opinion interested in the sphere of education. Replies were received from many of them. The Commission acknowledges its thanks to all those who-have sent, their replies to the questionnaire.

Itinerary

Soon after its inauguration, the Commission met in New Delhi, and considered the scope of its functions with reference to the terms under which it was appointed, the manner in which it was to discharge its responsibilities and the extent to which it would be necessary for the Commission to elicit public opinion from educationists and other citizens all over the country.

It drew up a detailed tour programme to enable the members to visit various States. A copy of the tour programme is appended (vide Appendix 111). The Commission regrets that within the limited time at its disposal it could not accept invitations to visit other places but it feels that he ground covered has given it a reasonable opportunity to understand and appreciate the many problems of Secondary Education in the various States of the Indian Union.

Co-opted Members

In most of the States which the Commission visited, the Government of the State concerned nominated a member of the Education Department or a prominent educationist of the State as a co-opted member during the Commission's tour in the particular State. The following persons were co-opted as members of the Commission for the States mentioned:

- Shri C. L. Kapoor, Secretary, Education Department, Punjab
- Shri A. A. Kazmi, Director of Education, Jammu and Kashmir
- Shri S. N. Sahay, Vice-Chancellor, Bihar University, Patna

  and
- Shri J. C. Mathur, Secretary, Education Department, Bihar
- Shri S. C. Rajkhowa, Inspector of Schools, Assam
- Shri A. K. Chanda, Chairman, Secondary Education Board, West Bengal
- Dr. B. Prasad, Director of Public Instruction, Orissa
- Shri S. Govindarajulu Naidu, Director of Public Instruction, Madras

- Shri V. Sundararaja Naidu, Director of Public Instruction, Travancore-Cochin
- Shri J. B. Mallaradhya, Director of Public Instruction, Mysore
- Dr. D. Shendarkar, Deputy Director of Public Instruction, Hyderabad
- Dr. V. S. Jha, Secretary, Education Department, Madhya Pradesh
- Shri D. C. Pavate, Director of Education, Bombay
- Shri Nanabhai Bhatt, M. P., Gram Dakshina Murti, Saurashtra
- Shri S. N. Chaturvedi, Director of Education, Madhya Bharat
- Shri R. G. Gupta, Assistant Director of Education, Rajasthan
- Dr. A. N. Banerjee, Director of Education, Delhi

The Commission wishes to express its sincere thanks to the co-opted members who gave valuable advice and materially helped the Commission by arranging for visits to educational institutions and for interviews. The Commission had largely to leave it to the Directors of Public Instruction and to the co-opted members in these States to decide on the representatives who were to be interviewed. Besides the co-opted members, certain of the State Governments appointed also liaison Officers whose duty it was to help in arranging for the meetings of the Commission, for the interviews, and for visits to educational institutions and generally to make the work of the Commission profitable and pleasant.

The Commission wishes to express its thanks to these officers for the very efficient help that they gave, enabling it to discharge its duties satisfactorily. The Commission had the advantage, of interviewing a large number of distinguished educationists, members of Universities, representatives of teachers' organizations, representatives of managements, high officials of the Departments of Education and associated professions, Ministers of the States and Centre and leading representatives of the public. A list of such persons is given in Appendix IV. To all these persons the Commission is greatly indebted for the opportunity of a free and frank exchange of ideas on all important subjects connected with secondary education.

The Commission was gratified to note that in all the States that were visited, great interest and enthusiasm were evinced in problems of secondary education. In several States, Committees had already been appointed to enquire into and report on the working of Secondary Education in these States. The Commission wishes to add that it is particularly grateful to the State Governments, to the Ministers of Education and other Ministers of the States, to the Directors of Public Instruction and to the Ministry of Education at the Centre for their ready willingness to assist the Commission, and for the manner in which every possible co-operation was extended in the work that it had undertaken.

Raison D'etre of the Commission

In the course of our interviews the question arose as to the necessity for the Central Government to appoint an All-India Commission on Secondary Education since, under the Constitution, education is a responsibility of the State Governments. This is an important issue and we consider it necessary to state clearly the raison d'etre of such a Commission. We recognise that secondary education is mainly the concern of the States but, in view of its impact on the life of the country as a whole, both in the field of culture and technical efficiency, the Central Government cannot divest itself of the responsibility to improve its standards and to relate it intelligently to the larger problems of national life.

The aim of secondary education is to train the youth of the country to be good citizens, who will be competent to play their part effectively in the social reconstruction and economic development of their country. The Central Government is, therefore, naturally concerned about the type of education to be given to the youth of the country. It must make sure that secondary education will prepare young men for the various vocations that are open to them. Moreover, it is directly charged with the responsibility of maintaining proper standards in higher education. This cannot be done, unless careful consideration is given to the level of efficiency attained at the secondary stage.

All-India Problems

There are several other fields in which it is desirable that a clear policy should be laid down on an all-India basis. One of the fundamental rights guaranteed by the Constitution is the right of every citizen of the Union to free and compulsory education up to the age of 14. For the proper functioning of democracy, the Centre must see that every individual is equipped with the necessary knowledge, skill, and aptitudes to discharge his duties as a responsible and co-operative citizen. What James Madison said about his country, the United States, many years ago, holds good today in our country also. "A popular Government without popular information or the means of acquiring it is but a prologue to a farce of tragedy or perhaps both.

Knowledge will forever govern ignorance, and the people who mean to be their own governors must arm themselves with the power which knowledge gives." We should, however like to add that it is not only knowledge that is required, but also the right kind of social training and the inculcation of right ideals without which knowledge by itself may be sterile or worse. Training for democracy postulates a balanced education in which social virtues, intellectual development and practical skill all receive due consideration and the pattern of such an education must be envisaged on an all-India basis.

Another important question with which we were faced everywhere was the place of the different languages more particularly of Hindi and English in the scheme of secondary education. There is a great deal of confused thinking as well as wide difference of opinion on this subject. If educational progress is to be well planned and confusion is to be avoided, the tendency to adopt divergent and even conflicting policies in this matter has to be resisted. And it is not only in the matter of linguistic policy that this tendency to separatism has been in evidence. There has been an accentuation in recent years of certain undesirable tendencies of provincialism, regionalism, and other sectional differences.

This situation is fraught with serious consequences and it is as much the duty of statesmen as of educationalists to take steps to reorient people's mind in the right direction. If education fails to play its part effectively in checking these tendencies, if it does not strengthen the forces of national cohesion and solidarity, we are afraid that our freedom, our national unity as well as our future progress will be seriously imperilled. We feel that in the entire planning of education and to some extent, in the matter of its financial responsibility, there should be the closest co-operation and co-operation between the Centre and the States.

In some fields of secondary education, the Central Government should assume greater responsibility, e.g., in the training of teachers, the formulation of educational and vocational tests, the production and selection of better textbooks, and the training of technicians. The Centre has also a special obligation with regard to the physical welfare of the pupils. It has already organized a National Cadet Corps for schools. Consistently, therefore with the recognition of the role of the States in formulating educational programmes and implementing them, we have no doubt whatever that, in view of the crucial importance of education for the whole future and progress of the country in every sphere-economic, industrial, social and cultural-the Central Government should view education from an overall national angle and assume the duties of educational guidance and leadership. While there is everything to be said for local and State autonomy in education, it should not be interpreted to justify differences in basic educational policies and objectives.

Previous Education Commissions

A number of Commissions has been appointed in the past to survey Indian Education-the Indian Education Commission of 1882, the Commission of 1902, the Sadler

Commission of 1917 and the recent Radhakrishnan Commission, all of which dealt incidentally with certain aspects of Secondary Education.

But no Commission has so far been appointed to survey the problems of secondary education as a whole. We have been entrusted with this responsibility and, in discharging it, we found that we had also to give some consideration to primary as well as higher education. This in fact was enjoined on us by our terms of reference since they are both intimately linked up with Secondary Education and their standards and efficiency depend largely on the proper organization of secondary education. Reference has, therefore, been made from time to time to these two stages. In discussing the new pattern of secondary education organization we have indicated how it is to be linked up at one end with Primary Education and at the other with University Education and how the total duration of education in these three stages will be distributed.

We have the feeling that the appointment of the Commission has been made very opportunely because, in our tour, we found clear evidence of serious interest in this problem all over the country. Not only is this interest apparent amongst educational authorities and teachers but State Governments have also taken steps to have the whole problem of Secondary Education surveyed and examined by competent committees appointed for the purpose.

In some States their reports have already been submitted, while in others the matter is under active consideration. We have studied with interest and profit such reports as have been published and we have had the advantage of an exchange of views with some of the members of these committees. Because of this general awakening, there is reason to hope that the States and the Centre would take active steps to implement as far as possible, the approved recommendations made by this Commission and the various State Committees.

It was also pointed out that this Commission should have preceded the University Commission established in 1948. This is obviously not a matter for us to discuss. Actually it has been a great advantage for us to know exactly what the University Commission had to say. In fact every Commission on education has had necessarily to deal with Secondary Education to a very large extent. It cannot be otherwise. The Indian Education Commission of 1882, the Commission of 1902 with its more restricted terms of reference, the Commission of 1917, more popularly known as the, Sadler Commission and the latest University Education Commission of which Dr. Radhakrishnan was the Chairman have all dealt with some aspects of secondary education. Their reports have all been studied by us with interest and profit.

Implementation of Recommendations

Many recommendations of previous Commissions have not been implemented. Many responsible people have therefore questioned the likelihood of any steps being taken to examine and implement the recommendations of this Commission. In reply we would point out that India's needs today are different from what they were in the past.

India is now free and independent. The educational needs of a free country are different and ought to be different from what, they were under foreign domination. The implementation of a report in the days of foreign rule was the responsibility of an alien government and if nothing was done that Government was to blame. Today, however, in a self-governing democracy, the responsibility for implementing a sound educational policy rests with the people themselves and their chosen representatives.

If public opinion, therefore, proclaims clearly that a new educational policy is needed, the report which we are representing, if approved, will be preliminary to action, and not, as reports have too often been in the past, an alternative to action. We are not inclined to take a pessimistic view of the matter and, although we are aware of the conditions under which State and Central Governments will have to examine this report, we believe that the States and the Centre are most actively interested in the problems of education, more particularly of secondary education.

Basis of Recommendations

We are anxious to see that our recommendations are of such a nature that they can be implemented. For this reason, we have divided them into short-term and long-term recommendations. It is, however, essential that the general orientation of policy should be clear from the outset so that the refashioning of the educational pattern may proceed on right lines and, even where we are not able to put certain suggestions and recommendations into practice immediately, we should know in what direction we are moving. We realize that some of the specific recommendations that we have made may have a comparatively short range applicability, for changed conditions, social, political, economic and cultural—always postulate new educational objectives and techniques.

In a changing world, problems of education are also likely to change. The emphasis placed on one aspect of it today may not be necessary at a future date. It must, therefore, be clearly understood that these recommendations are not to be considered as recommendations for all time but they must necessarily be looked upon as recommendations for a fair period. They may have to be reviewed from time to time in the light of experience. In any case, educational reform must be undertaken in such a way that it remains permanent over a definite period of time. Our proposals should not be subject to frequent changes by those temporarily responsible for carrying on the democratic form of government. While we agree that experiments in education are to be continuous, we, feel that the general lines of reform should be such as would be conducive to a steady growth.

The Development of Secondary Education in Our Country during the Pre and Post-independent Periods

With the central government lobbing its ball to the state governments for the implementation of the several schemes for the revitalization of the system of the secondary education in the country, the schemes of the access, equity, Mahila Samakhya, and quality in the field of secondary education has lost its very essence. Basic issues of quality, equity and access to secondary education in India still unresolved besides the central legislations by the Ministry of Human Resource development Govt. of India. The expert committees were formulated by the Govt. to gauge the system and suggest the measures to universalize the whole system.

The central governments own figures indicate that many as two-thirds of those eligible for secondary education remain outside the school system today. A Central Advisory Board of Education (CABE) committee estimates that 88,562 additional classrooms was required in 2007-08 and over 1.3 lakh additional teachers. The CABE is the highest advisory body relating to policy making in education in India. Figures put out by the Ministry of Human Resource Development's Department of School Education and Literacy indicate that as many as two-thirds of those eligible for secondary and senior secondary education remain outside the school system today. While noting that adequate number of elementary schools is to be found at a reasonable distance from habitations, the ministry admits in its website that this is not the case with regard to secondary schools and colleges. The gross enrolment rate for elementary education in 2003-04 was 85 percent, but for secondary education, the enrolment figure stood at 39 percent.

Pertinently, the CABE report also notes that the benefits of India's reservation policy in higher education are unlikely to reach those it's intended for in the absence of a strong secondary education system. A large majority of children and youth belonging to SC and ST community do not have access to secondary education; less than 10 percent of the girls among SCs and STs have access to the plus two stage. Without secondary or senior secondary education, benefits of reservation to SCs/STs will remain elusive," the report says. These are questions that the CABE report tries to address. School systems, the report says, should strive for equality and social justice, transcending discrimination that may arise because of gender, economic disparity, societal norms on caste and community, location (urban area or rural), disabilities (physical and mental) and cultural or linguistic differences. However, these inequities seem bound to remain given the current circumstances, where the government involvement in secondary education is much less than what is expected of it. The Committee report says that almost 25 percent of the secondary schools today are private, unaided schools whose clientele comes only from the privileged sections of society.

Expert opines that Private education has always played an important role we have different types of private secondary schools, such as private unrecognized, private recognized but unaided schools, and private, recognized and aided schools. In Kerala and West Bengal, it's common to see private aided schools, which are schools run by private managements that receive government grants. Going by the Sixth All India Survey Data, the CABE report notes that private aided schools account for over 46 percent of all secondary school students. The overwhelming participation of the private sector in secondary education, however, in no way absolves the government of its many responsibilities. To improve access to secondary education, experts agree that the government should invest more money. Unfortunately, the Centre has baulked at involving itself even in primary education, more so when it has to be on a collision course with private schools.

Similarly, though the CABE committee report advocates a common school system, the government seems to have already shown its disinterest. The CABE report was accepted in principle, but soon after, the Planning Commission diluted our recommendation that the typical secondary school should be like a Kendriya Vidyalaya. The Commission started saying that instead of Kendriya Vidyalaya norms, SSA norms could be extended to secondary schools. Such a move would result in parallel streams of education with poor quality being accepted as a part of secondary education.

The CABE committee, incidentally, had worked out the expenditure that will be incurred if all secondary schools are managed like Kendriya Vidyalayas. The total costs in such a scenario do not exceed six percent of the GDP but that does not seem to have been enough to convince the government. The report does not mention how many additional schools will be needed to meet the future demand. However, it presents two estimates, one projection based on the 100 percent success of SSA and the other, the 75 percent success of the programme. In the case of the former, the report estimates that 88,562 additional classrooms will be required in 2007-08 and over 1.3 lakh additional teachers.

A worrisome trend in government schools, undoubtedly a factor contributing to their poor performance, is the fact that almost 95 percent of the government grants go into paying staff salaries. There is no money for buying teaching learning materials, for cleaning or blackboards," he explains. The ratio should be at least 80:20, with 20 percent of the grant being used for improving or creating infrastructure, he adds. To ensure that government schools are more efficiently managed, a committee comprising members from the neighbourhood could be asked to take decisions concerning the school, suggests several experts of CABE Committee. Experts opines that there are several examples of successful private-public partnerships. "There have been initiatives like DPS Delhi Public School being given the responsibility to run two-three government schools in Gurgaon in Haryana In this way, the private schools can manage the schools for a while and use their expertise to train teachers.

The educationists have a consensus that the children are actually walking out because there is no quality education. Poor children can ill-afford to spend their time in classes that are taken badly, or in schools that have no infrastructure or teachers. Instead of looking for the reasons that are behind the problem, the government appears to be trying to implicate parents or children for the 'drop-out' rates. The CABE committee report has already set down comprehensive norms that secondary schools should follow, ranging from having one classroom for 30 students, ensuring safe drinking water facilities and separate toilets for girls and boys to computer labs. Experts also suggest granting free ships or scholarships to those from disadvantaged backgrounds to encourage enrolment in secondary and senior secondary schools. The CABE report notes that expansion of secondary education can be achieved by setting up new schools, upgrading existing elementary schools into high schools by providing more infrastructure and adding to the facilities in existing secondary schools to accommodate more students.

In view of this, the Central and the State/UT governments must jointly initiate planning to implement the agenda of universal and free secondary education in the first phase by the year 2015 and then extend it to senior secondary education in the second phase by the year 2020. The conventional expectation from secondary/senior secondary education lies in its role in creating the necessary base for generating technical person power, raising the potential of a society in contributing to the growth of knowledge and skills and thereby enhancing the nation's capacity to face the challenge of global competitiveness.

The no of higher secondary schools has been raised to 50,273 with 1000112 teachers, and figure of secondary schools is 101,777 with 1082878 teachers. Official statistics reveal that the enrolment of secondary and higher secondary school level is 3.70 crore and the gross enrolment ratio is 39.91. The total dropout rate up to matric is 61.92 as on September 2004. The population of children in this age group has been estimated to be 88.5 million as per Census, 2001. Enrolment figures show that only 31 million of these children were attending schools in 2001-02.

However, Para 5.13 –5.15 of the National Policy on Education (NPE), 1986 (as modified in 1992) deal with Secondary Education. Para 5.13. of the NPE, inter alia states that access to Secondary Education will be widened with emphasis on enrolment of girls, SCs and STs, particularly in science, commerce and vocational streams. The disparity between boys' and girls' enrolment is particularly marked at the secondary stage. As per the latest data available, out of the total enrolment of 21.2 millions n 1991-92 (as on 30.9.91) at the secondary stage (Classes IX and above), the girls account for 7 millions only, i.e. mere 33 per cent of the total enrolment, whereas boy's enrolment at this stage of education is 67 per cent of the total enrolment.

Nevertheless, a significant progress is also made in all spheres of secondary education. More than 84 per cent habitations in 1993-94 had a secondary school/section within a distance of 8 km as compared to 70 per cent within 5 km. The number of unserved habitations declined from 21 per cent in 1986-87 to 15 per cent in 1993-94. During 1950-51 to 1999-2000, number of secondary & higher secondary schools increased from 7 thousand to 117 thousand. The increase (16 times) is much more rapid than the corresponding increase in primary (3 times) and upper primary (14 times) schools. In the latest decade (1990 to 99), more than 37 thousand secondary & higher secondary schools were opened. The ratio of upper primary to secondary schools also improved from 1.83 in 1950-51 to 1.69 in 1999-2000.

Keeping in view the dismal statistics of secondary education in the country, Ministry of HRD launched several schemes, like scheme for strengthening of boarding and hostel facilities for girl students of secondary and higher secondary schools. The scheme is being implemented by NGOs and of the state governments. A one-time grant non recurring grant @Rs.1500/-per girl boarder for purchase of furniture (including beds) and utensils and provision of basic recreational aids, particularly material for sports and games, reading room equipments and books. And recurring Rs.5000/- per annum per girl boarder for food and salary of cook.

Finally, The CABE Committee in June 2005 recommended that "there is no alternative acceptable to regular schooling of good quality to all the girls". The Committee also felt that "incentives offered for promotion of girls education need to be revisited and measures taken need to be of such nature, force and magnitude that they are able to overcome the obstacles posed by factors such as poverty, domestic/sibling responsibilities, girl child labour, low preference to girl's education, preference to marriage over the education of girl child, etc." The key issues relating to secondary education highlighted in the Tenth Plan are: greater focus on improving access; reducing disparities by emphasizing the Common School System; renewal of curricula with emphasis on vocationalisation and employment-oriented courses; expansion and diversification of the Open Learning System; reorganization of teacher training and greater use of ICT. After merging several schemes like ET & CLASS scheme, a new Scheme called ICT Schools was launched for which the Annual Plan Outlay for 2006-07 was Rs. 67 crore. The intervention of the Central Government in Secondary Education has primarily been in two areas, (i) through apex level bodies and (ii) through various Centrally Sponsored Schemes. Central Government supports autonomous organizations like NCERT, CBSE, KVS and NVS and CTSA, the first named body for providing research and policy support to the Central and State Governments; CBSE for affiliating Secondary Schools and the remaining three for their own school systems. There are 929 Kendriya Vidyalayas (KVS) and 507 Navodaya Vidyalayas (NVS), and 69 Central Schools for Tibetans (CTSA). Scheme of Vocationalistion of Secondary Education at secondary level to enhance individual Employability. Rashtriya Madhyamik Shiksha Abhiyan (RMSA) launched in 2007 is a mission-mode exercise to universalize secondary education in which the centre is all set to universalize the secondary education till 2020.

The irony is that the arguments on the part of HRD ministry on community participation in implementing such schemes are not encouraging. Government should initiate evaluation mechanism and core commission to evaluate the progress of the schemes and policies to support the education sector by community mobilization to revitalize the schemes and put the policies into practice.

UNIT-VII

Curriculum and Teaching & Learning at the Secondary Stage

Language Issue

Context

The main thrust areas of Indian school education, as mentioned in the *National Curriculum for Elementary and Secondary Education: A Framework*, 1988, demand a fresh look. Some of these merit reformulation in the light of the country's experience in the field of school education and the others have to be re-affirmed. Some new thrust areas may also need to be added in the light of the changes all around. School education in the present scenario has to have the main thrust on the following:

- Inculcation and sustenance of personal, social, national and spiritual values like cleanliness and punctuality, good conduct, tolerance and justice; a sense of national identity and respect for law and order and truthfulness.
- Elimination of poverty, ignorance, ill-health, casteism, dowry, untouchability, and violence, and ensuring equity, health, peace and prosperity.
- Thinking, experiences and innovations which are rooted in the Indian tradition and ethos and relating these with global thinking.
- Establishing uniformity of structures of school education, i.e., 10+2+3 throughout the country.

- Broad based general education to all learners up to the end of the secondary stage to help them become life long learners and acquire basic life skills and high standards of Intelligence Quotient (IQ), Emotional Qoutient (EQ), and Spiritual Quotient (SQ)
- A common scheme of studies for the elementary and secondary stages with emphasis on the skill of "learning how to learn" with flexibility of content and mode of learning to suit all learners including those with special needs.
- Inclusion of Fundamental Duties and the core curricular areas at all the stages of school education.
- Human Rights including the rights of the child, especially those of the girl child.
- Ensuring the minimum essential level of the acquisition of knowledge, understanding and skill at all stages, commensurate with the learners' abilities and the societal context.
- Freedom, flexibility, relevance and transparency in the selection of content, transaction and procedures at different stages of school education.
- Nurturance and sustenance of multiple talents and creativity among all learners in various domains of knowledge.
- Shift of emphasis from information-based and teacher centred education to process centred and learner friendly education.
- Development of a responsive and supportive system of evaluation.

Value Education

Since India is the most ennobling experiment in spiritual co-existence, education about social, moral and spiritual values and religions cannot be left entirely to home and the community. School education in the country seems to have developed some kind of neutrality toward the basic values and the community in general has little time or inclination to know about religions in the right spirit. This makes it imperative for the Indian school curriculum to include inculcation of the basic values and an awareness of all the major religions of the country as one of the central components.

Value education and education about religions would not form a separate subject of study or examination at any stage. These would be so judiciously integrated with all the subjects of study in the scholastic areas and all the activities and programmes in the co-scholastic areas that the objectives thereof would be directly and indirectly achieved in the classrooms, at the school assembly places, play-grounds, cultural centres and such other places.

A comprehensive programme of value inculcation must start at the very earliest stage of school education as a regular part of school's daily routine. The entire educational process has to be such that the boys and girls of this country are able to know 'good', love 'good' and do 'good' and grow into mutually tolerant citizens. The comparative study of the 'philosophies' of religions can be taken up at the secondary and higher secondary stages.

Common Core Components

The need for strengthening national identity is being felt now much more than ever before. As such there is a strong plea for promoting national integration, and social cohesion by cultivating values as enshrined in the Constitution of India through school curriculum. With this in view, the ten core components identified in the *National Policy on Education*, 1986 need to be reaffirmed.

They are as follows: The history of India's freedom movement; The Constitutional obligations; the content essential to nurture national identity; India's common cultural heritage; egalitarianism, democracy and secularism; equality of sexes; protection of the environment; removal of social barriers; observance of the small family norm; and inculcation of scientific temper. The Fundamental Duties as laid down in Article 51A of Part IVA of the Indian Constitution, also have to be included in the core components.

These are to:

(a) abide by the Constitution and respect its ideals and institutions, the National Flag and the National Anthem;

(b) cherish and follow the noble ideals which inspired our national struggle for freedom;

(c) uphold and protect the sovereignty, unity and integrity of India;

(d) defend the country and render national service when called upon to do so;

(e) promote harmony and the spirit of common brotherhood among all the people of India transcending religious, linguistic and regional or sectional diversities; to renounce practices derogatory to the dignity of woman;

(f) value and preserve the rich heritage of our composite culture;

(g) protect and improve the natural environment including forests, lakes, rivers, wild life and to have compassion for the living creatures;

(h) develop the scientific temper, humanism and the spirit of enquiry and reform;

(i) safeguard public property and abjure violence, and

(j) strive towards excellence in all spheres of individual and collective activity so that the nation constantly rises to higher levels of endeavour and achievement.

These core components need to be integrated in school curriculum in a suitable manner. It is envisaged that they would help in instilling a nationally shared perception and values and creating an ethos and value system in which a common Indian identity could be strengthened.

Towards an Indigenous Curriculum

In order to make education a meaningful experience, it has to be related to the Indian context. Now, more than ever before, there is a realisation of the fact that by intellectual standards,

India cannot flourish merely by importing or borrowing what is happening abroad, or by showing proficiency in solving problems that have been faced abroad.

In concrete terms, this shift in thinking calls for evolving an approach to curriculum preparation based on thinking, experiences and innovations rooted in its indigenous tradition. While doing so adequate attention shall have to be paid to the country's cultural plurality and the enormous amount of wisdom and experience that can be drawn from the various regions and sections of the

Indian society. It may also mean making judicious use of and drawing from traditional knowledge systems and solutions to issues of health, water management, population explosion etc. At a time when there is worldwide recognition and patenting of items like *neem* and turmeric, this kind of information must become an integral component of learners' knowledge. It is also desirable that learners are introduced to the advances made by the country in the past in various areas of knowledge. Besides, the knowledge and appreciation of folk cultures, songs, traditional dance forms, costumes, and musical instruments must become part of the school curriculum.

The Minimum Levels of Learning

In order to ensure access to the education of a comparable standard to all learners irrespective of caste, creed, location or sex, the concept of the *Minimum Levels of Learning* (MLLs) has emerged as one of the basic concerns. An effort to combine quality with equity, keeping in view the developmental needs of learners from all the sections of society including the disadvantaged and deprived ones, the dropouts and the working children and girls, has generated a need for identifying certain essential levels of learning for each stage of school education. These have been called the Minimum Levels of Learning.

The MLLs are expected to be achieved by one and all. Since the MLLs provide a sense of direction and a certain amount of accountability, these are considered to be an effective tool for programme formulation for school improvement. The quality of a school or educational system, in real sense, has to be defined in terms of the performance capabilities of its students. The Minimum Levels of Learning can be stated in a variety of ways to specify the learning outcomes.

One of the important ways of doing so is to state MLLs in terms of competencies. Whichever approach is followed, the specification of the MLLs should meet the purpose of enhancing the learning attainments and serve as performance goals for the teacher and output indicators for the system. Accordingly, the MLLs must have, apart from relevance and functionality, the attributes of achievability, understandability and evaluability.

Learning has to be seen as a 'continuum' in which units are sequenced in a functional manner. The approach must help the learners progress systematically through this continuum by mastering the specified sets of competencies in each unit before moving on to the next one. Learning each subsequent unit will then be enjoyable and meaningful. The concept of the MLLs is holistic rather than fragmentary in nature. MLLs should be envisaged as learning outcomes to be achieved at the end of a particular stage. Specifying further details and their gradewise sequencing need not be considered as a rigid prescription.

The concept provides enough room for flexibility. The marshalling or sequencing of skills representing learning outcomes is to be done in such a way that it involves in a balanced manner the analytico-synthetic processes. Moreover, 'learning' is to be understood in the broader sense of 'skill', 'quality', 'attitude', and 'value' too. That way, the term would embrace all the cognitive, psychomotor and affective area learning outcomes of education.

The emphasis on defining the MLLs highlights the importance of the integrative nature of learning and evaluation to ensure effective diagnostic interventions and assessment procedures. Thus, the MLLs do not merely serve as the indicators of a learner's progress or guide evaluation alone, these also help in identifying the appropriate sequencing of learning, suitable transactional processes and desirable assessment techniques which would enable a teacher to provide remedial teaching on the one hand and enrichment programmes on the other as per the needs of individual learners. Teachers can get very specific clues for organising peer learning, goal directed learning and encouraging self-learning in a conscious and concerted manner. The MLLs approach is based on the elements of mastery level learning, child-centred and activity-based teaching, continuous and comprehensive evaluation, diagnostic and remedial teaching, differential treatment to optimise achievement levels of all and action research. All these elements need to be practised to achieve the goal of quality elementary education for all. Emphasis has been laid on the introduction of the MLLs and the adoption of a common scheme of studies at the different stages. Simultaneously, flexibility is envisaged in the selection of strategy for curriculum transaction. This will make learning relevant to the needs and environmental contexts of the learners and allow scope for initiative and experimentation on the part of the teacher, the school and the local educational authorities. However, the scope for flexibility in the methodology and approach to curriculum transaction is not expected to be used for introducing differential courses or similar measures which would create disparities in the standards of education in different parts of the country.

General Objectives of Education

Education liberates human beings from the shackles of ignorance, privation and misery. It must also lead to a non-violent and non-exploitative social system. School curriculum, therefore, has to aim at enabling learners to acquire knowledge, develop understanding and inculcate skills, positive attitudes, values and habits conducive to the all-round development of their personality. Young girls and boys, are to be empowered through education to increase their capability. Paradigm shifts are therefore necessary to support a curriculum that values the interaction of the process and the content. Besides, the development of intrinsic values and the emotional intelligence of learners is also crucial.

School curriculum has therefore, to help to generate and promote among the learners: language abilities of listening, speaking, reading, writing and thinking and communication skills – verbal and visual-needed for social living and effective participation in the day to day activities; mathematical abilities to develop a logical mind that would help learners perform mathematical operations and apply them in every day life; scientific temper characterised by the spirit of enquiry, problem-solving, courage to question and objectivity leading to elimination of obscurantism, superstition and fatalism, while at the same time, sustaining and emphasising the indigenous knowledge ingrained in the Indian tradition; understanding of the environment in its totality both natural and social, and their interactive processes, the environmental problems and the ways and means to preserve the environment; appreciation of the sacrifices and contributions made by the freedom fighters and social workers from rural, tribal and weaker sections from all the regions of the Indian society, particularly from the North-East and the Andaman and Nicobar Islands, in India's freedom struggle and social regeneration, and readiness to follow their ideals; appreciation for the need of a balanced synthesis between the change oriented technologies and the continuity of the country's traditions and heritage; knowledge of and respect for the national symbols and the desire and determination to uphold the ideals of national identity and unity; deep sense of patriotism and nationalism tempered with the spirit of *Vasudhaiva Kutumbakam;* understanding of the positive and the negative impact of the processes of globalisation, liberalisation and localisation in the context of the country; qualities clustered around the personal, social, moral, national and spiritual values that make a person humane and socially effective, giving meaning and direction to life; knowledge, attitude and habits necessary for keeping physically and mentally fit and strong in perfect harmony with the earth, water, air, fire and the sky; qualities and characteristics necessary for self-learning, self-directed learning and life-long learning leading to the creation of a learning society; capacity not only to process information but also to understand, reflect and internalise and develop insight; willingness to work hard, enterpreneurship and dignity of manual work necessary for increasing productivity, obtaining job-satisfaction and creating wealth generating systems; acquisition of pre-vocational/vocational skills; appreciation of the various consequences of large families and over population and need for checking population growth; and cultivating proper understanding of and attitude toward healthy sex related issues and respectful attitude toward members of the opposite sex.

The emphasis on the 'learner-centred approach' necessitates careful determination of the objectives of education to be achieved at a particular stage/class in keeping with the norms of physical, mental, social, and emotional development of the learners of the relevant age-group. However, the level of achievement with regard to a particular objective will be rising from one class to another in a spiral fashion.

The Learners' Profile

Learners are not passive objects. They are active and inquisitive persons. It is not that only the environment shapes them, rather they too shape the environment to a great extent. The learners do not come to school with a blank mind but with pre-conceived ideas. Their classroom experiences are interpreted in the context of these pre-conceived notions. Thus, the prior experiences, beliefs and emotions affect the individual's perception and interpretation of events. This knowledge acquisition is a constructive or generative process and each student's knowledge is personal and unique. For long, the child or the learner was viewed as a natural or given category. This undermined the importance of the fact that the development of the learner is intimately linked to changes in the socio-cultural and historical conditions in a given society. Thus, differences across groups and changes within a group may affect the nature of the learning. As such, a monolithic view of the learner and learning is untenable. On the other hand, an integrated approach for understanding the characteristics of learners seems appropriate and helpful. During the pre-primary stage, enormous changes take place in the children's physical growth and mental development. From a state of dependence and helplessness the children gradually attain independence and become curious learners. As their bodies grow and respond to the social and cultural cues, their nervous systems mature and their cognitive experiences are enhanced.

The children demonstrate in their behaviour a desire not to depend on others, but the crystallisation of this desire takes place gradually through the years of secondary education. In the normal course, learners, during the secondary stage of education, are expected to develop a philosophy of life that would provide them appropriate motives and directives of behaviour as future adults. Toward the end of the upper primary stage, the learners start critically evaluating the contradictions they observe in the words and deeds of individuals and the society. The awareness that one needs to stand on one's own and choose an appropriate career is normally reflected in the learner's behaviour. These developmental features indicate the need for gradual introduction of learning experiences.

related to ideas, attitudes and skills associated with moral values, national ideals and priorities, socio-cultural cohesion and global fraternity. Systematic provision of information and guidance that would help the youth in making right choices of career and vocation for themselves must be ensured toward the end of the upper primary stage and particularly during the secondary stage of education. For a large number of students, some kind of orientation to work education may be required as a part of their curriculum during the secondary stage.

During the period of secondary education, emergence of desire and inclinations of sexual nature is a normal feature of students' psycho-physical development. This dimension deserves careful attention of the curriculum organisers. The idea that the Indian society does not approve of promiscuity and that self-control or '*Samyam*' is one of the highly valued qualities ought to be underlined. This will generate among the youth healthy attitudes toward sex and respect for members of the opposite sex.

Curriculum designers could hardly afford to overlook the emotional dimensions of the child's life during the school period and the importance of emotional maturity in the life of a person. It is only gradually, through growth, that the child achieves emotional stability and emotional independence. There are occasions upper primary and during the secondary education, when the learner has to face intense stress and strain which may result in emotional crisis. Curriculum should provide for appropriate activities and experiences, of scholastic and co-scholastic nature, and counselling and guidance in this regard.

Importance of Mathematics and Humanities and Social Sciences

Scheme of Studies

The general objectives of education will be realised through the content and learning experiences related to different subject areas. However, the emphasis would shift from factual knowledge to the process of understanding, thinking and internalising. Toward all-round development of personality, value education, health and physical education, art education and work education, have to be given appropriate importance in the school curriculum. The inter-connections among various subject areas have to be clearly established. A common scheme of studies, therefore, is advocated for Classes I to X.

The core component areas and values shall form an integral part of the curriculum at all the stages and may suitably be integrated in different subject areas. Flexibility in the selection of content and organising learning experiences must be inbuilt in the system.

Secondary Stage (2 years)

(a) Three Languages — the mother tongue/the regional language, modern Indian language and English

(b) Mathematics

(c) Science and Technology

(d) Social Sciences

(e) Work Education

(f) Art Education (fine arts: Visual and Performing)

(g) Health and Physical Education (including games and sports, yoga, NCC and scouting And guiding)

Curricular Areas

Imaginative and discreet planning of appropriate learning experiences makes it possible for the curriculum objectives to be realised. Well planned activities and teaching-learning strategies facilitate these experiences which ought to make an integrated whole. However, for the sake of convenience, these have to be classified under various subject areas. The nature of various stages of education and the learners' profile have their bearing on the planning of objectives, learning activities and strategies under each curricular area. The curricular areas and their stagewise treatment for this purpose are proposed as follows:

Language

Language learning at secondary and the higher secondary stages. Language education has the greater potential as a means to develop, progressively through various stages, attitudes and values related to all the core components by incorporating appropriate themes and adopting suitable teaching learning strategies. Language education must aim at encouraging independent thinking, free and effective expression of opinions and logical interpretation of the present and the past events. It must motivate learners to say things their way, nurture their natural creativity and imagination and thus make them realise the basic difference between their verbal language and the language of Mathematics. These are the reasons why learning of language ought to find a central place in the total educational process. In this context the following focal points merit serious consideration:

Despite general acceptance of the central importance of language education in principle, practical effort for improving it has yet to be made at all levels in the country.

The oral aspect of language has to be duly emphasised in language education and oral examination in language must be made an integral part of the evaluation process. Emphasis will have to shift from the teaching of textbooks to extensive general reading and it would need continuous guidance and monitoring.

Due stress is to be laid, in all language education programmes, on the ability to use the language in speech and in writing for academic purposes, at work place and in community in general.

The Three Language Formula

Even about four decades after the formulation of 'Three Language Formula', it is yet to be effectively implemented in true spirit. Despite all the changes in the socio-economic scenario, market pressures and the behaviour pattern of the Indian youth, the three language formula still remains relevant.

Under this Formula: The First language to be studied must be the mother tongue or the regional language.

The second language —

(i) in Hindi speaking states will be some other modern Indian language or English, and

(ii) in non-Hindi speaking states will be Hindi or English.

The Third language —

(i) in Hindi speaking states will be English or a modern Indian language not studied as the second language, and

(ii) in non-Hindi speaking states will be English or a modern Indian language not studied as the second language.

Since the basic objective behind the Three Language Formula was, and continues to be, national unity and facile intra-state, interstate and international communication adherence to it must be ensured by the Central as well as State/ Union Territory governments. Minor modifications in the formula and its implementation in complex linguistic situations, as in some northeastern states for example, could, however, be allowed as per the needs and discretion of these states and within the overall spirit of the formula. Every child's mother tongue or regional language has to be taught right from the first standard. In the cases where the children's home language is different from the school language or the regional language, gradual and smooth transition to the regional language is to be effected within a reasonable time at the primary stage itself. In states where because of plurality of regional languages the official or the associate official language of India has been accepted as the state language or first language, it will have to be taught from the first standard. Provision for the teaching of mother tongue would be made for children from linguistic minorities wherever they are in adequate numbers.

Creative expression and the ability to think on one's own must be encouraged and nurtured through language teaching with the oral form of language finding important place in language curriculum. Applied or practical grammar also has to be given at this stage so that it may develop the students' insight into the nature, structure and functions of the languages. The study of the third language would also begin at the upper primary stage. However, the choice of a particular class/grade of its introduction may be left to the States/UTs or organizations themselves. The study of all the three languages, then, has to continue up to the end of the secondary stage, i.e., Class X.

At the secondary stage (Classes IX and X) in the first language full mastery over the applied form of language and good acquaintance with literary language would be aimed at. Learners have tom achieve maturity in oral and written expression in response to what they read or listen to. Understanding and appreciating the depth and diversities of human mind through the literary texts in prose and poetry must be ensured among the students. Teaching of grammar is to be systematically strengthened to facilitate the understanding and use of the subtle usages of language. Desirable attitudes and values must be inculcated through carefully selected language materials. Thus, high order communication skill in the first language, with grammatical accuracy and appropriateness of style must be adequately underlined as the main objectives of first language learning at this stage. In

English, Hindi and other modern Indian languages studied as second language at this stage, the capacity to use the language in speech and writing whenever needed in life, and read it with reasonable speed for information and pleasure would be the most important objective. Grammar is not to be taught as a theoretical subject per se, but it would be taught as practical or functional grammar in context with the minimum of theory.

Sanskrit

Sanskrit has a special claim on the national system of education because it: Has consistently been need in India for thousands of years and is still inextricably linked with the life, rituals, ceremonies and festivals of vast Indian masses; contains great store of knowledge and wisdom that needs to be revived, reformulated and enriched with whatever is the best in modern disciplines of knowledge; has the universal appeal all over the country; has very close structural, lexical and semantic relationship with Hindi and most other regional languages of India which makes the learning of these languages easier and better; and has been internationally accepted as the most scientifically structured language and is being increasingly acknowledged as the best suited language for computer use.

Therefore, it is extremely important to provide for and encourage the study of Sanskrit. It may be introduced as part of a composite course of Hindi and the regional languages as mother tongue at a suitable point of the primary or the upper primary stage. The course has to be so planned that the study of Sanskrit may not be ignored. At the secondary stage Sanskrit may be made available as an additional option and at the higher secondary stage, suitable elective courses in Sanskrit may be made available to all the students who wish to study it. Open school courses for Sanskrit may also be designed for learners at all levels. A major shift in designing Sanskrit courses and transacting curriculum in the subject is that the language is to be treated as a living phenomenon which is still relevant to the general life needs of the people of India, and which has caught international attention because of the global interest in subjects like yoga, vedic mathematics, astronomy and ayurveda.

Hindi

All the languages of India are equally important and all the citizens of this country must love and respect all of them. Hindi is different in the sense that the Indian Constitution has given it the place of the Official language of the Indian union. As originally envisaged, it is fast becoming ligua franca of country. As such, it is necessary that courses in Hindi are suitable for opening of chanenels of integral communication in all parts of India and ensuring acquisition of a high level proficiency in it. In order to achieve these targets, more and more functional courses in Hindi, besides those of literature, are to be made available in the regular school systems as well as in the form of Open School course.

Foreign Languages

In view of the fast increasing international interaction and cooperation in socio-political, educational, cultural and economic fields, a growing need for learning more and more foreign languages like Chinese, Japanese, Russian, French, German, Arabic, Persian and Spanish has recently been felt. These languages cannot be accommodated within the Three Language Formula. However, depending on the demand for the study of any number of these and the infrastructural resources available with the schools, these languages may be offered as additional options at the secondary stage.

Mathematics

One of the basic aims of teaching mathematics in schools is to inculcate the skill of quantification of experiences around the learners. Toward this, carrying out experiments with numbers and forms of geometry, framing hypotheses and verifying these with further observations form inherent part of mathematics learning.

It would also include generalising these findings with proof and developing competence to solve problems. Mathematics helps in the process of decisionmaking through its application to real life situations in familiar as well as non-familiar situations. It contributes in the development of precision, rational and analytical thinking, reasoning, positive attitudes and aesthetic sense. Apart from being a distinct area of learning, it helps enormously in the development of other disciplines which involve analysis, reasoning and quantification of ideas. Study of mathematics also provides ample opportunities for making conjectures, testing and building arguments about their validity and also in asking new questions. Understanding of the basic structure of mathematics leads to a much better appreciation of the scope and power of mathematics. The mathematics curricula must develop an appreciation and understanding of the contribution of Indian mathematicians along with that of others. This would develop a sense of self-esteem and self-confidence amongst the learners.

While determining the curriculum in mathematics for the secondary stage it must be kept in mind that majority of learners would leave school at the end of the stage. They would need to apply mathematical skills and competencies in their work situations. A smaller number of students, of course, would go for higher education.

At the Secondary Stage, the teaching-learning of mathematics has to serve two complementary purposes. Firstly, the aim should be to further enhance the capacity of the students to employ mathematics in solving problems that they face in their day-to-day life. Secondly, a systematic study of mathematics as a discipline has to be started here and continued further. The curriculum may include the study of relevant arithmetical concepts, number system, algebra, geometry, trigonometry, coordinate geometry, mensuration, graphs, statistics etc. The idea of proofs should be developed with thrust on deductive reasoning. Emphasis is to be laid on wider applications of mathematics by way of making data based problems pertaining to actual data on population, agriculture, environment, industry, physical and biological sciences, engineering, defence, etc.

Also the students should attain proficiency in presenting information available in their environment in the form of graphs and charts, and be able to do calculations with speed and accuracy. Further the students should acquire the ability to solve problems using algebraic methods and apply the knowledge of simple trigonometry to solve problems of heights and distances etc. The history of mathematics with special reference to India and the nature of mathematical thinking should find an important place. The students may be encouraged to enhance their computational skill by the use of *Vedic Mathematics*.

Mathematics learning should be imparted through activities from the very beginning of school education, i.e., from the primary stage itself. These activities may involve the use of concrete materials, models, patterns, charts, pictures, posters, games, puzzles and experiments. The importance of using learning aids needs to be stressed. To help exploration of mathematical facts through experimentation, a mathematics corner could be set up in the existing science laboratories.

For this existing science laboratories need to be converted into science-cum-mathematics laboratories. This may be done by involving students and teachers by mobilizing community resources to this end. This should be treated as an exploratory centre for science and mathematics. Indigenous experiences and innovations in mathematics, based on real life situations be given an important place. In terms of scheme of evaluation of such mathematical learning, this has to be given weightage equal to that in science. While developing the instructional materials, the content and language of problems included in the textbooks should highlight core components like gender equality, protection of environment, removal of social barriers, observance of small family norm etc. At the secondary level, evaluation should lay stress on testing the understanding and application of concepts rather than testing the rote memory of the concepts.

Science and Technology

Science is the creative response to the curiosity and capacity to wonder present amongst every human being. Learning of science in schools augments the spirit of enquiry, creativity and objectivity along with aesthetic sensibility. It aims to develop well-defined abilities of knowing, doing and being. It also nurtures the ability to explore and seek solution of the problems related to environment and daily life situations and to question the existing beliefs, prejudices and practices in society. Science concerns itself with the fundamental knowledge of universe, world and its environment. Technology deals with numerous ways and means of pressing science into the service of mankind, thus enhancing and improving the quality of human life. Learning of science in general education up to secondary stage, therefore, needs to be replaced by learning of science and technology in view of the strong organic linkages between the two. Scientific pursuits have primarily attempted to comprehend the physical world, the technological initiatives that have tended to manipulate and control the same. Science is universal and its principles and laws could be verified anywhere.

The technology takes appropriate shapes depending upon various factors including economic, geographical, social and political conditions. The twenty-first century citizens will have to acquire the basics of scientific and technological literacy. The learners have to understand how basic scientific principles are applied in finding solutions to problems in the field of agriculture, weather, energy, health and nutrition, industry, defence, information processing and other areas of human concern. It would help them discover the relationship between science and technology in these areas besides acquiring problem-solving and decision-making skills. Science operates through its processes. Consequently, teaching and learning of science needs to be characterised by focused emphasis on processes, i.e., experimentation, taking observations, collection of data, classification, analysis, making hypothesis, drawing inferences, and arriving at conclusions for the objective truth. The process skills so acquired would help in developing attitudes and values that constitute the spirit of scientific temper. Science has to be learned more in familiar environment and not in alien and contrived situations.

An important purpose of science and technology teaching in general education up to secondary stage is to familiarise the learner with various dimensions of scientific and technological literacy. These would include — understanding the nature of science; ability to properly apply appropriate science concepts and their technological applications; capacity to understand values that underlie science and technology, willingness to understand and appreciate the joint enterprise of science, technology and society, ability to develop rich and satisfying views of the universe and to continue science and technology education throughout life, and development of certain manipulative skills which are required in day-to-day life situations. In addition to the support available to develop these skills within and outside the laboratories it would be imperative to make use of tools of information technology such as computers and multimedia packages.

Science and technology education should have something of value to offer to all students.

Particularly, rural and tribal oriented technology will have to be made an important part of the educational package and its connectivity will have to be ensured. Science must cut across traditional subject boundaries and open itself to issues such as gender, culture, language, poverty, impairment, future occupation and environment and observance of small family norm. It is also necessary to familiarise children with Indian traditions of scientific and technological learning and contributions of Indian scientists both in the past and the present. The achievement of India in various fields through scientific and technological enterprises would develop and nurture self-confidence and self-assurance amongst the learners.

At Secondary Stage, this is the stage after which majority of the learners will enter the world of work. Scientific attitudes and skills developed at this stage would become foundation for further growth. They need to be exposed to the nature and the structure of science and the support it provides to the technological developments. At this stage, learning of science would continue to be built around natural and social elements of environment. Focus would continue to be on understanding of concepts and applications in the areas of matter and its properties, energy, relationship of various physical processes and the technological applications of principles of science. The biological sciences will deal with living organism, their organisation and life processes. An integrated approach to science and technology leading to their application in areas like health and nutrition, industry, agriculture and animal husbandry and allied areas would establish linkages of science to societal aspirations. Science, technology, society and environment would coalesce in teaching and learning of science at this stage. Practical activities to be chosen should have relevance for future life through acquisition of skills and values. The learners need to be encouraged to work both individually as well as in the groups. Critical, creative and generative thinking has to be developed. Improvisation should be encouraged but designing would also be provided for as a component in exploration. Flexibility in experimentation needs to be widely promoted. Teachers could help the learners devise appropriate experimentation and activities within the school and also outside school involving immediate environment such as farming, factories, industries and community.

Social Sciences

The component of social sciences is integral to the total quantum of general education upto secondary stage. It helps the learners in understanding the human environment in its totality and developing a broader perspective and an empirical, reasonable, and humane outlook. It also helps them grow into well-informed and responsible citizens with necessary attributes/skills so that they could participate and contribute effectively in the process of development and nationbuilding. The social sciences curriculum in schools will draw its content mainly from geography, history, civics and economics. It may also include some elements of sociology. Together they provide different dimension of studying the human society — over space and time and in relation to each other. It helps the learners in understanding the contemporary society better. Social sciences education aims at providing students essential knowledge, skills and attitude necessary for self-development and also for becoming an effective and contributing member of the society.

In order to make the social sciences education meaningful, relevant and effective, the concerns and issues of the contemporary world need to be kept in the forefront. To this end, the quantum of history may have to be substantially reduced. Past developments could be studied as a backdrop for understanding the present. As such, the needs and challenges of today must be responded suitably. Globalisation and liberalisation on the one hand and localisation on the other, are going to have tremendous impact on the future society. These have also brought in their wake many economic and social challenges and opportunities which need to be addressed effectively for building a strong cohesive Indian Society. It also calls for developing emotionally intelligent learners, who are prepared to face new challenges and adjust to unfamiliar situations.

In a democractic set-up with decentralisation of power, local governance such as 'Panchayati Raj' has gained importance. It aims at raising the levels of participation and involvement of people. In order to make optimum utilisation of resources for development, the local governance has to be more responsive and efficient. The learners, therefore, are to be equipped well to understand the process of development, its need and implications as well as the system of governance — at all levels — local, state and national, and their own place in it. This would necessitate considerable increase in the coverage of courses in civics. Academic as well as social skills such as critical thinking, reading and interpreting tables, diagrams and maps, cooperating with others, responding to other's problems and providing leadership need to be developed in a systematic manner. A well-designed social sciences curriculum would help learners 'think globally and act locally'.

In a world of ever-increasing knowledge, selection and organisation of the content areas assume great importance. The social sciences curriculum has to be comprehensive and not yet heavily loaded with information. Interrelatedness of ideas and their comprehensibility must be kept in view. It would also be desirable to emphasise the process of learning and thinking rather than mere acquisition of facts. Learners need to be given meaningful learning experiences through well-planned activities. This will help them acquire basic competencies and skills. Keeping these in view, the themes/issues could provide a sound basis for the selection and organisation of the content areas. While number of topics/areas may be few, the depth of treatment should be more to optimise the learners' experiences. These themes may be drawn from geography, history, civics, economics and sociology in a balanced manner and suitably graded — simple to complex and immediate to remote. Some of these issues and themes may be as follows:

Study of Indian civilisation and its rich cultural heritage along with other world civilisations and their interconnections may be the major area of study drawn from history. It ought to include the different cultural movements and revolutions in the life of the country and also the spread of its culture in other lands. Food security, population growth, poverty, water scarcity, climatic changes and cultural preservation are some of the major issues of the twenty-first century, which have relevance for the social sciences curriculum. As such 'Environment, resources and sustainable development' and 'man-environment interaction' would be drawing their content mainly from geography, economics, sociology and other related areas. Social, economic and political institutions and their functioning and administrative system especially with reference to India would draw content from civics and economics. Emphasis has to be laid more on the economic, political and social aspects of human environment especially the contemporary world that too with focus on India. The Europe-centred view of the world must change. This would render topics like the discovery of India or America by Europeans irrelevant for Indian students. Social sciences are the most suited areas of study for integrating almost all the core components indicated earlier. For example, the history of India's freedom movement, the constitutional obligation, content essential to nurture national identity, equality of sexes, removal of social barriers, fundamental duties and human rights including right of the child may be integrated appropriately. Suitable content and approach to ensure infusion of these vital areas may have to be followed at different stages. Similarly, many values may be inculcated through the teaching of social science.

Teaching of social sciences ought to promote a humane and national perspective, and inculcate a sense of pride in the country and in being an Indian. It needs to strengthen the national identity and develop an appreciation for cultural heritage. It should promote communal harmony and social cohesion. Its teaching must be objective and free from all kinds of stereotyped images, biases and prejudices.

Fieldwork, project work and group activities should form the basis of teaching-learning in social sciences. Projects having direct link with the local community may be encouraged. Economic and politico-legal literacy, grievance redressal system and consumer education should be promoted.

At Secondary Stage, Contemporary India may be the focal theme. It may include the processes and patterns of man environment interaction and the issues related to environment, its resources, and development. Major developments in the recent past including India's struggle for freedom and the contributions of various sections/regions/groups especially the role of women and weaker sections in the movement having bearing on the social, economic and political developments and challenges in the post-independent India will also be covered. Issues and challenges of India such as poverty, illiteracy, corruption and anti-social practices, fundamental rights, fundamental duties and economic development will be covered appropriately. In addition, India's role in the world especially world peace, international cooperation and decolonisation may be included. Contributions and achievements of Indians in other countries may be given due place. At the end of the secondary stage, the students may develop the ability to use their knowledge, understanding and skills by undertaking wide range of studies at various scales-local, regional, national. By now they may develop the ability to describe interaction within natural and human processes and recognise patterns. They may also be able to look for sources of information and analyse problems/issues rationally and scientifically. It would be useful if students take up a few case studies/project work as it would help them investigate and consider the issues that arise from people's interaction with their environment.

Place of History in School Curriculum and Life

Concept of History: History is what historians see it. The term history is derived from the Greek word historic which means "information "or 'An enquiry to designed to elicit truth." Modern concept of history-Until recently the history in schools consisted, mainly a record of battles, conquest, and history of the dynasties of ruling kings. But with a change and advancement of civilization and an adoption of the various aims of education, the subject of history and the organization of the matter have undergone a change History is no longer a record of battles and life histories of ruling dynasties or kings The modern concept of history emphasizes its concern with the evolution growth and development of human civilization through the ages History is the intellectual form in which a civilization renders account to itself of its past.

Definitions of history-History is the transmission of our mental, moral, technical and aesthetic heritage as fully as possible to as many as possible, for the enlargement of and mans' understanding, control, embellishment and enjoyment of life....Ariel and Willdurant.

History is the record of what one age finds worthy of note in another....Buckhardt

History is a continuous process of interaction between the historian and his facts and unending dialogue between the present and the past...Carr,E.H.

History is the past politic....Freeman

Place and importance of teaching history-History in the school curriculum-History as an independent subject or a part of environmental studies or social sciences forms an important part of the high school curriculum In classes XIth and XIIth, it is included as a separate subject The primary purpose of inclusion of history broadly, is to widen the horizons of the students. History is a continuous process and the present is a part of it and which is linked to the past. Hence the present can only be understood only as a part of the process. Thus the context of time is crucial to an understanding of the present. Like wise, the present helps in shaping the future. Social environment and History Curriculum—The study of social sciences should have three dimensions, namely learning about the social environment, learning through the social environment and learning for the social environment. A pupil will learn about the social customs cultural heritage history of society etc. through observation, exploration and scientific study of social phenomena and events and will thereby develop genuine interest in, and an urge for, preservation of what is good in our culture and improvement of existing socio-economic cultural set-up.

History at Secondary stage-At the secondary stage the study of social sciences should sciences should comprise elements of history, geography civics and economics to promote an understanding of contemporary India. The teaching of history should be objective and free from any communal parochial and other prejudices. The perspective of the past should help in understanding the contemporary developments. At the secondary stage significant movements events from the ancient, medieval Indian history, and other countries of the world and modern world history may form an important part of the curriculum.

Objectives Of Teaching History At Secondary Level

The objectives of teaching history at the secondary stage as apart of general education may be as follow:-

- to develop an understanding of the evolution of human societies and civilizations in general and of Indian society and civilization in particular
- to develop an understanding of the processes through which human societies have changed and evolved
- to develop an understanding of the integrated nature of historical development and of the homogeneity of civilization

- to inculcate an appreciation of the contribution of different peoples to the progress of mankind as a whole
- to develop an appreciation of the growth of various components Indian culture and legitimate pride in the achievement of the Indian people in different periods and in different parts of the country
- to develop an historical perspective for understanding contemporary India and the contemporary world of current problems and contemporary processes of change
- to develop an integrated view of Indian history and civilization of human civilization as a whole
- to help develop a spirit of enquiry and the ability to think critically and creatively and to differentiate between the obsolescent and the dying and the living and the emerging
- to develop critical appreciation of the past so that the pupils' personality is free from parochialism irrational prejudices bigotry communalism and every kind of chauvinism and is imbued with a rational scientific and forward-looking outlook
- question of the skills and habits of self learning.

Instructional objectives-

- Knowledge
- understanding
- critical thinking
- practical thinking
- interests
- attitudes.

Knowledge

The pupils should acquire knowledge of terms concepts, facts, events, symbols, ideas, conventions, problems trends personalities, chronology and generalizations, etc., related to the study of history. The pupil should be able to; Recall facts terms, concepts, events etc. Recognize facts, terms concepts, events etc. Show information on maps, charts, diagrams etc. Read information presented in various forms Understanding The pupil should develop understanding of the term, facts, principal events, trends, etc. related to the subject of history. The pupil should be able to – classify illustrate, compare and contrast, explain, discriminate, identify, arrange, detect, interpret extract from the different courses in history Critical thinking.

The subject should enable the pupils to develop critical thinking The should be able to identify the problems analyze the problem, collect the evidence, sift evidence facts and opinion, select relevant evidence and facts and weigh them, establish relationship and marshal facts, draw conclusion advance arguments in support of his contention verify the inferences.

Practical Skills

The subject should enable the pupils to develop practical skills helpful in the study and understanding of historical facts. The pupils should be able to draw maps, charts, diagrams, etc. prepare model, tools etc.

Interest

The subject should enable the pupils to develop interest in the study of history. The pupil, on his own, should be able to collect coins and other historical materials, prepare illustrative material aids, participate in historical dramas and mock sessions of historical events visit places of historical interest archaeological sites, museums, and archives, read historical documents, maps and charts write articles on historical and other related topics.

Attitudes: The subject should enable the pupils to develop healthy social attitudes. The pupil should posses the sense of patriotism, show respect towards other people opinions, ideas, beliefs, and ways of life read about other faiths and religions establish friendship with pupils of other communities and faiths practice the spirit of noble ideas cooperate with others in the social and civic activities.

Objectives at higher secondary level —

NCERT suggested the following objectives of teaching history in classes lx and x.

- To promote an understanding of the processes of change and development through which human societies have evolved.
- To promote an understanding of the foundations of human civilization and appreciation of the basic unity of mankind.
- To develop an appreciation of the contributions made by various cultures to the total heritage of mankind.
- To foster the understanding that the mutual interaction of various cultures has been a major factor inhuman progress.
- To develop a world historical perspective necessary for the understanding of the contemporary India.
- To facilitate the study of the history of specific countries and regions in the general perspective of world at a later stage.

Physical Education—Socially Useful Productive Works

Upper Primary and Secondary Stages Work Education Work Education is viewed as purposive and meaningful manual work, organised as integral part of the learning process and resulting into goods or services useful to the community besides the pleasure of self-fulfillment. It should be an essential component at all stages of education and be provided, through well-structured and graded programmes. The competencies to be developed in this field should include knowledge, understanding, practical skills and values through need based life activities. Major categories of work which need to be specifically stressed include: (a) work pertaining to needs of the individual such as health, hygiene, clothing, cleanliness, etc.; (b) work in home to be performed as a growing member of the family; (c) work in the classroom, school and in the out of school activities integrated with school life as well as learning of other subjects such as physical education, art education, social studies, science and others specifically designed to foster certain learning objectives of work education; (d) work in the community focused on selfless service or *seva*; and (e) work relating to vocational development, production, social usefulness and exploration of the world of work.

The activities pertaining to work education should be so organised as to realise the objectives of work education such as inculcation among learners of respect for manual work, values for selfreliance, cooperativeness, perseverance, helpfulness, tolerance and work ethics besides developing attitudes and values-related to productive work and concern for the community.

The theory and practice have to be such that it enables learners to understand the facts, terms concepts and scientific principles involved in various forms of work situations, know the sources of raw-materials, understand the use of tools and equipments in production and service processes, acquire skills needed for technologically advancing society and conceptualise their role in productive situations. The programme should develop among learners the skills for identifying, selecting, arranging and developing innovative methods and observing, manipulating and participating in work practices and thereby enhancing productive efficiency.

At the secondary stage, the complexity of the activities needs to be increased keeping the nature of essential activities, by and large, the same. Pre-vocational courses will get a prominent place at this stage which will facilitate choice of the vocational courses at the higher secondary stage and help them acquire the knowledge and skills required for entry into the world of work. While many teachers may function as work education teachers, a large number of activities may require specialist personnel. Teachers undertaking work education need to be properly oriented and trained in the specific area of work. It would be desirable to utilise community resources for effective implementation of the programme both in terms of man and material. Services of experts available in the community need to be utilised by seeking their involvement in the programme.

Art Education

Art education constitutes an important area of curricular activity for development of the personality of the learners. The aim of art education may be perceived as development of aesthetic sensibility among learners so as to enable them to respond to the beauty in line, colour, form, movement and sound. The study of arts and understanding of cultural heritage may go side by side and reinforce appreciation and understanding for one another. The experiences gained by learners at primary stage in the area of fine arts under the *Art of Healthy and Productive Living* would have developed enough motivation and interest among learners toward the subject. The curriculum at upper primary and secondary stages need to aim at developing awareness and interest in a wide variety of arts both at the classical and folk level so that the learner is both the performer and the recipient of pleasure. Art education can provide the most satisfying medium of creative expression which has to be given due importance in the best interest of the society.

Even among fine arts, music has a special claim in the overall scheme of education at all levels. It begins charming a child through lullabies in the cradle and permeates the entire life subsequently. Music teaches children not only the rhythm of life but also finer emotions, values and standard and pleasant pronunciation.

The secondary stage is apt for refining aesthetic sensibilities and social values through projects on conservation of natural and cultural heritage by providing opportunities for study of Indian culture working with artists/artistes in the community, organising festivals and celebrations of the community at large, display of physical environment and surrounding landscape and the like. Art education at this stage should comprise, study of visual and aural resources and their exploration; projects leading to creative expression and exhibition of the works in visual and aural forms; intergroup inter-school art activities; study trips and interaction with artists in the community; and exploration of traditional art forms including theatrical arts available in the community and neighbourhood.

Art education programme should concentrate on exposing the learner to folk arts, local specific arts and other cultural components leading to an awareness and appreciation of national heritage. Activities and programmes and themes should also be chosen and designed so as to promote values related to other core components like India's common cultural heritage, history of freedom movement and protection of environment. Learning by doing and a wide exposure to art forms is a must for self-expression and widening of the learner's own experience. Art education should not be fragmented. It should adopt an integrative approach at all stages up to Class X.

Health and Physical Education

Health and physical education has to be concerned with total health of the learner and the community. It will include mental and emotional health besides physical health of the learners. The main aim of health and physical education programme should be to develop desirable understanding, attitude and practices with regard to nutrition, health and sanitation so as to improve health status of the self, family and the community. Learners need to be helped to develop an awareness about the health and sanitation at the community level and their role in that context. Physical education has to concentrate on developing health, strength and fitness of the body.

Games and sports have to find a prominent place in the total scheme of things. Emphasis should be on acquisition of adequate neuro-muscular coordination commensurate with their developmental stage. Yoga and meditation can be very well-organised under the regular school schedule to help children acquire concentration and relaxation. Other important activities concerning the area of health and physical education include Scouting and Guiding, NCC, and Red-Cross which can help in cultivation of such basic qualities as endurance, courage, decisionmaking, resourcefulness, respect for others, truthfulness, faithfulness, loyalty to duty, and concern for the common good. Students' involvement in these activities would constructively channelise their energies and also promote and integrate learning in different curricular areas directly or indirectly. This would promote the latent curriculum of an institution. With a view to promoting healthful living and solving major health problems of the country, the general education of first ten years must help develop a system which promotes an integral development of body, mind and spirit. Medical inspection and check-up should be compulsory at all the stages with adequate follow up in cases in which deficiencies are noticed. Health and physical education including games and sports should be considered an integral part of the learning process and be included in the evaluation of performance.

Physical education should include more vigorous activities of various sorts including athletics, major games including indigenous games, gymnastics, yogic exercises, meditation, combatives, judo and swimming. The NCC, scouting and guiding and social service should be encouraged in addition to the compulsory programmes of physical education. In Classes IX and X, health education should enable the students to learn, in comparatively great detail, about personal health, impact of environmental pollution on health, food and nutrition, control and prevention of diseases, first aid, home nursing, and safety measures. The knowledge of and activities related to personal and community health assume great importance. An awareness of HIV and AIDS may be given. Students may also be acquainted with evils associated with promiscuity and child and drug abuse. Adolescence education and sex education may also be provided in a suitable manner. It would be desirable to generate suitable self-instructional material in this regard for different age groups of learners addressing to their needs and requirements and matching to their level of growth and maturity. It should be provided to all learners. Provision for separate teacher and classes may need not be encouraged. The whole approach should be such that each learner participates and learns ways of healthful living.

Instructional Strategy

For effective transaction of the curriculum and achievement of curricular objectives, appropriate strategies should be used in organising activities for students and in providing learning activities. Instructional strategies may assume a variety of modes and may involve activities such as observation, collection of materials and information, demonstration and experimentation, project assignment, fieldwork and educational excursion and visits to museums, fairs and industrial units and places of historical importance. Playing games, participating in community singing, role playing, dramatisation, discussion, debate, problem solving, discovery learning, creative writing, and supplementary reading may also form an important part of the total instructional strategies.

A number of factors need to be considered while making use of a particular strategy: learners' capabilities, availability of resources, entry behaviour, school environment, objectives to be achieved, the nature of content and the teachers' own preparation and mastery. The immediate environment of the learner, both natural and human, should be used for making learning concrete and meaningful. Effective learning takes place when teachers are able to involve the students in the process of learning, by taking them beyond the process of listening to that of thinking, reasoning and doing. In order to promote self-study skills use of library and resource centres needs to be encouraged.

Receiving regular feedback for teaching and learning should be an in-built component of teaching-learning strategy. Continuous and comprehensive evaluation plays an important role in providing regular feedback. It should be used for remediation.

Different kinds of strategies are needed for slow, average and fast learners. Diagnostic and remedial instruction should be used for the slow learner. Enrichment materials and goal-directed teaching-learning strategies would help fast learners. Co-scholastic areas of learning should be handled adopting appropriate strategies and they be given due importance for developing the child's personality. Several school activities such as morning assembly, cultural and recreational activities, school beautification, activities in community living, celebrations of days of national importance, special days and weeks, and creative activities, may be organised/conducted with proper planning and well-directed goals.

Medium of Instruction

The mother tongue is the most vital factor for the children's intellectual, emotional and spiritual growth. The mother tongue is the 'mother tongue' not because it is the mother's tongue but because, like the mother, it is central factor behind the nurturance of the children's mental and emotional make up. Their perceptions, comprehension, responses, creative expressions thinking and analysis — all are maximally developed, therefore, through the medium of the mother tongue. The medium of instruction ideally, therefore, ought to be the mother tongue at all the stages of school education.

In the case of learners whose mother tongue is also the regional language or state language, it must continue as the medium of instruction ideally at all the levels of schooling or at least up to the end of the elementary stage. However, in the case of those students whose mother tongue is different from the state language or regional language, the regional language may be adopted as a medium only from the third standard onward. In the earlier years the students' mother tongue ought to be used in such a manner that a smooth transition from the students' operations in the mother tongue to those in the regional language naturally takes place at the earliest.

Instructional Time

All possible efforts should be made to ensure that the stipulated number of working days are actually available to schools for instructional activities. Loss of instructional time due to unspecified reasons should be prevented or minimised through better educational management. After taking into account the number of days required for organising evaluation activities/tests/examinations, school functions, etc. a minimum of 180 days in a year should be available for effective instruction.

For the upper primary and secondary schools, the duration of a school day should be six hours out of which five hours should be kept for instruction and the rest for the other routine activities. The duration of a class period may be around 40 minutes. It should be impressed upon schools that every subject and activity should be given the number of hours/periods and adequate time. Time once allocated for one subject area/activity should not be encroached upon as per the individual or institutional perception of the relative 'importance' of different subjects.

Open Learning System

The Open Learning System, at the school and the university levels, is now established fully both at the centre (National Open School) and in states (States Open Schools). The mission statement of the open learning system is to take education to the doorsteps of the learner, enhance social equality and create flexibility for lifelong learning. This system at the school level utilises to a great extent information and communication technologies through the use of computers and radio and television broadcasts. Along with the use of satellite-based communication technologies, it provides many structural flexibilities which seem to have an edge over the conventional formal system. These flexibilities relate to the place of learning, time of learning, eligibility criteria, students' choice in selecting combinations of subjects, and the scheme of examination.

Alternative Schooling through open learning system seems to be a viable strategy for reaching the unreached and may contribute toward universalisation of elementary education. Open schooling, through its bridge courses and foundation courses, and undifferentiated curriculum, can contribute in a big way to achieve the goals of general education especially in equipping the learners with necessary life skills for becoming self-confident individuals and contributing citizens of the nation.

Techniques of Teaching at Secondary Stage; Teaching Models—Team Teaching—Individualized Instruction—Programmed Instruction

There is no return from the 21st-century journey; survivors are going to be institutions with extraordinary attention to taking advantage of technology, with clear strategies in educational planning, with strong knowledge about design process of teaching and learning, and with a proactive attitude for achieving activities that we have so far only dreamed about. In the information society era, the art and science of redesigning the process of teaching and learning is as important as correct utilization of technology. Teachers are in need of more options to teach in order to have free time for evaluation of the quality of teaching and learning and enough time for research in the field.

We need to empower our students in the learning activities and their dependence on a single source (teacher) for learning. Students are in need of learning-while-doing with multiple options of learning resources. Our students must be self-directed and life-long learners in order to survive tough expectations of job markets. The change from process-oriented to outcome-oriented and change from teacher-centred to student-teacher-centred curriculum are wish of every higher education institutions. These changes need commitment, leadership, and precise planning by whole institution. I try to explain the roles of technology and process in the ideal model of teaching and learning.

Technology

These days everybody is talking and writing about computer and communication technology and their magical contributions to better educational programmes. The centre stage of this attention is Internet and its tools such as FTP (File Transfer Protocol), Telnet (remote access), Gopher, and the most exciting of all World Wide Web (WWW). World Wide Web is a global interactive, dynamic, distributed, graphical hypertext information system which brought a new beginning and imagination for how to redesign the process of teaching and learning. The main purpose of technology is to provide students and teachers with more options to learn, to teach, to research, to communicate, and to share knowledge. Utilization of technology needs a major planning in training of faculty and students, a major planning in providing opportunity for communication, and a major commitment in the changing the culture of operations. In the traditional way of teaching and learning, higher education institutions designed a programme based on the text book and lecture which is framed with time and place for students. In this model, the main purpose is to satisfy requirement for mastery of a body of knowledge for a life long career. Explosion of technologies in the education and work places have changed the requirements in education for a successful career. In addition to mastery of a body of knowledge a college graduate must develop specific competencies and abilities. With the help of technology, learning these abilities can be included in the process of teaching and learning.

Critical thinking ability-computer resources and applications in form of case study, simulation, problem solving, and intelligent system can help to extend this ability. This ability is very important quality for the success in the information society.

Process design ability-finding the correct way to communicate and access needed resources is very important in the accomplishment of assignment. Learning to design an effective process for accessing and analyzing information is very essential for students in today's multi-resource environment. Students need to design process with a clear strategies for accessing, manipulating, and utilization of information in order to accomplish the desired tasks.

Team work-in today's work places accomplishment of all the assignments are based on the team work. Students should learn how to be a team member, how to contribute to the process, how to use computer for communication with team members, and understand what is the role of the other members in the team. Outcome oriented process-in today's multi-resources environment, it is important for students to design process based on the expected outcome (down-to-top design), a design from expected outcome to process.

Communication skills-knowledge of how to use computer and communication tools and how to utilize them for accomplishment of process are very important part of students competency. In addition to electronic communication, students should develop human communication skills as a team member. Computer and communication technologies can solve two of the strongest barriers to the teaching and learning, where (place) and when (time). Computer-based education is gaining more and more popularity and role in the higher education institutions. Already most of higher education institutions are active in the offering computer-based classes for distance education students. My prediction is in a few years the traditional students (undergraduates) also will have the opportunity to choose some courses independent of place (campus) and time (class schedule). Technology not only brought new way of teaching and learning, but also provided opportunity for everybody from anywhere to teach and learn (virtual classroom).

The Chronicle of Higher Education in December, 1995 issue had an article 'Campus in Cyberspace'. The main point of article was, governors of 11 western states have agreed to explore the creation of a 'virtual university' in their region, one that would deliver courses through computer networks, television, or other technologies, and would award degrees on its own. With the existing demands for virtual classes and capability of technology, I would be surprised if this 11 states have not already established the idea of this virtual university. This is a simple example of independence of teaching and learning from time and place. The learners are not anymore a specific group or groups in society. In the information society everybody needs to be a learner. There is also good opportunity for everybody to be a learner. There is multiple options of resources for everybody in the information society. Synthesis of computers and telecommunications provide options for various design of teaching and process of learning which can help everybody to learn. In this new pedagogical model, teaching and learning is not limited to the classroom and lectures, it can take place in the home, work place, hotel room, and even airplane.

In the future, the individual objective of students, their desired outcome, their styles of learning are going to have major roles in the design of curriculum. With internet and advent of information superhighway, a new definition of teaching and learning is easier to design and implement. Finally, technology provided the following changes for a more realistic and productive teaching and learning environment.

- It allows students to have an active role in the teaching and learning process.
- It provides teachers with more options to teach and more time to evaluate progress of activities.
- It prevents barrier such as when, where, and limited resources.
- It changes teacher-centred to teacher-student-centred, or student-centred education.
- It changes from process oriented to outcome oriented teaching and learning.
- It helps students to be ready for the tough global economy.
- It helps students to be a more effective member of the information society.
- It provides opportunity for virtual university.
- It provides opportunity for joint study of researchers from around the world.

Process

Technology power can provide us with opportunity in designing process of teaching and learning which so far only dreamed about it. National Information Infrastructure presents a global access and communication to every home, school, and work place in utilization of computer technology for teaching and learning. National Learning Infrastructure supports and facilitates technology-oriented teaching and learning in the teacher-learner-centred environment. The stage is ready for designing of practical application of teaching and learning with a new idea in higher education institutions. Before I discuss my new model of teaching and learning, I briefiy explain the characteristics of our learners. Most of today's new generation of learners are adult learners who have need for a specific competency and skills. Most of these adult learners are employed in an organization and the new competency is for advancement in the job, completion of new assignment, or improvement of performance. Only 43 percent of our traditional students are under 25 years of age. It means that we are dealing with learners who have experiences to contribute and objectives for participation.

The following is an idea with a proactive thinking which can be an alternative way for producing the desired outcomes for students and organizations. This process of teaching and learning is designed based on the objective of learning and learner has an active role in the designing of the process of teaching and learning. Example one, in traditional way of teaching, university offers a general course in C++ programming language which has the same process of teaching and learning for World Wide Web (JAVA) programmer, window application developer, and UNIX simulation programmer. Example two, English Literary Theory class is designed for general audiences without attention to the needed skill of high school teacher in feminism or Marxism.

In the new process, the start point is needed skill which is the main initiative for design of process of teaching and learning. Teaching and learning are the other two points of ideal model. In this model both teacher and student are in the control of teaching and learning. I try to explain each in more detail with an example in the following sections.

Needed Skill

The student provides information about objective of learning and needed skills. In some cases employers might also provide additional information about the purpose of an employee's learning. The related department evaluates the objective of learning and arranges different groups of students with similar objectives in the class. I will present two examples in each section of process design in order to clarify this model. Example one: students in the C++ course are divided to three groups, first group's objective is to learn C++ in Window application, the second group's objective is to use new competency for the Web interaction (JAVA), and third group's objective is to develop applications on UNIX machine. Example two: students in English 409, Literary Theory are divided to three groups, first group's objective is to learn about a feminist approach, second group's objective is to learn about a Marxist approach, and the last group's objective is to learn a psychoanalytical approach.

Process Design

In the ideal model, the department which offers the course will design the process of teaching and learning based on the desired outcomes of students. The course can be offered on campus, computer-based off campus, or combination of both of them. As a adult learner with many barriers related to the time and place, I wish for computer-based classes. If computer technology and communication are available, I think most of the adult learners prefer computer-based classes. The major part of design is assignment of teacher and students to the course in order to provide learning opportunity for the desired skills. By year 2000 computer-based classes will be a dominant means in the educational delivery, specially in the adult and continuing education.

Teaching

Each course has a pre-determined number of weeks for general teaching and learning. For example, during the first nine weeks of the semester teacher will provide a general knowledge about C^{++} programming language. If the teacher has experiences in Windows application, WWW application, and UNIX application, the same teacher will continue to work with each group separately for needed skills. After first nine weeks of general learning sessions, it is better to have multiple teachers in order to teach specific needed skills. For example, the teacher who is expert in window application will continue to work with the group who want to use C^{++} for development of widow application.

The same way the other two groups continue working with course teacher or new expert teachers who are specialist on those needed skills. In most cases two teachers can provide and satisfy all different expertise needed by students. In the first seven weeks of semester Literary Theory will be a general discussion about subject matter. From this point the expert teacher will work with smaller group which needs to learn about feminism. The main concepts in multi-teachers is to provide opportunity for learners to gain needed competency and expertise that can be used immediately in the work places or satisfy a specific need. I understand the design of teaching in the multi-teacher environment is complicated, but we should remember computer and communication technology can contribute to the second part of teaching and learning of the course. The second part of the course is mainly assignments and team work. The projects and team works are for gaining practical experiences. Students have opportunities to communicate, share, and accomplish tasks as a member of the team with each other and teacher. The qualities such as human and electronic communication, team work, accomplishment of task, and using computers are essential for every employee in the work place. With this model we can provide our students with the competency that they need and pay for it. This is a practical way of preparing our students for information society and to participate in a tough global economy.

Learning

In the first few weeks, students can participate in the classroom setting, listen to the lecture, and based on the assignments use computer technology for accessing information, preparing assignments, or using learning tools such as simulation, case study, and intelligent system. The last few weeks of skill-oriented activities can be designed to help students to gain needed skills.

The learners can have a few classes on the campus and some of the general sessions and skill-oriented sessions can be arranged by the internet (WWW). It is very important for today's learners to be empowered about learning process and not to be limited by time and place. By year 2000, technology will provide many additional choices for dream process of teaching and learning in the higher education institutions.

Evaluation of the outcomes of these types of classes is very important for students, organizations, teachers, and universities. With follow up questionnaire, universities can collect data about effectiveness of new skills in the work places. These findings can improve design of the future skill-oriented classes.

Kaufman (1995) writes, "to focus only on the means—delivery methods, means, and locations—and not the ends—what learners must know and be able to accomplish in and beyond the conventional classroom—is to squander this great opportunity."

Practical implementation of these types of classes will be sooner or later part of curriculum development. This model has good potential for adult continuing education. As a part of reengineering effort, I suggest that two prototype classes should be designed with this model. A graduate class in computer science with maximum 20 students with 10 weeks of general sessions and 6 weeks of two groups of skill-oriented sessions. Two teachers will contribute to the teaching and will facilitate learning, the main teacher who teaches general sessions will continue with one of the skill-oriented group. The second skill-oriented group will work under direction of a second teacher. The second prototype class which is very proper to be arranged, is for a computer-based distance education class.

For the journey of 21st-century we need to be proactive and aggressive. If we do not start evaluating and planning for this types of classes, we might miss a major opportunity for being a model for other university to follow. I know this model needs a lot of detail work and need assessment, but we should remember technology and time is ready for dramatic changes and transformation of process of teaching and learning to the new level which we could only dream about just a few years ago.

Characteristics and Functions

One set of characteristics of good teaching, extracted from research studies and summarised from the individual lecturer's point of view (Ramsden, 2003) includes:

- A desire to share your love of the subject with students
- An ability to make the material being taught stimulating and interesting
- A facility for engaging with students at their level of understanding
- A capacity to explain the material plainly
- A commitment to making it absolutely clear what has to be understood at what level and why
- Showing concern and respect for students
- A commitment to encouraging independence
- An ability to improvise and adapt to new demands
- Using teaching methods and academic tasks that require students to learn actively, responsibly and co-operatively
- Using valid assessment methods
- A focus on key concepts, and students misunderstandings of them, rather than covering the ground
- Giving the highest quality feedback on student work
- A desire to learn from students and other sources about the effects of teaching and how it can be improved.

A similar set of characteristics has been derived from feedback from students at UTS, and is summarised in the following section.

The Students' Choice

The Planning and Quality unit run a Student Feedback System at UTS. The system uses a questionnaire which gathers both numerical ratings and student opinions about teaching strengths and improvements. Systems for generating and analysing student feedback questionnaires have been used at UTS since 1988, although the questionnaires themselves have changed over time.

In the early 1990s, some research was carried out to look at staff who had been very highly rated by students. Highly rated staff come from a wide range of disciplines and teaching situations, but they share a number of characteristics which students consider to be strengths in teaching in lecture and tutorial classes. The following information was obtained from the students' responses and through interviews with the lecturers. A project on 'effective interaction' carried out in 2003 suggested that the qualities which students value have changed little over time.

Teaching Skills and Practices

The most frequent comment made by students was that highly rated lecturers explained in a way which was clear and helped students to understand. They made difficult work comprehensible without oversimplifying, and used simple language. If technical language was used, it was clearly defined. In lectures, visual media, such as overheads, slides, handouts and blackboard diagrams were used to assist in explanation or clarification where appropriate. Abstract concepts were illustrated with examples, and the distinction between concept and example was made clear.

Highly rated lecturers were well prepared, structured their lecture content effectively, and communicated the structure to students. They clearly defined the subject objectives and emphasised important points. They spoke clearly and at an appropriate speed and allowed adequate time for students to both take notes and listen, indicating when note-taking was and was not required. They often provided handouts to assist students to take notes without furious copying. They used questions and activities to engage students' thinking and interest.

They were highly knowledgeable and up to date in their subject area, but did not pretend to "know it all" and were willing to learn from their students, recognising that work experience makes many part-time and senior students a valuable resource. Students commented that the lecturers tried to make the work interesting. They related new concepts to students' experiences by means of case studies, relevant examples or anecdotes, and placed a high priority on varying student activities during lecture sessions.

Student participation was encouraged, in lectures as well as tutorial or laboratory sessions. These lecturers knew that most students gained a better understanding from active involvement than from passive note-taking. They therefore made a conscious effort to release time from "lecturing" for student analysis, problem solving, questioning, discussion or "buzz group" activities relevant to the topic for the lecture. During lectures, they made frequent opportunities for questions from, or discussion by, students, and attempted to answer all questions promptly and clearly. They treated all student questions seriously and did not intimidate or ridicule. They also asked direct questions of students in order to check understanding before or during a lecture.

Giving time for students to actively engage with the subject matter means reducing time available to cover new content. The lecturers' most frequent strategies for gaining time without compromising course objectives were:

- Providing students with printed subject notes and/or summary handouts, thus reducing note writing, and encouraging students to highlight key points, add comments and note insights generated during class interactions.
- Thoroughly explaining key concepts and examples in short lecture segments, and encouraging students to access texts and references for further details and multiple examples.
- Reducing the content covered in lectures to central areas, and encouraging wider reading and/or the integration of work experience through carefully designed assignments and tutorials.

Attitude towards Students

Highly rated lecturers genuinely wanted students to learn, understand and develop critical thinking abilities, as well as master content or learn skills. They demonstrated an empathy with student thinking, anticipating misconceptions and allowing students to develop understanding in a variety of ways. They observed students in class for signs that they were failing to keep up, were bored, or were not understanding, and were flexible in responding to student needs. They encouraged student feedback on their teaching, and often sought informal feedback during classes.

Outside class time, they made a point of being approachable and willing to help students. They tried to avoid "spoon-feeding" and encouraged students to take an active role in working through their difficulties, but would take time to work though concepts in detail with those who genuinely had difficulties.

Personal Qualities

Highly rated lecturers showed enthusiasm for their subject, professional area and teaching role. Students found this motivating and commented that they looked forward to coming to classes. The most frequently mentioned personal attribute of the highly rated lecturers was their "easy going", "relaxed" or "open" manner, and the relaxed atmosphere that this brought to the classroom. Students also appreciated appropriate humour and an attitude which suggested that learning was enjoyable.

In summary...

Highly rated lecturers saw their teaching role as vitally important They worked hard at making the most of their class contact time to maximise student learning and interest in the subject. While some felt that they were fortunate in having "natural" teaching ability, they all emphasised the considerable amount of time they had spent in lecture and resource preparation.

Teaching as a function of learning: Voices of NGO.

Teachers need to learn that teaching is to support the children. Teachers need to provide ample interactions of children with things; people and environment are required both through action and language multiple interpretations..

A FOCUS group discussion, which worked as a group interview, was held on teacher development in which the key resource trainers of two non-government organisations (N=8, discussion time: one hour) took part.

The key statements of the participants were noted down which worked as discursive data or teachers' voices for analysis.

Voices:

- Teachers are central to the qualitative improvement in education.
- Teachers' motivation hinges on children's achievement and motivation. The teachers' energy level rests on the ways children enthuse and infuse energy into the teacher.
- For enthusing teachers, the administrative will and rigour are also equally important. The educational administrators must also be trained and benefit from existing body of knowledge on teacher motivation and learning which is being regarded a common human potential.
- The teacher development model is based on three aspects: (a) Equity framework of learning, i.e, every child learning in the classroom irrespective of the background of the child which requires freedom of pacing diversity and inclusive learning; (b) Creating a learning environment emphasising supportive relationships, innervations, child's participation through group work; (c) The assessment leading to child level planning for support and affirmative action.
- The constructive perspective of learning with human beings as generations of knowledge requires to be emphasised at all levels. Also, an understanding of not only how children learn is important, but also the educational functionaries need to understand how children get put off from learning and how schools push out students. Lecturing, cramming, instructing, preaching and mechanical activities put off children from learning.
- When we talk of teacher development, we assume that teacher too is an active learner, the self-motivation and self-development aspects become important for all the activities of teacher development. Then their training

is one of the multifarious activities of the system to support learning of teachers.

- The broad focus of any teacher training programme and module needs to be the teacher is a pivot of learning which also means the educational management structures also the become the learning organisations.
- In cash we wish to develop teacher as a learner, the natural implication is that all component of the educational system also become learners. In such a situation, teaching becomes a concept dependent on learning.
- The teacher's main function is teaching, but teaching too requires learning. The teacher cannot function effectively if she is not a good learner herself. Thus, lecturing, preaching and ordering are not learning.

Analysis

In seems that in the NGO functionaries working in the area of education and alternative modes of learning, the concepts of 'teacher as a learner has been accepted and constructivist approach to learning is gaining currency.

With the emphasis on constructivist model of learning in National Curriculum Framework (NCF) of 2005, there is a need for shifting the prevalent teacher training models and approaches, both pre-service and in service trainings, into teacher development models emphasising teacher as a learner assumption.

Teachers need to learn that teaching (hence the function of the teacher) is to support the children.

Conclusion

If recent education reform of Sarva Shiksha Abhiyan (SSA) has to make a proper headway, the whole system of teacher education and training would require to revamped based on the premise of 'teacher is a learner' and 'teaching as a function of teacher that induces learning'. The emphasis has to shift to constructivist pedagogy for the classroom reform and critical pedagogy for the systematic reform if the SSA has to make a lasting impact.

Special Educational Needs of Exceptional Children

Throughout the world, Children With Special Needs (CWSN) were a neglected lot till the 18th century, when the ideas of fraternity, equality and liberty sweeping France and America inspired political reformers and leaders in medicine and education to turn their attention towards the educational needs of such individuals. France played a pioneering role in the area of special education. It was in Paris that Valentine Huay started a School for the Blind in 1785 and Father De L'epee developed an early version of finger spelling for the deaf. Jean Marc Gaspard Itard's case study of 'The Wild Boy of Aveyron' is a pioneering work in the field of education for the mentally retarded.

Special Schools in India

Along with other parts of the world, India too, witnessed the emergence of special schools for people with disabilities. The first school for the deaf was set up in Bombay in 1883, and the first school for the blind at Amritsar in 1887. There was rapid expansion in the number of such institutions. Today, there are more than 3200 special schools throughout India.

However, these special schools have certain disadvantages which became evident as the number of these schools increased. These institutions reached out to a very limited number of children, largely urban and they were not cost effective. But most important of all, these special schools segregated CWSN from the mainstream, thus developing a specific disability culture.

Integrated Education

The emergence of the concept of integrated education in India during the mid 1950s was seen as a solution to these problems. Small experiments in this area were begun by the Royal Commonwealth Society for the Blind, and the Christopher Blind Mission. The Ministry of Education, too, launched a comprehensive scholarship scheme in 1952 — a rudimentary beginning of the integrated education initiative by the Government.

Integrated Education for Disabled Children (IEDC)

Consequent on the success of international experiments in placing children with disabilities in regular schools, the Planning Commission, in 1971, included in its plan a programme for integrated education. The Government launched the IEDC scheme in December 1974. However, educational administrators have been slow in grasping the value of IE.

The aim of IEDC is:

- to provide educational opportunities to CWSN in regular schools,
- to facilitate their retention in the school system, and
- to place children from special schools in common schools.

The scope of the scheme includes pre-school training, counselling for the parents, and special training in skills for all kinds of disabilities. The scheme provides facilities in the form of books, stationery, uniforms, and allowances for transport, reader, escort etc. Inspite of all these facilities, IEDC met with limited success — only a little more than one lakh CWSN have been covered. However, it was successful in creating awareness on the importance of integrating CWSN in the mainstream of education, a fact noted in the National Policy on Education — 1986.

Project Integrated Education for the Disabled (PIED)

The next step was another experiment on IE in India. There was a shift in strategy, from a school based approach to a Composite Area Approach — and in 1987 the Ministry of Human Resources Development, along with UNICEF launched another experiment: Project Integrated Education for the Disabled (PIED).

In this approach, a cluster, instead of the individual school approach is emphasised. A cluster, usually a block of population is taken as the project area. All the schools in the area are expected to enrol children with disabilities. Training programmes were also given to the teachers. This project was implemented in one administrative block each in Madhya Pradesh, Maharashtra, Nagaland, Orissa, Rajasthan, Tamil Nadu, Haryana, Mizoram, Delhi Municipal Corporation, and Baroda Municipal Corporation. The approach is an improvement over the special schools in many ways and appears to be the only way towards universalising education of the disabled children. It is more cost effective and easier to organise, since existing school infrastructure is to be made use of.

Inclusion is a philosophy built on the belief that all people are equal and should be respected and valued, as an issue of basic human rights an "unending set of processes" in which children and adults with disabilities have the opportunity to participate fully in ALL community activities offered to people who do not have disabilities. (UNESCO-at the UN-Committee on Rights of the Child, October 6, 1997-Centre for Human Rights, Geneva).

Under PIED, there has been a significant increase in the number of not only mildly disabled, but also severely disabled children, with the number of orthopaedically handicapped children far outstripping other disabled children. All these perform at par with non-disabled children; in fact their retention rate is higher than that of non-disabled children and absenteeism is low. PIED has also had a positive impact on the attitudes of the teachers, the heads of schools, as well as parents and the community in general. Also, the interaction between the disabled and the non-disabled children is good.

Inclusive Education

Another important paradigm shift in this area was initiated with the thinking that any difficulty that a child exhibited in learning was to be attributed not to a problem within the child, but to the school system. The organisation and management of schools, and the various programmes of teaching and interventions could also be one of the causes of children's learning difficulties. The new whole school policy is also referred to as the social or environmental model and rests on the theory that the child is a product of his/her experiences and the interventions the child has with various environments that impinge upon him/her. Thus to a great extent a child's growth and development depends upon this.

Inclusive Education in DPEP

This policy dictated the philosophy of inclusive education in DPEP. Moreover, DPEP also addressed core issues related to curriculum such as what factors limit the access of certain children to curriculum; what modifications are necessary to ensure fuller curriculum access. Thus, with its child-centred pedagogy, DPEP set a stage where children with special needs could be provided learning opportunities tailored to their needs.

IED was formally added in DPEP in 1997. By 1998, many DPEP states had conducted surveys, assessment camps and evolved strategies to provide resource support to those children with special needs who were enrolled in DPEP schools.

The IED guidelines in DPEP clearly menton that, "DPEP will fund interventions for IED of primary school going children with integrable and mild to moderate disabilities". Towards this end DPEP supported:

- Community mobilisation and early detection
- In-service teacher training
- Provision of resource support
- Provision of educational aids and appliances
- Removal of architectural barriers.

IED was initially introduced in the states in a small way by taking one block/cluster as a pilot project in each DPEP district. From a few hundred blocks in 1998, IED is currently being implemented in 2014 blocks of 18 DPEP states. Ten states of Gujarat, Haryana, Himachal Pradesh, Karnataka, Kerala, Madhya Pradesh, Maharashtra, Orissa, Tamil Nadu and Uttaranchal have upscaled the IED programme to all the blocks.

DPEP estimates clearly showed that there were a large number of disabled children in the relevant age group. Gradually realisation dawned that UPE could not be achieved unless children with special needs were also brought under the ambit of primary education. This led to more concrete planning and strategisation of providing resource support and remedial assistance to children with special needs. As the programme progressed many models of service delivery evolved with the sole aim of providing supportive learning environment to children with special needs. The thrust was on imparting quality education to all disabled children. Constitutional and legal obligations and policies at the international and national levels:

- UN Convention on the Rights of the Child, 1989
- UN Declaration on Education for All, 1990 (Jomtien Declaration)
- UN Standard Rules on Equalisation of Opportunities for Persons with Disabilities, 1993
- The Salamanca Declaration, 1994
- Article 45 and 93rd Amendment.

National Policy on Education, 1986:

"...Future emphasis shall be on distance and open learning systems to provide opportunities and access to all the major target groups, especially the disadvantaged, viz., women, scheduled castes and scheduled tribes, the adult working class, and people serving in the far-flung remote areas."

Rehabilitation Council of India Act, 1992

Passed by Parliament in 1992, this act makes it mandatory for every special teacher to be registered by the council and lays down that every child with disability had the right to be taught by a qualified teacher. In fact it provided punishment for those teachers who engaged in teaching children with special needs without a license.

Education Policy of Government of India, 1992 (Modified)

Persons with Disabilities (Equal Opportunities, Protection of Rights & Full Participation) Act, 1995 A composite act covering all aspects, it mainly deals with education and employment.

National Trust Act (National Trust for the Welfare of Persons with Autism, Cerebral Palsy, Mental Retardation and Multiple Disability), 1999.

A landmark legislation, this trust seeks to protect and promote the rights of persons who within the disability sector, have been even more marginalised than others. The salient features are:

- First of its kind in the category of persons addressed
- Recognition of range of independence in Skills, Daily Living and Financial Management
- Protection-dominant, rather than autonomy-dominant
- Local Level Committee-District Level Coverage
- Decision making powers to Persons with Disabilities
- Legal Guardianship-even for parents
- Stake-holdership of Registered Organisations
- Legality/ Responsibility linked to Bequests.

Open learning has emerged with a promise to make education a really effective tool for the process of democratisation and social justice. It is particularly characterised by removal of restrictions, exclusions, and privileges; by the accreditation of students' previous experiences, by the flexibility of the management of the time variable; and by substantial changes in the traditional relationship between teacher and students. It offers unique educational opportunities free from the constraints of time and space as well as rigidity of curricula.

Inclusive education goes beyond physical presence of a child in the classroom situation; going through the same curricula as the non-disabled, appearing at the same examination with them and acquiring the same certificate.

National Institute of Open Schooling is promoting inclusive education by registering children with disabilities through Accredited Institutions (AI), Accredited Vocational Institutions (AVI), Special Accredited Institutions for the Education of the Disadvantaged (SAIED) and Open Basic Education (OBE). Some of the disabled learners may like to stay at home or study at their working places. Open schooling may reach any group of person at any given circumstance. Learning materials, audio-video cassettes, or working kit may reach at the doorsteps of disabled learners.

In spite of in-built flexibilities in the open learning system and concessions given in the tuition fee, it could not attract a large number of the children with disabilities. The reasons may be numerous. Perhaps, the existing curriculum is not relevant or the evaluation system or often procedures need revision.

To enhance the access, retain them in the learning process and achieve development of the children with disabilities, NIOS has established a Cell for the Education of the Disabled (CED) in the year 2000. In the dynamic changing environment and rapid technological advancement, open learning has to play a significant role not only to provide access, but to retain persons with disabilities in the learning process and achieve success.

It is felt that the issues pertaining to relevant programmes, curricula and pedagogy are important and initiatives in these directions, specially for catering to the needs of learners with disabilities and the marginalised groups of children need to be addressed with seriousness.

The formal, non-formal, adult education, vocational education, special education and open schooling systems all have to optimise their services and support to promote the full and equal participation of persons with disabilities. There was need for supportive materials for use by resource teachers and general teachers, and decentralisation of training at block level and cluster level with more practical input.

The objective of the training is to develop Multi category Resource Persons (MRP) who can orient other teachers to promote the development of inclusive education in schools in rural society.

Inclusion Means

- **educating** children with disabilities in the schools they would attend if they did not have disabilities

- providing services and support that parents and children with disabilities need in order to be in normal settings
- supporting regular education teachers and administrators
- having children with disabilities follow the same schedule as other children
- encouraging friendships between children with disabilities and their classmates/peers without disabilities
- teachers and administrators taking these concerns seriously
- teaching ALL children to understand and accept differences.

Direct Services to Children. The first step is identification of CWSN for micro-planning of IED in terms of Visual Impairment, Hearing Impairment, Locomotor Impairment, Mental Retardation, Learning Disabilities and Others. The next step involves formal and functional assessment of each identified child to determine the nature and extent of disability. This should be followed by preparation of individualised need based profile which delineates all the needs, special services required, duration of such services and evaluation procedures. After this the most suitable learning environment is to be identified for each child. All necessary required support, aids and appliances and learning material suitable to the special need of a challenged child should be provided. Finally, all schools must not only be barrier free and provide easy access to CWSN, but also be equipped with other facilities to take care of their special needs.

Support Services

There is need to generate awareness and appreciation of the potential and utility of the education of CWSN, and educate and sensitise parents, teachers, community leaders and the community as a whole. Parents of CWSN also need to be trained in coping with the disabilities of these children and helping them. Teacher training should form the backbone of inclusive education. Support services in the form of physiotherapy, occupational therapy, speech therapy, counselling etc. should be provided in the resource room. SSA missions may also plan for Vocational Education of disabled children at Upper Primary Level. The planning of IED may include extra curricular activities like drawing, painting, dance, music, sports, craft and indoor games. Use of technology is also advocated in the shape of special aids and appliances, computer assisted instruction and development of low cost/no cost Teaching and Learning Aids using indigenous material. While taking care of the special educational needs of CWSN, it is also necessary to consider adaptations in the evaluation system.

Monitoring and Evaluation. This is an important aspect for assessing progress and providing improvement in the process. Therefore, an adequate and efficient mechanism needs to be in place for this purpose.

Guidance and Counselling

Guidance is assistance given to an individual to help him, to adjust to himself, to others and to his own peculiar environment. Guidance helps him to understand himself. It helps him in his acquaintance with the things and the world around him. Finally, it helps the person to seek harmony between his personal needs and ambitions with peculiarities of his own environment. In this way, guidance can be described as a process of assisting an individual with his adjustment problems. Thus, according to Jones, "Guidance is the help given by one person to another in making choices and adjustments and in solving problems". While Skinner says "Guidance is a process of helping young persons learns to adjust to self, to others, and to circumstances".

Guidance aims to prepare an individual for his future life. It helps him to acquire essential skills, abilities and capacities for the tasks to be accomplished in future. It also helps the individual in selecting a proper future profession and role in the society and enables him to play his role successfully. Guidance has personal and social significance. It aims to help an individual in the process of his adjustment with himself and his environment. It helps him to develop his strengths and abilities, to achieve utmost personal and social efficiency. It also aims to stop wastage of human power and physical resources by helping the individuals to find their place in society.

Thus, we can say that Guidance is the process of helping an individual to help himself and to develop his potentialities to the fullest by utilizing the maximum opportunities provided by the environment.

On the other hand, Counselling is the service offered to the individual, who is undergoing a problem and needs professional help to overcome it. The problem keeps him disturbed, high strung, under tension and unless solved, his development is hampered or stunted. Counselling therefore, is a more specialized service requiring training in personality development and handling exceptional groups of individuals. For example, individuals suffering from sensory handicaps like, visually handicapped, deaf and mute, speech disorders, or from physical handicaps like malfunctioning of glands or vital organs; orthopaedically handicapped; personal-social handicaps like, neurotics, psychotics, depressed isolates or from intellectual retardation or exceptionally high talent and so on. In other words, when the development is not normal because of certain handicaps, the individual needs help to be able to adjust to the environmental pressures and learn to overcome his handicaps or at least accept them squarely.

Counselling services are therefore, required for individuals having developmental problems, because of the handicap they suffer in any area of growth like, physical, mental, moral, social and emotional, either because of hereditary factors or environmental conditions.

Counselling therefore is offered to only those individuals who are under serious problem and need professional help to overcome it, while guidance is needed by all at any time.

Both guidance and counselling assist the individual to know about himself, to adjust himself, with others and the environment and thus lead the individual to become a Wholesome Person.

Philosophy of Guidance

Guidance is universal and the basic principles of the philosophy of guidance are common to all countries with a slight modification to suit the locally accepted beliefs and the specific guidance services offered. The eight principles of the philosophy of guidance are:

1. The dignity of the individual is supreme.
2. Each individual is unique. He or she is different from every other individual.
3. The primary concern of guidance is the individual in his own social setting. The main aim being to help him to become a wholesome person and to gain fullest satisfaction in his life.
4. The attitudes and personal perceptions of the individual are the bases on which he acts.
5. The individual generally acts to enhance his perceived self.
6. The individual has the innate ability to learn and can be helped to make choices that will lead to self-direction, and make him consistent with the social environment.
7. The individual needs a continuous guidance process from early childhood through adulthood.
8. Each individual may, at times, need the information and personalized assistance best given by competent professional personnel.

The Goals to Achieve in Guidance

At present, Guidance has taken an unprecedented lead over all the other helping professions, for it empowers an individual to charter his life successfully, inspite of all odds.

The main goals are:

1. *Exploring-self:* The basic aim is to help an individual increase his understanding and acceptance of self; his physical development, his intelligence, aptitudes, interest, personality traits, attitudes and values, his

achievements in scholastic and other spheres, his aspirations and life-style preferences and above all his here-and-now needs which keep him highly motivated to behave positively *or otherwise.*

2. *Determining Values:* The second aim is to help an individual recognize the importance of values, explore different sets of values, determine personal values and examine them in relation to the norms of society and their importance in planning for success in life.
3. *Setting Goals:* This aim is to help an individual set goal for him self and relate these to the values determined by him so that he recognizes the importance of long-range planning.
4. *Explore the World of Work:* The aim here is to help the individual explore the World of Work in relation to his self-exploration, his value system and goals that he has set for himself to achieve success in life.
5. *Improving Efficiency:* The individual is helped to learn about factors which contribute to increase effectiveness and efficiency and to improve his study habits.
6. *Building Relationship:* The aim is to help the individual to be aware of his relationship with others and to note that it is a reflection of his own feelings about himself.
7. *Accepting responsibility for the future:* The individual is helped to develop skill in social and personal forecasting, acquire attitudes and skills necessary for mastering the future.

To sum up, guidance empowers him to be an integrated individual, actualizing his potential to the fullest.

Why Guidance?

Guidance is needed at every stage of development right from the beginning of life till the end. Everyone needs guidance at one time or the other. If properly guided, every individual will be satisfied in life.

Aim and Meaning of Spiritual Guidance

It is good to know how properly to practice asceticism in spiritual life: asceticism to be practiced in knowledge; spiritual ascent and transformation to be in knowledge; repentance in knowledge, obedience in knowledge, prayer in knowledge, deeds in knowledge, as the Holy Fathers say.

Awareness of where we stand at all times. To know what we strive after and in which direction we move every single moment. Christ to be our touchstone. Many times, in different contexts and studying the process of spiritual maturation from various aspects, we point out that there are three stages (levels) in the spiritual development of a person. The ascetical-hesychastic living Tradition names them as:

- First stage-purification of the heart from passions
- Second stage-illumination of the mind
- Third stage-deification of man's person.

Why is it necessary to repeat already said and even adopted things? Because we forget! Knowledge is preceded by ignorance, which is the greatest sin, as the Holy Fathers say. And, it is followed by forgetfulness! Knowledge is not a mental category in the Church. Knowledge is grace! It is a gift of the Holy Spirit by the prayers of the spiritual father. We acquire knowledge, it is given to us only through practice, through the graceful experience in the practice of obedience during which at first the energy of the mind is purified and then the mind is illumined and deified to its very essence or getfulness happens in the instance of repeated fall, falling away, losing grace, when we return to the life and deeds according to the passions of the old man.

Thus, to each of the above-mentioned stages there is a certain corresponding process of purification, of prayer, of temptations. To each of these three stages there is a corresponding priestly rank, when it comes to canonical ordination. To each of these stages there is also a corresponding mode of organisation of monastic life: Community (cenobium), Skete, Desert. At each of these three stages also occurs certain, specific and different for each level, spiritual relationship of the spiritual child with the spiritual father, which depends, among other things, on the stage in which each of them is. This relationship is dynamic. It passes from one level to another. It transforms.

The spiritual father gives birth (spiritually, by grace) to his spiritual child. And he has to raise him, to educate and bring him up, to set him free. This development is inevitable and takes place only in the Holy Mystery of the personal relationship between them, in the Church. Such a relationship can be unique, deep, sincere, loving. When the spiritual child is in the first stage of spiritual growth, the quality of this relationship depends, first of all, on the openness and the unreserved trust and obedience of the spiritual child to his father, and not as much on the holiness of the spiritual guide. Starting point of this relationship is the degree of darkness of ignorance and captivity by passions of the spiritual child, especially by the main one-vainglory.

It is necessary to reach the level at which the spiritual child experiences purification and opening of the heart (as a spiritual centre of our being) and gushing forth of the mind-and-heart prayer. Then their relationship most frequently becomes communion and exchange, in humility, of the graceful experience between brother and brother, brother and sister, in Christ. St. John the Baptist says: *He must become greater; I must become less.* So it is in the spiritual relationship of the spiritual father with his spiritual child: his supervision and guidance are diminishing more and more, in proportion of Christ's revelation and growth in the heart of the spiritual child.

Hence, the meaning of guidance in spiritual life through the personal relationship spiritual father-spiritual child is a new quality of relationships, growing in Christ, in the image and likeness of God: the Holy Trinity. And it is not a relationship as some understand it and which is most frequently found in the philosophic-religious systems of the Far East, in the form of once for all given idolatrous relationships: guru (master)-disciple.

Counselling

A counsellor can meet with you on a one-to-one basis, with you and your partner or with members of your family, to talk through issues that are concerning you.

Group Therapy

A counsellor leads the discussion for a group of people (with or without similar issues of concern) who get together on a regular basis to share their experiences or concerns.

Online and Telephone Counselling

Working with a counsellor online, by telephone, by Email, chat-room or instant messaging is certainly not as good as face-to-face counselling but can be very effective when there are long distances involved. This is especially relevant in India, USA, UK & France.

Self-help Groups

People who are experiencing similar problems, such as loss and grief, trauma, divorce and illness, meet to discuss common issues and problems (with or without a counsellor to lead the discussion).

Meaning Given in Counselling

The following headline caught my eye on CNN some time ago: "Uncontacted tribe sighted in Amazon". I assume by "uncontacted" CNN meant that we have no form of communication with this tribe, we are isolated from them. This got me thinking about the process in counselling where one person (the counsellor) meets with another (the client) and they somehow come into contact. They have a connection because meaning is shared.

My idea of counselling starts with the client showing the counsellor what the client's meaning is: How the client sees the world and himself in it. This is what some call a person-centred approach; the counsellor takes the lead from the client and strains to see and feel the client's worldview. Other approaches to counselling also do this. Cognitive Behavioural Therapists (CBT) examine the meanings clients carry around with them in order to understand why they feel and behave in certain circumstances. Gestalt therapy uses a certain picture (which can be viewed as an old lady or a young woman, depending on the perspective) to show that we give different meanings to the same things.

But counselling does not stop at understanding a client's meaning. Many would agree that the purpose of counselling is to achieve awareness and change. But change in what direction? If we can somehow communicate with the Uncontacted Amazon tribe, are they to change in line with our meaning, our perspective, or vice versa? And what if the two are irreconcilable? Logotherapy places great importance on changing the way clients think about things, but how are we to assess whether that change is helpful for the client?

The narrative approach, such as that advocated by Michael White, would call this re-authoring a client's story Perhaps we are all uncontacted tribes, isolated from each other until we make the effort to somehow share each other's meaning. But once we have shared these meanings, where do we go from there?

Definition of Counselling

Counselling takes place when a counsellor sees a client in a private and confidential setting to explore a difficulty the client is having, distress they may be experiencing or perhaps their dissatisfaction with life, or loss of a sense of direction and purpose. It is always at the request of the client as no one can properly be 'sent' for counselling.

By listening attentively and patiently the counsellor can begin to perceive the difficulties from the client's point of view and can help them to see things more clearly, possibly from a different perspective. Counselling is a way of enabling choice or change or of reducing confusion. It does not involve giving advice or directing a client to take a particular course of action. Counsellors do not judge or exploit their clients in any way.

In the counselling sessions the client can explore various aspects of their life and feelings, talking about them freely and openly in a way that is rarely possible with friends or family. Bottled up feelings such as anger, anxiety, grief and embarrassment can become very intense and counselling offers an opportunity to explore them, with the possibility of making them easier to understand. The counsellor will encourage the expression of feelings and as a result of their training will be able to accept and reflect the client's problems without becoming burdened by them.

Acceptance and respect for the client are essentials for a counsellor and, as the relationship develops, so too does trust between the counsellor and client, enabling the client to look at many aspects of their life, their relationships and themselves which they may not have considered or been able to face before.

The counsellor may help the client to examine in detail the behaviour or situations which are proving troublesome and to find an area where it would be possible to initiate some change as a start. The counsellor may help the client to look at the options open to them and help them to decide the best for them.

Models of Counselling

Although there is considerable consensus about the core content of a counselling course, there are nevertheless distinct methods of counselling. Most courses start from a theoretical base-typically humanistic, psychodynamic, cognitive or behavioural. Before enrolling on a course it is advisable to be aware of its theoretical emphasis and what that means in terms of the learning experience offered and the skills acquired.

Characteristics of Effective Counselling

Effective counseling is a two way street. It takes a cooperative effort by both the person receiving counseling and the counsellor. And it takes a commitment to make sometimes difficult changes in behaviour or thinking patterns.

What you expect to achieve with your counsellor should be clearly defined as you begin your counseling. You and your counsellor should discuss realistic time frames for reaching your goals and agree on how you will measure your progress.

It's important that you and your counsellor establish a good relationship that allows you to be completely honest about your thoughts and feelings. Often, this requires an elusive "chemistry" between both of you in which you feel comfortable with your counsellor's personality, approach and style. If after the first few sessions you don't feel this chemistry, look for another counsellor with whom you feel more comfortable.

Once you think you've found the right counsellor, how do you tell if your relationship is effective? Here are some signs to look for:

While you are responsible for making changes in your life, an effective counsellor can help pinpoint the obstacles in your way. If you have control over these obstacles, a counsellor can suggest behavioural changes to help you overcome them. If these obstacles involve factors outside of your control, your counsellor can teach you coping mechanisms that will foster your well being in trying circumstances.

An effective counsellor can identify negative thinking patterns that may be feeding feelings of sadness, depression or anxiety. By encouraging you to build upon personal strengths and suggesting skills that can overcome self-inflicted feelings of hopelessness, a counsellor can help you develop a more positive attitude. A good counsellor can assist you in making positive changes in your relationships with others, helping you recognize behaviors that may be contributing to a troublesome relationship. Your counsellor can teach you effective ways of communicating, clearing the way for honest exchanges with people in your life who may be causing you emotional pain.

You can determine whether your work with your counsellor is effective if you begin to obtain insights about your own thoughts and behaviors that may have eluded you before. Over time, you should be able to recognize patterns in the way you act, trace their sources and identify stumbling blocks to your happiness that you may have unwittingly created. The end result is personal growth that empowers you to control your life and enjoy positive, life-affirming relationships with others.

Objective

Primary Objectives: To provide a well founded Counselling Service, available to students and staff, in the university by:

- offering one-to-one counselling for personal and educational issues
- offering therapeutic group work
- offering a variety of personal skills training (e.g. examination preparation, assertiveness training) on a workshop basis
- developing awareness amongst staff of issues of concern to students
- contributing to providing training in tutoring and other skills relevant to staff in meeting their responsibilities to students

Secondary Objectives: To contribute to the creation of a positive environment for learning within the University by:

- using the knowledge gained through the nature of counselling to help the University identify and address areas of stress
- participation in policy making and policy implementation in areas directly related to student support

Objectives of Genetic Counselling

The results of a survey published in the Journal of Public Health Medicine [Michie, S. et al. (1998) J. Pub Health Med. 20, 404-408 (Abstract)] suggest that, although purchasers, providers and users of genetic services are in broad agreement about the aims of such services, purchasers differ from providers and users in the relative priorities they assign to these aims. The study used the 'Delphi' technique to survey the attitudes of public health doctors and GPs (purchasers), clinical geneticists and genetic counsellors (providers) and users (outpatients and members of a support organisation). There was broad agreement that the five most important aims were to give information, give support, facilitate decision-making, enable risk assessment, and achieve understanding. However, purchasers assigned relatively higher priorities to facilitation of decision-making and risk assessment, while providers and users ranked giving information and support more highly.

Comment: There are several possible explanations for the difference between purchasers and the other groups, but at least on the surface it appears that those responsible for commissioning genetic services tend to value 'active' outcomes from these services, while those directly involved in the service, either as providers or users, value the more neutral aims of providing information and support. This difference may assume increasing importance as the potential range of genetic services widens.

Need Career Counselling?

What do you want to be when you grow up? Which one of us hasn't faced that question when we were younger? Most of us probably had an answer. Teacher! Fireman! Astronaut! The choices seemed endless then. But the question takes on a whole new significance for students fresh out of Class X or Class XII.

In a world filled with career choices ranging from medicine to mass communications, engineering to event management, marine biology to information technology, the confusion teenagers face over which career to pick is understandable. A large number of students continue to choose a career based merely on the fact that their friends are doing the same thing or because their parents told them to do so. This, however, may not be the best way to go about it.

If you've just taken your Class X/ Class XII board exams, and are trying to decide on a profession, the first thing you need to realise is that every individual is different. Not everyone can be a doctor or an engineer (not everyone wants to be one!)—and that's okay!

Choosing a field of study that is not really suited to your interests or skills could prove disastrous. And that's where career counselling comes in.

What is Career Counselling?

Career counselling helps students discover their true potential and interest in various subjects in order to help them choose the right career. Several institutes, including schools and colleges, today offer career counselling through a series of aptitude and IQ tests. The tests usually have multiple-choice questions, which don't need to be prepared for in any way.

Then comes a face-to-face interview with a career guidance counsellor. The interview provides the student with the opportunity to clear any doubts or queries he/ she may have regarding career options and educational courses. It also allows the counsellor to further judge the aptitude of the student, thus building on the preliminary results of the written tests.

Varsha Rebelló, manager and senior counsellor, Career Launcher India, says, "Career counselling is the guidance given to a student on the road he/she should take to achieve his/her goals. The advice and counselling provided is based on three deciding factors — personality, aptitude and interest. The counsellor is trained in administering tests that determine the aptitude and skills of a child, his/her personality traits and subjects of interest."

Classroom Climate

Teachers transmit information to students who are made to act as passive recipients of it in the name of discipline. There is a need to combat this view that knowledge needs to be stored into various compartment of students' minds.

Despite the fact that mere acquisition of wordy knowledge is a harmful idea, it is the most popular method of learning in most schools. Teachers transmit information to students who are made to act as passive recipients of it in the name of discipline. There is a need to combat this view that knowledge needs to be stored into various compartment of students' minds.

Mere acquisition of knowledge, without understanding and a sense of value is of no use. In most educational institutions we are teaching the subject matter or content and not educating students. A mere plastering of facts and figures of various subjects on the minds of student is being done. We are mistaking information acquisition as learning. Most teachers are perpetuating this classroom hoax year after year.

Some of the most common concerns about the current teaching method in the classroom are given below. These concerns have been very often voiced in the media and critiques of education.

- We cannot undervalue knowledge and subject matter as teachers will be teaching in subject – but issue is how to use the knowledge for making pupils think, to respond with sensitivity, and to develop pupils' sense of value.
- The subject matter must provide food for the mind, i.e., thinking, imagining, expressing, modifying etc.
- Good teaching promotes the activity of the mind; bad teaching is mechanical and lifeless.
- Intolerant use of abstractions mechanically in teaching is the major vice of the intellect. In teaching, a sense of values, sensitivity and the right personal attitudes are equally important.
- Questioning and dialoguing have a special value, they train the mind. A teacher's questions can play on a child's mind spurring it to become independent, enterprising and perhaps creative.
- Knowledge is not the sole end of teaching; because it is pupils master their subject and utilize knowledge that matters.
- It requires a good deal of faith to put information in the second place and learning in the first, to have patience to let the child's mind grow.
- Far too many teachers are so intent on teaching the subject matter and say that they have no time for high flying ideas about inspiring pupils for the joy of learning. They say that they have to get their pupils bass the Board Examination. In fact, they do not have even

enough common sense, if the joy of learning and the process of learning are emphasised, the pupils' will do better in the Board's examination.

- Even so called good teachers are more concerned with what the pupils must know and how their faculties must be trained rather than pupils' sense of values and their knowledge of good and evil.
- Too much of lecturing as a substitute of teaching makes the minds of pupils inert and sterile.
- The test of a successful education is not the amount of knowledge take away from the educational institution but their appetite to knowledge and awakened capacity to learn. And, this not happening in educational institutions.

A model of classroom processes: From the above-motioned concerns, a model of good classroom teaching without undermining the importance of Board Examination can be constructed to have the following features:

- Creating a learning environment of good relationships of mutuality and value-orientation.
- Using activities and subject matter analytically so as to promote thinking
- Demystifying the process of learning and emphasising self-study skills
- Giving training in examination skills by making students to construct their own questions

This model of teaching can be easily adopted for classroom teaching and can be helpful in making pupils independent learners. The teacher in such a situation acquires the role of facilitator who arranges for the learning environment and learning opportunities.

UNIT-VIII

Administration of Secondary Education

Decentralization and Centralisation

Secondary education serves as a bridge between elementary and higher education and prepares young persons between the age group of 14-18 for entry into higher education or work situations. The population of children in this age group has been estimated to be 88.5 million as per Census, 2001. Enrolment figures show that only 31 million of these children were attending schools in 2001-02, which means that two-third of the population remained out of school. Given the liberalization and globalization of the Indian economy, the rapid changes witnessed in scientific and technological world and the general need to improve the quality of life, it is essential that school leavers acquire a higher level of knowledge and skills than what they are provided in the eight years of elementary education. The average earnings of secondary school certificate holders are significantly higher than those with primary school education.

Secondary Education in India

Steps have been taken in the last few years to universalize elementary education. Towards that end Sarva Siksha Abhiyan (SSA) is being implemented all over the country in collaboration with the State Governments. Mid-day Meal Scheme is a part of this programme. As a result of these steps, the number of "out of school" children (6-14 years) has come down to less than 5% of the total population in that age group. The Sarva Shikha Abhiyan at the elementary level to universalize elementary education for the age group 6-14 has already set the stage for an exponential growth of demand for secondary education. While the growth of enrolment in the secondary school, had increased at an annual rate of 2.83 per cent during 1990s, it increased at 7.4 per cent, per annum between 2000 and 2003. The full impact of SSA is likely to be reflected during the terminal years of the Eleventh Plan. If the goal of universal retention at the elementary level is achieved by 2010, steps will have to be taken to expand facilities for secondary education in a big way.

Agencies of Secondary Education—Secondary Education Boards/Councils—Staff-Personnel Administration

- The Central Board of Secondary Education (CBSE)
- The Council of Indian School Certificate Examination (CISCE)
- The State Government Boards
- The National Open School.
- The International School.

Central Board of Secondary Education

A trail of developments mark the significant changes that took place over the years in shaping up the Board to its present status. U P Board of High School and Intermediate Education was the first Board set up in 1921. It has under its jurisdiction Rajputana, Central India and Gwalior. In response to the representation made by the Government of United Provinces, the then Government of India suggested to set up a joint Board in 1929 for all the areas which was named as the ' Board of High School and Intermediate Education, Rajputana. This included Ajmer, Merwara, Central India and Gwalior.

The Board witnessed rapid growth and expansion at the level of Secondary education resulting in improved quality and standard of education in institutions. But with the advent of

State Universities and State Boards in various parts of the country the jurisdiction of the Board was confined only to Ajmer, Bhopal and Vindhya Pradesh later. As a result of this, in 1952, the constitution of the Board was amended wherein its jurisdiction was extended to part-C and Part-D territories and the Board was given its present name 'Central Board of Secondary Education'. It was in the year 1962 finally that the Board was reconstituted. The main objectives were those of: serving the educational institutions more effectively, to be responsive to the educational needs of those students whose parents were employed in the Central Government and had frequently transferable jobs.

Jurisdiction

The jurisdiction of the Board is extensive and stretches beyond the national geographical boundaries. As a result of the reconstitution, the erstwhile ' Delhi Board of Secondary Education' was merged with the Central Board and thus all the educational institutions recognized by the Delhi Board also became a part of the Central Board. Subsequently, all the schools located in the Union Territory of Chandigarh. Andaman and Nicobar Island, Arunachal Pradesh, the state of Sikkim, and now Jharkhand, Uttaranchal and Chhattisgarh have also got affiliation with the Board. From 309 schools in 1962 the Board today has 8979 schools on 31-03-2007 including 141 schools in 21 countries. There are 897 Kendriya Vidyalayas, 1761 Government Schools, 5827 Independent Schools, 480 Jawahar Novodaya Vidyalayas and 14 Central Tibetean Schools.

Decentralisation

In order to execute its functions effectively Regional Offices have been set up by the Board in different parts of the country to be more responsive to the affiliated schools. The Board has regional offices in Allahabad, Ajmer, Chennai, Guwahati, Panchkula and Delhi. Schools located outside India are looked after by regional office Delhi. For detailed jurisdiction of regional offices of CBSE click here. The headquarter constantly monitors the activities of the Regional Offices. Although, sufficient powers have been vested with the Regional Offices. Issues involving policy matters are, however, referred to the head office. Matters pertaining to day-to-day administration, liaison with schools, pre and post examination arrangements are all dealt with by the respective regional offices.

Financial Structure

CBSE is a self-financing body which meets the recurring and non-recurring expenditure without any grant-in-aid either from the Central Govt. or from any other source. All the financial requirements of the Board are met from the annual examination charges, affiliation fee, admission fee for PMT. All India Engineering Entrance Examination and sale of Board's publications.

Major Activities and Objectives

The Central Board of Secondary Education was set up to achieve certain interlinked objectives:

- To prescribe conditions of examinations and conduct public examination at the end of Class X and XII. To grant qualifying certificates to successful candidates of the affiliated schools.
- To fulfil the educational requirements of those students whose parents were employed in transferable jobs.
- To prescribe and update the course of instructions of examinations
- To affiliate institutions for the purpose of examination and raise the academic standards of the country.

The prime focus of the Board is on:

- Innovations in teaching-learning methodologies by devising students friendly and students centred paradigms.
- Reforms in examinations and evaluation practices.
- Skill learning by adding job-oriented and job-linked inputs.
- Regularly updating the pedagogical skills of the teachers and administrators by conducting in service training programmes, workshops etc.

The Council of Indian School Certificate Examination (CISCE)

The Council has been constituted to secure suitable representation of governments responsible for schools (which are affiliated to it) in their states/territories; the Inter-State Board for Anglo-Indian Education; the Association of Indian Universities; the Association of Head of Anglo-Indian Schools, the Indian Public School Conference; the Association of Schools for the ISC Examination and eminent educationists. The objects of the Council is educational, and includes the promotion of science, literature, the fine arts and the diffusion of useful knowledge by conducting school examination through the medium of English. The Council exists solely for educational purposes and not for purposes of profit.

Early Beginnings

In 1952, an All India Certificate Examination Conference was held under the Chairmanship of Maulana Abul Kalam Azad, Minister for Education. The main purpose of the conference was to consider the replacement of the overseas Cambridge school Certificate Examination by an All India Examination. This set the agenda for the establishment of the Council.

In October 1956 at the meeting of the Inter-State Board for Anglo-Indian Education, a proposal was adopted for the setting up of an Indian Council to administer the University of Cambridge, Local Examinations Syndicate's Examination in India and, to advise the Syndicate on the best way to adapt its examination to the needs of the country. The inaugural meeting of the Council was held on 3rd November, 1958.

In December 1967, the Council was registered as a Society under the Societies Registration Act, 1860. In 1973, the Council was listed in the Delhi School Education Act 1973, as a body conducting "public" examinations.

The Work

The Work of the Council: The Council for the Indian School Certificate Examination conducts three examinations, namely, the Indian Certificate of Secondary Education (ICSE-Year 10); The Indian School Certificate (ISC-Year 12) and the Certificate in Vocational Education (CVE-Year 12). The subject choices and syllabuses prescribed for these examinations are varied and aimed at nurturing the unique gifts of individual pupils.

The ICSE (YEAR 10)

The Indian Certificate of Secondary Education has been designed to provide an examination in a course of general education, in accordance with the recommendations of the new education policy 1986, through the medium of English Private candidates are not permitted to appear for this examination.

The ISC (YEAR 12)

The Indian School Certificate Examination is an examination, through the medium of English, designed in accordance with the recommendations of the new education policy 1986, after a two-year course of studies beyond the Indian Certificate of Secondary Education (Year 10) examination or its equivalent.

The C.V.E (Year 12)

The Certificate of Vocational Educational (CVE-12) has been created as an examination, in accordance with the recommendations of the Ministry of Human Resource Development (MHRD) through the Joint Council of Vocational Education (JCVE) established under the National Policy of Education 1986. This examination can be taken by candidates after a two year course of studies beyond the Indian Certificate of Secondary Education (Year 10) examination or its equivalent, through the medium of English.

The State Government Boards

Many parents are unaware of the risk involved in sending their children to dubious and unrecognized Boards of School Education being operated in different states of India. To help them, through this section we in coachingindians.com endeavor to furnish the list and related information of all the recognized

State Boards of India. Not only the parents and we believe this information will benefit all those desirous of dealing with recognized Boards.

Following are the list of State Boards of School Education in India, recognized by the Department of Higher Education, Ministry of Human Resource Management, Government of India. Some of the states are having more than one School Education Boards. The state wise list is given as under:

Andhra Pradesh: Andhra Pradesh Board of Secondary Education

Assam: Assam Board of Secondary Education; Assam Higher Secondary Education Council

Bihar: Bihar School Examination Board; Bihar Intermediate Education Council

Goa: Goa Board of Secondary & Higher Secondary Education

Gujarat: Gujarat Secondary Education Board

Haryana: Haryana Board of Education

Himachal Pradesh: Himachal Pradesh Board of School Education

Jammu & Kashmir: J&K State Board of School Education

Jharkhand: Jharkhand Academic Council

Karnataka: Karnataka Secondary Education Examination Board; Karnataka Board of the Pre-University Education

Kerala: Kerala Board of Public Examinations

Maharashtra: Maharashtra State Board of Secondary and Higher Secondary Education

Madhya Pradesh: Madhya Pradesh Board of Secondary Education

Manipur: Manipur Board of Secondary Education; Manipur Council of Higher Secondary Education

Meghalaya: Meghalaya Board of School Education

Mizoram: Mizoram Board of School Education

Nagaland: Nagaland Board of School Education

Orissa: Orissa Board of Secondary Education; Orissa Council of Higher Secondary Education

Punjab: Punjab School Education Board

Rajasthan: Rajasthan Board of Secondary Education

Tamil Nadu: Tamil Nadu Board of Secondary Education; Tamil Nadu Board of Higher Secondary Education

Tripura: Tripura Board of Secondary Education

Uttar Pradesh: UP Board of High School & Intermediate Education

West Bengal: West Bengal Board of Secondary Education; West Bengal Council of Higher Secondary Education.

The National Open School

The National Institute of Open Schooling has a pivotal roie to play in the promotion and development of Open Schooling in the country. In a diverse country like India, it is not possible for the NOS alone to cater to the regional requirements. The NIOS has therefore evolved alternate models of State Open Schools and State Centres for Open Schooling. The NIOS has also been providing professional and technical support to States in order to set up and develop State Open Schools, particularly with regional medium. In order to systematise the interaction between the NIOS and the State Open Schools and other agencies, it was considered appropriate to establish a forum under the NIOS in the form of a Consortium.

The National Consortium for Open Schooling (NCOS) was therefore launched in September, 1997, with a view to facilitate better co-operation, collaboration and expansion of activities in the Open Learning System.

The International School

It controls the schools, which are accredited to curriculum of international standard.

Education for the elite has been a tradition in India since the beginnings of its civilization. Great Buddhist universities at Nalanda and Taxila were famous far beyond India's borders. Withholding education from the nonelite, including women, has also been a tradition. The lowest caste members, including the Harijans and non-Hindu tribal groups, were denied the right even to hear the Vedas, sacred Hindu texts, recited.

State governments control their own school systems, with some assistance from the central government. The Indian education system is based on 12 years of schooling, which generally begins at age 6 and includes 5 years of primary school, 3 years of middle school, 2 years of secondary school, and 2 years of higher secondary school.

Completion of higher secondary education is required for entry to institutions of higher education, which include universities and institutes of technology. While most students enrol in government schools, the number of private institutions such as international schools in India is increasing at all educational levels. Indians have a right to establish institutions to provide education in their native language and with a religious or cultural emphasis, although the schools must conform to state regulation of teaching standards. Students begin specializing in subjects at the level of higher secondary school. A university typically has one or more colleges of law, medicine, engineering, and commerce, and many have colleges of agriculture. Prestigious and highly selective institutes of management have been established. The educational establishment also includes a number of high-level scientific and social science institutes, as well as academies devoted to the arts.

Decentralization

From Class to Masses: Journey of Educational Development in India Context: Education affects subterranean domain of human psyche in a very subtle manner and helps in surfacing hidden treasure of potentialit ies and capacities which result into reduction of ignorance, exclusion, injustice and poverty. It is seen as indispensable for progress of a country and quality of life of its citizen, it holds ideals which may lead a nation towards the attainment of development, peace, equity and social justice. It is also considered principal responsibility of a society to nurture its offspring-future generation and give a positive direction to their developmental needs through education. In the words of Gabriel Mistral, famous poetess –

Many of the things we need can wait. The child cannot. Right now is the time his bones are being formed, his blood is being made, and his senses are being developed. To him we cannot answer 'Tomorrow,' his name is today."

The government of India recognizing the pivotal role of education in development made several resolutions to provide free Elementary education to all. Indian Constitution stated:

The State shall endeavour to provide, within a period of ten years from the commencement of this constitution, for free and compulsory education for all untill they complete the age of fourteen years (Article 45)

This centrality of education remain alive in all plans made by Government of India and plans after plan focused on education, Science and Technology and stressed their crucial relationship with the economic and human resource development. It was, however, the Kothari Education Commission (1964-66) which highlighted the relationship between education and productivity and the crucial role of education in the progress of the country.

The commission stated:

"Education as an investment in human resources plays an important role among the factors which contribute to economic growth". *The commission also recommended* a *common school system for all children, without discrimination for providing quality education.*

Secondary Education-a Broken link in Integrated Educational Development: Given the rapid changes witnessed in scientific and technological world and the general need to have unbroken chain of schooling after elementary education to improve the quality of life, it is imperative that school leavers acquire a higher level of knowledge and skills than what they are provided in the eight years of elementary education. It has been established beyond doubt that the rate of return to secondary education is not only positive but also very large.

> *"The secondary education which serves as a bridge between primary and higher education is expected to prepare young persons between the age group 14-18 in the world of work and entry into higher education. The secondary education starts with classes 9-10 leading to higher secondary classes 11 and 12."*

The secondary education system of India is under the administrative control of the Union Department of Education and is supported by organizations-NCERT, CBSE, NIOS, KVS, NVS, CTSA, etc. The development of this sector is also supported by the specific centrally sponsored schemes.

Schemes and Programs

The development of Secondary Education sector is also supported by the following specific Centrally Sponsored Schemes:

- Vocationalisation of Secondary Education
- Integrated Education for Disabled Children
- Computer Literacy and Studies in Schools (CLASS)
- Education Technology
- Improvement of Science Education in Schools
- Promotion of Yoga in schools
- Strengthening Culture and Values in Schools
- Strengthening Boarding and Hostel Facilities for Girls
- Environmental orientation to School Education.

Universalization of Secondary Education: Can it be Achieved in the Near Future?

Ever since the Constitution was adopted in 1950, the focus of educational programmes was concentrated on elementary education. Since the constitutional commitment is free and compulsory education to all children up to the age 14, all efforts were focused on achieving the goal of universal elementary education. But development of Secondary education has never been out of sight for policy maker and people engaged in educational planning and development. The Government recently constituted a task force on secondary education development. Due to this specific attention there has been expansion in the educational facilities at the secondary level too; enrolment has improved significantly and allocation of teachers has seen significant improvement, facilities in secondary schools over time have also improved impressively. The majority of secondary schools have now got school buildings. The plan allocation on secondary education increased from Rs. 20 crore during the First Plan to more than Rs. 2,600 crore in the Ninth Plan. However, expenditure on secondary education always remained below one per cent of the GDP.

Analysis of the current scenario shows that secondary education rarely is a meaningful terminal level of education. The most significant set back in secondary education refers to the extremely slow growth of vocational and technical education. Serious attention was not paid to vocational education, partly because of the need for heavy investments on the one hand, and lack of sufficient demand for such education on the other. Vocational education, particularly in secondary schools, did not really take off, as it was planned to be of a second rate, meant for the poor, and as a terminal one having inter-connectivity neither with higher education nor with the industrial or agricultural sector. It is also viewed as a strategy to reduce demand for higher education. Vocational education is costlier than general secondary education. Employment opportunities have not been particularly better for vocational school graduates and as a result, economic rated of return to vocational education were generally less than those to secondary general education.

NGOs in Educational Development – In Search of Solutions

Widely acknowledged as the political actors in the developing world, the emergence of NGOs has been called the global 'associational revolution' that could prove to be as significant as the rise of Nation state. Non-governmental organizations working in education in India have participated as professional resource centres and innovators able to reach children who are educationally disadvantaged. The Indian government could improve the effectiveness of primary education by increasing its collaboration with such organizations. NGOs extend education to underprivileged children in India and develop innovations that improve the quality of primary education. Though we will be delving on their role in educational development in India, with specific reference to Rajasthan in the later part of this paper, to cite few areas, where NGOs could really play very crucial role are-

Targeting under-served Children

- The government could support the efforts of NGOs to bring out-of-school children into schools through timely supply of teachers, classroom space, and other resources.
- Targeted action is needed to reach different types of out-of-school children-those who work, those who live in slums, those on the streets, those who are members of tribes or of migrant families and those who live in places without schools.
- To encourage young, first-generation learners to stay in school requires a supportive and nurturing environment. To help make learning interesting and worthwhile for such children, teachers in government schools could receive special training in new methods developed by NGOs.

Enhancing Quality

- Improving the quality of education requires working closely with key agents of change, such as teachers, school heads, school management committees and village education committees.
- To develop a cadre of trainers for primary school teachers, teacher training institutes would do well to evaluate and learn from NGO models for teacher training.

- Teachers need a range of knowledge and skills to teach underprivileged children effectively. Here again, NGO models would be a useful tool for teacher training institutes.
- NGOs and the government could collaborate in developing appropriate and flexible learning assessment tools, in line with innovative teaching and learning methods.
- But without safeguards, large-scale replication by the government of such NGO innovations as the "alternative school" and the "voluntary teacher" could lower the quality of education.

Government-NGO Links

- The government and NGOs will need to share a common vision on how to achieve universal primary education if India is to reach this goal.
- NGOs can be credible partners with the government in shaping policies for education. This entails collaboration rather than parallel initiatives by NGOs.
- To stay at the cutting edge in education, NGOs should continually evaluate and refine their models.
- If NGOs are to play a policy role in education, two areas that have been neglected will need to be addressed-NGO capacity building and organizational development.

Public-private Partnerships in Education – Collaboration for Realising Dream

The abysmal picture of public education system in rural as well as urban India has led to mushrooming of private education system. Middle class is increasingly looking up to private education system to address its aspiration and fulfil need of providing quality education.

Alongside various non-governmental organisations and civil society organisations have been making efforts of various kinds to reach out to marginalised sections of society who have been hitherto unserved or underserved by the public education system. Thus, state governments, communities and civil society organisations have been engaging in individual and lone efforts since several decades in past.

In economic terms there are four types of schools in private sector: very expensive, expensive, less expensive and moderately charged. Most schools in private sector are so called 'English Medium' schools since they enjoy higher social status in the society and therefore attract more students than 'Hindi Medium' schools.

Private sector schools cater to those segments of the population who have spare money. Some families, which do not have spare money, even cut down on the necessity items in order to be able to send their children to a private school which in quality necessary occupies the lowest rung of the 'Private School' ladder.

The school which is considered inferior to all others in the private sector is run by untrained and ill educated entrepreneurs who have no idea of even the basic principles of learning and teaching.

Their only concern is to make money. Teachers in these schools are also untrained, very poorly paid and thoroughly exploited. The minimum infrastructure essential for teaching-learning is also not present in theses schools. Sometimes there is not even enough space for children to sit and work, not to speak of open space for playing.

Children as also schools are socio-economically differentiated. In a nation where 40% of its population still continues to live below poverty line the focus on equity and social justice becomes imperative. Development planners have been grappling with issue of how to break this vicious cycle of underdevelopment comprising of lack of access to basic services like health, nutrition, education and employment.

Taking cognisance of the paramount deprivation and demand for provision of facilities and mobilising communities to proactively participate in various developmental initiatives it is now time that various initiatives collaborate and join hands together. The government has so far controlled the entry/ exit points of private sector. Other alternatives have largely remained unexplored so far particularly with a view to develop partnerships. Apart from ever expanding system of private education, there is yet another positive dimension of public private partnership i.e. more and more private organization joining hands under corporate social responsibility – CSR for the development of human capital through education. The argument is not in favour of developing an alternative system of private system of education and a substitute to public education.

Rather than fostering perpetuation of a dual system this kind of public private partnership is argued to support and reinforce state initiatives. The collaborative of non-governmental agencies, social development initiatives by social responsibility recognising corporate units and various government departments can bring about the necessitated change of appreciable quality in the scenario of public education in favour of equitable quality care and education for all children.

Some states have shed their inhibitions about accepting donor assistance for primary education and taken a positive inclination.

Teacher Morale—Job-satisfaction

Growth in Number of Teachers

During 1950-51 to 1999-2000, number of teachers at primary, upper primary and high/higher secondary level increased at an annual rate of growth of 2.20, 4.76 and 4.62 per cent. In absolute number, teachers increased by 4, 15 and 14 times respectively at the primary, upper primary and high/ higher secondary level. There were more than 1,720 thousand secondary/higher secondary teachers in 1999-2000 (Table). Over time, pupil per teacher also increased to a significant effect. In 1950-51, pupil teacher ratio at the primary, upper primary and high/higher secondary level were 24:1, 20:1 and 21:1. This has now been increased to 43:1, 38:1 and 32:1 in 1999-2000.

Table: Growth in Number of Teachers at the Secondary Level: 1950-51 to 1999-2000

Year	Primary	Upper Pri.	High/Hr. Sec.	Pupil Teacher Ratio		
				Primary	Upper Pri.	High/Hr. Sec.
1950-51	538	86	127	24	20	21
1960-61	742	345	296	36	31	25
1970-71	1060	638	629	39	32	25
1980-81	1363	851	926	38	33	27
1990-91	1616	1073	1334	43	37	31
1998-99*	1904	1278	1747	42	37	31
1999-2000	1919	1298	1720	43	38	31

• Provisional thereafter.

Source: MHRD, 2001.

In 1993-94, rural and urban areas constitute 64 and 36 per cent of the total secondary school teachers. On an average a government school had 5 teachers compared to 13 and 11 teachers respectively in case of the private aided and unaided schools. More than 95 per cent teachers in 1993-94 were in the position against the sanctioned posts in the secondary schools. The percentages of SC, ST, OBC and female teachers were 6.46, 3.57, 22.46 and 34.68 per cent respectively.

Private aided (35.84 per cent) and unaided (52.24 per cent) schools had much higher percentage of female teachers than in the government (29.74 per cent) and local body (24.40 per cent) run schools.

Similarly, rural areas (23.09) had a much lower percentage of female teachers than in the urban (55.45 per cent) areas. However, in addition to regular teachers, a few voluntary, contractual and part time teachers were also in existence in schools both in the rural and urban areas spread over different managements.

Teachers Attrition & Stay Arrangements

At the beginning of 1993-94, a total of 814 thousand teachers were in the position in secondary schools (Table). However, about 25 thousand teachers left the profession because of the retirements, resignation, terminations, transferred and deaths. This gives an attrition rate of 3.07 per cent. It is general belief that if the teacher is staying in the village/town where the school is located, it improves functioning of school.

The data suggests that a vast majority of secondary school teachers, especially in the rural areas (38.34 per cent) were not staying in a place where schools were located compared to which about 16 per cent teachers in the urban areas were not staying in the same town. So far as the provision of housing facilities to teachers are concerned, secondary school teachers were better placed than their counterparts in the primary and upper primary schools. A little more than 5 per cent of the total secondary schools in 1993-94 were provided with the housing facilities. However, only 2.37 per cent of the total secondary teachers were benefited with the housing facility. Teachers under the private unaided managements had the higher percentage (6.53 per cent) of housing facilities than the private aided (5.31 per cent), government (5.75 per cent) and local body (1.82 per cent) schools.

Table: Status of Secondary School Teachers (I): 1993-94

Management	% of Sanctioned Posts Filled In	% of Female Teachers	% of Schools Providing Housing Facility	Average Experience of Teachers (in Years)	% of Teachers Teaching Subject of PG
Government	92.07	29.74	5.75	16	55.07
Local Body	94.81	24.30	1.82	18	67.10
Pvt. Aided	96.89	35.84	5.31	15	67.81
Pvt. Unaided	102.18	52.24	6.53	7	71.24
Total	95.49	34.68	5.28	14	62.84

Source: NCERT, 1998.

Table: Status of Secondary School Teachers (II): 1993-94

Area	% of Teachers Staying Outside Village/Town	% of Trained Teachers & above	% of Teachers with PG
Rural	38.34	89.41	29.45
Urban	15.97	93.39	38.00
All Areas	30.33	91.03	32.91

Source: NCERT, 1998.

Teachers Training

About 91 per cent secondary school teachers were trained in 1993-94. A much lower percentage of SC, ST and OBC teachers were trained.

In the rural areas (89.41 per cent), comparatively a lower percentage of secondary school teachers were trained than in the urban areas (93.39 per cent). The majority of secondary teachers both in the rural (69.32 per cent) and urban areas (61.06 per cent) were the graduates.

However, more female teachers were graduates in the rural areas (73.12 per cent) than in the urban areas (60.64 per cent). A good number of teachers both in rural (29.45 per cent) and urban (38.00 per cent) areas were the postgraduates and above. Only, 11.62 per cent secondary stage teachers attended two or more in-service or refresher courses.

On an average, a secondary stage teacher had experience of 14 years. However, teachers in the private unaided schools had experience of only 7 years. The average experience was highest in case of the local body schools (18 years).

Teachers Qualifications & Subject Specialization

Only 63 per cent secondary school teachers possessing postgraduate degrees were teaching subject of their post graduation. This otherwise means that about 37 per cent teachers were teaching a subject other than their postgraduate subject. Of the 286 thousand teachers teaching science at the secondary stage, 65 per cent were the science graduates and another 8 per cent had a post graduate degree in science. About 27 per cent of the total teachers teaching at the secondary stage studied only up to the higher secondary level. Similarly, 36 per cent teachers studied mathematics only up to the higher secondary level but they were teaching mathematics at the secondary stage.

School Budget—Sources of Income

The expenditure on education in general and secondary education in particular consistently increased during the period 1950-51 to 1997-98. The expenditure increased from a low Rs. 114 crore in 1950-51 to Rs. 42,027 crore in 1997-98; thus showing an increase of 17.84 per cent per annum.

The expenditure on education by other departments, if included, comes out more than Rs. 52,465 crore in 1997-98. But much of the increase in the expenditure is eaten by the high inflation.

Compared to 369-fold increase at current prices, the increase in constant prices during 1950-51 to 1997-98 was only 18 times. The per capita and per pupil cost (at constant prices) in 1997-98 were only Rs. 104 and Rs. 553 (Azad, 2001).

Average Annual Expenditure (Rs.) Per Student* NSSO 52nd Round: 1995-96

Level	Government	Local Body	Private Aided	Private Unaided	Total
Primary	257	338	1181	1424	501
Middle	622	726	1346	2156	915
Sec./Hr. Secondary	1236	1349	1861	3061	1577
Higher Education	2559	2415	3143	5296	2923
All Levels	580	628	1615	1904	904

*Other than public expenditure.

Source: NSSO, 1998.

The percentage expenditure on education to GDP in 1997-98 was much lower (3.7 per cent) than the targeted GDP (6 per cent) recommended by the Kothari Commission (1964-66). The plan expenditure on education increased from Rs. 153 crore in the first plan to Rs. 24,909 crore in the ninth plan. But percentage of plan allocation on education during the same period declined from 7.86 to 2.90 percent.

The plan allocation on secondary education increased from Rs. 20 crore during the first plan to Rs. 2,604 crore in the ninth plan. During the same period, the percentage to total allocation on secondary education declined from 13 to 10.5 percent. However, allocation to elementary education increased from 56 per cent in the first plan to 66 per cent during the ninth plan.

A close look at the percentage expenditure on secondary education to GNP reveals that the same remained below 1 per cent throughout the period 1974-75 to 1997-98. In the latest year, it was only 0.87 per cent.

The percentage expenditure on elementary education to GNP was 1.47 per cent. The total expenditure on education to GNP during the same period however increased from 2.10 per cent in 1974-75 to 2.92 per cent in 1997-98. In 1989-90, government and local body schools together contributed more than 95 per cent of the total expenditure on education. During 1950-51 to 1989-90, allocation on account of fees and other private sources declined sharply from 32 per cent in 1950-51 to 6.6 per cent in 1989-90.

In 1989-90, more than 79 per cent of the total expenditure on higher secondary education was incurred on salaries of teaching staff. Together with the salaries of non-teaching staff, it comes out to be about 92 per cent. A significant decline is also noticed in the budgetary allocation for education under both the state and union governments. While the state government budgets declined from 21.4 per cent in 1970-71 to 19.7 percent in 1997-98, central government budget estimates declined from 28 per cent in 1970-71 to 2.1 per cent in 1991-92 but increased to 3.4 per cent in 1997-98.

Table: Average Annual Expenditure by Items: Per Student NSSO 52nd Round: 1995-96

Items	Primary	Middle	Sec./Hr. Secondary	Above Higher Secondary
Tuition Fee	100	124	197	721
Other Fee	39	64	106	303
Books	67	153	272	506
Stationery	63	126	190	290
Uniform	118	212	248	84
Transport	31	42	98	351
Pvt. Coaching	48	125	326	307
Other Expanses	25	45	74	187
Exam Fee	11	24	66	174
Total	501	915	1577	2927

Source: NSSO, 1998.

The NSSO 52nd Round data on average annual expenditure per student at secondary/higher secondary education in 1995-96 reveals that it was Rs. 1,577. A significant difference in unit cost is noticed in schools under different managements. It was highest in case of the private unaided (Rs. 3,061) managements followed by private aided (Rs.1,861), local body (Rs. 1,349) and government (Rs. 1,236) managements.

A further break-up of annual expenditure per secondary/ higher secondary student reveals that chunk of the amount was incurred on private coaching (Rs. 326). While a student in the government and local body school incurred (all levels) Rs. 84, students under private aided and unaided schools incurred an expenditure of Rs. 284 and Rs. 186 respectively. Further, it has been noticed that on an average a secondary/higher secondary student incurred an amount of Rs. 272 on account of books and another Rs. 248 on uniforms. The same on account of tuition fee and stationery was Rs. 197 and Rs. 190. Other major items of expenditure were the examination (Rs. 66) and transport (Rs. 98) fee.

The analysis presented above clearly indicates that secondary education has never been the priority area of investment. It was the elementary education, which has got the lion's share all through the plan periods. The second area of concern is the expenditure incurred on salaries (92 per cent). Practically no money is left for the developmental work. Third, the share of secondary education in the ninth plan stands only at 10.5 per cent. In 1997-98, its percentage to GNP was well below the one per cent. Whatever meagre increase the secondary education has got was eroded by the inflation and in real terms the increase is somewhat illusory. The UEE by 2010 will generate rapid demand for secondary education to expand. In that case, it would demand a quantum jump in allocation than what is it receiving today.

Growth in Enrolment

Enrolment during 1950-51 to 1999-2000 at different levels of school education is presented in Table. A perusal of table reveals that irrespective of the level of education, enrolment has shown consistent and significant increase throughout the period 1950-51 to 1999-2000. This is also true for the increase in girl's enrolment, which increased at much faster rate than the increase in boy's enrolment. Enrolment at the primary level increased from 19.2 million in 1950-51 to 97.4 million in 1990-91 and further to 113.6 million in 1999-2000.

This shows that the same increased by more than six times in a period of about fifty years. The girl's enrolment during the same period increased from 5.4 million in 1950-51 to 48.5 million in 1999-2000, thus showing an average annual growth rate of 4.63 per cent or 9.1 times in absolute terms. In percentage terms, the share of girls enrolment increased from 28.13 per cent in 1950-51 to 41.48 per cent in 1991 and further to 43.58 per cent in 1999-2000, the year for which the latest enrolment data is available. The share of girl's enrolment at upper primary and high/higher secondary level increased from 16.13 to 40.38 per cent and 13.33 to 38.99 per cent during the same period. In the latest decade (1991 to 2000), enrolment at the primary level increased at an annul rate of 1.72 per cent compared to

2.40 and 4.43 per cent increase in the upper primary and high and higher secondary enrolment.

Like the increase in primary enrolment, upper primary enrolment is also increased but at much faster rate which is because of the low enrolment base in the initial year. Enrolment in upper primary classes increased from 3.1 million in 1950-51 to 34.0 million in 1990-91 and further to 42.1 million in 1999-2000. During the last decade, upper primary enrolment increased at the rate of 2.46 per cent per annum, which is slightly higher than the increase in the primary enrolment. During the same period, girls enrolment also increased significantly from a low 0.5 million in 1950-51 to 17.0 million in 1999-2000; thus showing an impressive 34 fold increase. The overall upper primary enrolment also increased by 14 times or at the rate of 5.47 per cent per annum. All together, the country had more than 156 million children in elementary classes in 1999-2000 compared to 28 million children in secondary and higher secondary classes.

Redefining Universalisation

The analysis presented above reveals that at all levels of school education, a significant progress in enrolment is made but a large number of children still remain out-of-school (the estimated number in 1999-2000 was about 67 million of age group 6-14 years, see Mehta, 2002). Unless these children are brought under the education system, the goal of universal enrolment cannot be achieved.

It may however be noted that without attaining the status of universal primary enrolment, the goal of universal elementary education cannot be achieved. Primary enrolment depends on 6-11 years population but the same is not true in case of the upper primary enrolment.

Upper primary enrolment is not a function of 11-14 year population but is a function of primary graduates. Only primary graduates can be admitted in the upper primary classes. It is quite possible that many children of age group 11-14 year are out of the system and there may also be dropped out children and a few of them may still be in the primary classes. A never enrolled or dropped out child of age 13 or 14 cannot be enrolled in upper primary classes for whom some sort of alternative system of education would have to be evolved. Without bringing these children under the formal or non-formal system of education, the goal of universal elementary enrolment cannot be cherished. Therefore, upper primary level of education cannot be expanded in isolation of the primary level. This is also true for secondary level, which cannot be expanded independent of upper primary level. All the children of age group 14-16 cannot be brought under the system in Classes IX-X unless the goal of universal elementary education is achieved. Many children of this age group may still be in the primary or upper primary classes or may even be out of school.

Transition Rates: 1970-71 to 1998-99

YEAR	Grade V/VI			Grade VIII/IX		
	BOYS	GIRLS	TOTAL	BOYS	GIRLS	TOTAL
1970-71	86.80	74.08	82.56	-	-	-
1980-81	92.11	81.77	88.35	88.58	83.16	86.89
1981-82	93.77	86.41	91.10	88.67	81.67	86.47
1982-83	95.11	87.18	92.22	85.95	79.72	83.92
1983-84	92.89	86.71	90.62	86.14	81.56	84.64
1984-85	91.90	86.84	90.02	88.24	83.55	86.69
1985-86	90.79	82.01	87.45	83.93	79.02	82.28
1986-87	93.61	85.49	90.50	87.63	81.47	85.55
1987-88	91.59	83.56	88.50	84.13	79.75	82.63
1988-89	94.48	84.15	90.45	85.67	82.67	84.65
1989-90	98.32	91.30	95.56	89.37	84.64	87.72
1990-91	95.20	93.22	94.42	84.93	79.56	83.01
1991-92	87.00	83.00	85.00	79.30	70.49	76.05
1997-98	89.00	91.00	86.00	86.34	82.64	84.89
1998-99	95.59	90.33	93.37	83.15	82.66	82.95

Thus, availability of graduates' (primary and upper primary) along with the transition from primary to upper primary and upper primary to secondary level would decide the future expansion of upper primary and secondary levels of education. So far as the demand for upper primary is concerned, it is more likely to be in educationally disadvantage areas where primary education has not been fully expanded. Further expansion of primary education in these areas and high transition from primary to upper primary level will generate more intensive demand for upper primary education to expand. Further improvement in transition may result into rapid demand for upper primary education in year that follows. Once the goal of universal elementary enrolment is realized, the secondary level may then expect to receive a quantum jump in enrolment. This may happen in the year 2010, if the goal of newly launched *Sarva Shiksha Abhiyan* is realized in that year.

Transition Rates

As mentioned above, enrolment at the upper primary level depends upon the number of students completing primary level and transiting to upper primary levels of education. Similarly, enrolment in secondary classes depends on upper primary graduates. The inter stage transition rates i.e. transition from Grade V, the terminal grade of primary to Grade VI, the initial grade of upper primary education and transition from terminal grade of upper primary level i.e. Grade VIII to Grade IX, initial Grade of secondary level are presented in Table.

A close scrutiny of Table reveals that transition from primary to upper primary level has been reasonably high to start with and improved consistently. The high transition rate is also evident from the increasing share of girl's enrolment to total upper primary enrolment. The improvement in transition rate is also associated with a decline in gender differences. In the latest year 1999-99 (provisional), the transition rate is 95.59 per cent with boy/girl differential only 5 per cent. Like transition from primary to upper primary level, transition from upper primary to secondary level also remained high throughout the period 1970-71 to 1998-99. In the latest year 1998-99, it was as high as 83.15 per cent with negligible boy/girl differential. This is quite evident from the increasing share of girls enrolment to total enrolment at high and higher secondary level. The relatively high transition from primary to upper primary level and low gender differences suggest that unless primary education system is improved, the goal to attain universal elementary education cannot be realized. This is also true for enrolment at the secondary level of education, which cannot cover all the children of age group 14-16 years, unless the goal of universal elementary enrolment (covering all children of age group 11-14 years) is realized. Thus, efficiency of primary education system has direct impact on upper primary and secondary education system to expand. An inefficient primary education system will continue to send fewer primary graduates to upper primary level. Till then, Universalisation of primary graduates will be treated as achieving Universalisation of elementary education.

Grade-to-Grade Transition Rates between Secondary & Higher Secondary Grades

Year	Sex	IX to X	X to XI	XI to XII
1990-91	Boys	87.13	-	-
	Girls	89.56	-	-
	Total	87.95	-	-
1991-92	Boys	84.32	-	-
	Girls	81.74	-	-
	Total	83.44	-	-
1997-98	Boys	87.39	43.28	94.10
	Girls	90.66	44.22	93.79
	Total	88.62	43.63	93.98
1998-99	Boys	85.13	43.19	93.82
	Girls	89.19	46.06	98.30
	Total	86.68	44.29	95.52

Source: Calculated by author based on the MHRD data.

The transition between secondary and higher secondary grades reveals that majority of children promote from Grade IX to Grade X but the same is not true in case of promotion from Grade X to XI and Grade XI to XII. It has also been noticed that more girls transited from Grade IX to X and also from Grade X to XI. The promotion rate from Grade IX to X in 1998-99 was as high as 86.68 per cent (Boys 85.13 and Girls 89.13 per cent). However, only 44.29 per cent children transited from Grade X to XI; thus contributing a lot to wastage in the system. Compared to this, majority of children transited from Grade XI to XII (95.52 per cent). Here again, more girls transited from Grade XI to XII than their boys counterparts. The low transition from Grade X to XI has serious implications for Universalisation of senior secondary education, which cannot be achieved unless all these children transit from Grade X to Grade XI.

Conclusion

Since free and compulsory education to all children up to the age fourteen is the Constitutional commitment in India, all efforts in the past were focused on achieving the goal of universal elementary education. It is upper primary and secondary level of education that is now in the focus. Over time, secondary schooling facilities improved to a significant level but still there are a few areas of concern. Schooling facilities to a large number of habitations were not available (unserved habitations, 15.18 per cent) in 1993-94. In about 161 thousand habitations, the same was not available even within a distance of 8 km. About 24 per cent schools were independent secondary schools and 5 per cent were integrated with the primary, upper primary and higher secondary schools. Majority of secondary schools had got school buildings but only 65 per cent of them had *pucca* (permanent) buildings. Government schools had lower percentage of buildings than the schools under the private managements. Only 75 per cent schools owned buildings and 65 per cent needed additional instructional rooms. A large number of secondary schools did not have ancillary facilities like urinal, drinking water and lavatory in schools. A little more than 50 per cent secondary schools in 1993-94 did not have library. About 6 per cent schools had shortage of blackboard and another 11 per cent furniture for students. A large number of schools even did not have science laboratory; majority of which were the Government schools. Government schools also had lower average number of teachers than the schools under other managements. More than 95 per cent teachers in 1993-94 were in position against the sanctioned posts. Percentage of female teachers was much lower than their male counterparts and the difference was more pertinent in the rural areas. Majority of the secondary school teachers were not staying in the village/town where schools were located. Only 5 per cent teachers were provided with the housing facilities. About 91 per cent teachers in 1993-94 were trained. Majority of secondary school teachers were graduates and a good number of them were postgraduates. However, about 37 per cent of them were teaching a subject other than their postgraduate subject. A number of teachers teaching at secondary level themselves studied up to secondary level only. On an average, a secondary school teacher had an experience of 14 years but the same in case of the private aided schools was only 7 years.

Over a period of time number of secondary schools, teachers, enrolment, and investment on secondary education increased significantly. During 1950-51 to 1999-2000, high/higher secondary schools increased from 7 thousand to 117 thousand; thus showing a growth rate of 5.92 per cent per annum. During the same period enrolment and teachers increased at the rate of 6.17 and 4.62 per cent per annum. In the more recent decade (1991-2000); schools, teachers and enrolment increased at the rate of 4.33, 3.43 and 4.43 per cent. The ratio of high/higher secondary to upper primary schools in 1999-2000 was 1.69; thus indicating a high/higher secondary school for every two upper primary schools.

The share of girls enrolment at the high/higher secondary level increased from 13.33 per cent in 1950-51 to 38.99 per cent in 1999-2000; thus indicating that a large number of girls still out of the system. The rate of increase in girls' enrolment at the secondary level was higher than the increase at the other levels of education. The girls' enrolment increased at much faster rate than the increase in boys' enrolment, which is because of the low enrolment base in the initial period. The overall enrolment at high/higher secondary level increased from 1.5 million in 1950-51 to 28.2 million in 1999-2000. The gross enrolment ratio in 1998-99 remained low at 41 per cent. The net attendance ratio in 1995-96 (Grades IX-X) was only 26 per cent. The transition rate from upper primary to secondary level in 1998-99 was 83 per cent but ratio of Grade IX to I (eight years back) was low at 37 per cent. Only 27 children could reach Grade X in 1992-93 out of 100 in Grade I in 1983-84. This indicates that in process over 18 million children dropped out from the system; thus contributing a lot of wastage in the system. The pass percentage from Grade X to XI in 1992-93 was as low as 44 per cent. However, the transition rate between the Grade XI to XII was high at 96 per cent. So far as the investment on education is considered, secondary education has never been the priority area of investment. However, plan expenditure on secondary education increased from Rs. 20 crore during the first plan to Rs. 2,604 crore in the ninth plan. The percentage to the total allocation on secondary education during the same period declined from 13 to 10.5 percent. The percentage expenditure on secondary education to GNP is below 1 per cent. More than 90 per cent of the total expenditure is being incurred on salaries of teaching and non-teaching staff. The average annual private expenditure per secondary/higher secondary student in 1995-96 was Rs. 1,577; chunk of which was incurred on private coaching (Rs. 326).

The goal of universal secondary enrolment cannot be achieved unless the goal of universal elementary education is achieved. Enrolment in secondary classes is a function of upper primary graduates. The demand for secondary schools is expected to increase once the goal of universal elementary education is achieved.

Management Innovations in Secondary School—Community Relationships

The majority of secondary schools in 1993-94 were in the rural areas and most of these were co-educational schools. Of the total 66 thousand schools, rural areas had more than 47 thousand schools (71.21 per cent). Schools distributed according to management reveals that the majority of schools had either the government (37.46 per cent) or private management (51.25 per cent). Majority of private schools were aided schools (68.62 per cent). On the other hand, percentage of schools run by the local body and private unaided managements were only 11.29 and 16.08 per cent respectively. A close look at the distribution of schools according to enrolment reveals that the highest percentage of enrolment was in schools run by the private aided management (46.04 per cent) followed by the government (37.67 per cent), private unaided (8.72 per cent) and local body schools (7.57 per cent). It may however be noted that private schools had higher enrolment and the government schools lower enrolment than their share in the total number of secondary schools.

Type of Secondary Schools

Across the country, a variety of secondary schools are available. The majority of secondary schools in 1993-94 were integrated with the upper primary schools (33.99 per cent) followed by the independent secondary schools (23.79 per cent). On the other hand, about 17.37 per cent secondary schools were the integrated with either primary or upper primary schools. Only 5.44 per cent secondary schools in 1993-94 were integrated with the higher secondary schools. Upper primary integrated with secondary and higher secondary (13.95 per cent); and primary integrated with upper primary, secondary and higher secondary (5.46 per cent) were the other types of schools. Further, it has also been revealed that private managements (aided 29.12 and unaided 40.45 per cent) had the majority of independent secondary schools. More than 62 percent secondary schools under local body managements were integrated with the upper primary schools. Schools under private managements also had the highest percentage of integrated schools from primary to higher secondary level. Future expansion of secondary education should be viewed in the light of the existing arrangements of secondary schooling, as well as, the management type. With the limited set of data, it is not possible to know which arrangement is the most economic one. It may also be recalled that Secondary Education Commission (1952) recommended a national system of education covering 11 years of education and the Kothari Commission 10+2 pattern. The states have accepted 10+2 pattern but still the system is not uniform across the country.

Facilities in Schools

School Buildings: The distribution of schools according to buildings reveals that unlike the primary schools, the majority of secondary schools have got the school buildings. Only 0.51 per cent of the total 66 thousand schools were functioning either in the tents or in open space. The majority of such schools were the government run schools. About 64 per cent schools in the rural areas had the *pucca* (permanent) buildings compared to 82 per cent in the urban areas. About 65 per cent government schools had pucca buildings compared to 26 per cent *partially pucca* and another 7 and 2 per cent schools were functioning in the thatched huts and tents. On the other hand about 72 per cent schools run under the local body managements had *pucca* school buildings. A little more than 70 per cent private aided and unaided schools had pucca buildings and not a single school under this category was functioning in the open space.

Further, it has also been noticed that about 74 per cent schools owned buildings and rest of the 26 per cent schools had either rented or they rent-free buildings. Schools in the urban areas (63.71 per cent) had lower percentage of owned buildings than schools in the rural areas (78.63 per cent). On the other hand, it has been noticed that the majority of government and local body schools had their own buildings but the same is not true in case of the schools run by the private aided (59.49 per cent) and unaided (47.17 per cent) managements. Most of the private schools had rented buildings.

It has also been noticed that the majority of secondary schools require additional classrooms, which is true for all types of school managements. Comparatively, percentage of private schools that need additional classrooms is a bit lower than the requirement in case of the government and local body schools. Compared to the primary (2 rooms) and upper primary (5 rooms) level of education, the average number of instructional rooms were quite high (8 rooms) in secondary schools. Government run schools (2 rooms) had the lowest number of rooms than the rooms under other managements. On an average secondary schools under local body management had 2 instructional rooms. Schools under the private managements (aided 4 and unaided 5 rooms) had much higher number of rooms than the schools under the government and local body managements. Disparity in number of instructional rooms is also noticed in case of the rural (2 rooms) and urban (4 rooms) areas. Both within the rural and urban areas, schools under the private managements had much higher number of rooms than the other managements. A close look at the number of rooms distributed according to enrolment size reveals that higher is the size of school, higher is the number of instructional rooms. Schools having more than 600 enrolment had an average of 10 and 16 rooms respectively in the rural and urban areas.

Urinal & Lavatory Facilities

So far as the ancillary facilities in secondary schools are concerned, still a large number of schools did not have urinal and lavatory facilities. This is also true in case of the separate urinal and lavatory facilities for girls. Comparatively, schools in the urban areas were more equipped with such facilities than schools in the rural areas. Only 71 and 47 per cent secondary schools in the rural areas had the urinal and lavatories facilities. It has also been observed that private aided and unaided schools are more equipped with these facilities than the government and local body schools. All the secondary schools even did not have drinking water facility in the school. In rural areas, such schools in 1993-94 were only 79.72 per cent. A good number of private schools too did not have drinking water facility in the school.

Furniture

Only 63.44 per cent secondary sections had furniture for teachers, urban areas had more such sections (81.36 per cent) than the sections in the rural areas (58.20 per cent). Similarly, private schools had got higher percentage of furniture for teachers than in the government and local body schools. Almost 50 per cent schools did not have provision for contingency funds. More government schools had such provisions than the private schools. Only 80.24 per cent schools had playground facilities in schools. However, only 69.89 per cent of them found it adequate. More than 47.56 per cent secondary schools in 1993-94 had at least one physical teacher.

Blackboard

Only 94.44 per cent secondary schools had usable blackboards and 5.56 per cent had the shortage of blackboards. Private schools had a bit higher percentage of usable blackboards than the government and local body schools. Further, it has been noticed that 11.21 per cent secondary schools even did not have mats/furniture and another 11.36 per cent schools found it inadequate. About 51.82 per cent secondary schools had got both almirahs and boxes/trunks compared to 40.39 and 2.39 per cent schools having almirahs and boxes.

Science Laboratories

The distribution of secondary schools according to availability of science laboratories reveals that as many as 40.65 per cent schools did not have laboratories, which in the absolute number come out to be 35 thousand schools. A little less than one-fifth (21.13 per cent) schools had separate laboratory for physics, chemistry and biology. While 42.98 per cent schools had combined laboratory for physics, chemistry and biology; another 4.13 per cent had combined laboratory for physics & chemistry and separate for biology. A large number of government (14,696), local body (4,885), private aided (11,205) and unaided (4,347) schools did not have science laboratory. Irrespective of the school management, guidance services in secondary schools were rarely available in 1993-94.

Library Facilities

Only 79.03 and 85.04 per cent secondary schools had library facilities in 1993-94. About 70 per cent government and local body schools had library facilities compared to 80 per cent had the same in the private managed schools. Even the school has got library, it does not guarantee that it has also got a Librarian. Only 10.56 per cent schools in the rural areas and 19.32 per cent in the urban areas had a Librarian. However, a few schools have also got the part-time librarians (8.40 per cent). About 75.40 per cent secondary schools were subscribing newspapers and another 47.81 per cent magazines. Percentage of private schools subscribing newspapers and magazines were much higher than these facilities in the government and local body schools. More than 51 per cent secondary schools had the textbook banks.

Incentive Schemes

Mid-day meal scheme was in existence in about 8.73 per cent secondary schools. Similarly, about 16.77 per cent schools had incentive scheme of free uniforms and about 40 per cent schools free textbooks. More than 10 per cent secondary schools had the scheme of attendance of scholarship for girls.

Bibliography

Aggarwal, Santosh : *Three Language Formula: An Educational Problem*, New Delhi, Sian, 1991.

Allen, G. : *Pre-Primary Education*: *American Opinion*, May issue, 1971.

Altbach, Philip G. and Gail Kelly : *New Approaches to Comparative Education,* Chicago, The University of Chicago Press, 1986.

Applebee, Arthur N.: *Curriculum as Conversation: Transforming Tradition of Teaching and Learning,* Chicago, University of Chicago Press, 1996.

Barnes, D.: *From Communication to Curriculum,* London, Pelican, 1990.

Beane, J. A.: *Toward a Coherent Curriculum*, Alexandria, VA: Association for Supervision and Curriculum Development, 1995.

Bender, S. J., and G. S. Smith: *Teaching Archaeology in the Twenty-First Century,* Society for American Archaeology, Washington, D.C., 2000.

Bentley, T. : *Learning beyond the Classroom: Education for a Changing World*, London, Routledge. 1998.

Bentley, T. : *Learning beyond the Classroom: Education for a Changing World*, London, Routledge. 1998.

Brown, J. D.: *The Elements of Language Curriculum: A Systematic Approach to Program Development,* Boston, Heinle & Heinle, 1995

Burnaford, G.: *Teachers Doing Research,* Mahwah, Lawrence Erlbaum.

Carl R. Rogers: *Client-Centered Therapy: Its Current Practice, Implications and Theory*, Boston, Houghton Mifflin, 1965.

Carr, W. & Kemmis, S. : *Becoming Critical: Education, Knowledge and Counselling*, London, Falmer, 1986.

Chumbow, B.S. : *The Place of Mother Tongue in the National Policy of Educational Guidance,* Port Harcourt, Nigeria, 1990.

Clifton, C., & Grant Haworth, J.: *Curriculum in Transition: Perspectives on the Undergraduate Experience,* Needham Heights, MT: Ginn Press, 1990.

Compton, Mary F. & Horace C. Hawn: *Exploration: The Total Curriculum*, Columbus, National Middle School Association, 1993.

Curtain, Helena A. & Carol Ann Pesola: *Languages and Children - Making the Match*, White Plains, Longman Publishing Group, 1994.

Diller, D.: *Literacy Work Stations: Making Centers Work,* Portland, Stenhouse, 2003.

Donaldson, Gordon A. : *Cultivating Leadership in Schools*, New York, College Press, 2001.

Donoghue, M.: *Foreign Language and the Elementary School Child*, Dubuque, William C. Brown, 1968.

Ehrman, M. E.: *Understanding Second Language Learning Difficulties,* Thousand Oaks, Sage, 1996.

Elliott, J. : *Action Research for Educational Change*, Milton Keynes, Open University, 1991.

Evers, C. & Lakomski, G. : *Knowing Educational Administration*, Oxford, Pergamon, 1991.

Fogarty, Robin: *How to Integrate the Curricula,* Palatine, IRI/ Skylight, 1991.

Galbraith, M.W. : *Education Through Community Organizations*, San Francisco, Jossey-Bass, 1990.

Gardner, H. : *The Unschooled Mind: How Children Think and How Schools Should Teach*, New York, Basic Books, 1991.

Gaudiani, Claire: *Teaching Writing in the FL Curriculum*, Washington, Center for Applied Linguistics, 1981.

Genesee, F. , & Upshur, J. A.: *Classroom-based Evaluation in Second Language Education,* New York, Cambridge, 1996.

Gibson, R. : *Critical Theory and Education*, London, Hodder & Stoughton, 1986.

Giroux, H. : *Critical Theory and Educational Practice*, Geelong, Australia, Deakin University, 1983.

Glatthorn, Allan: *Developing A Quality Curriculum*, Association for Supervision and Curriculum Development, Alexandria, VA, 1994.

Goodlad, John I. : *Educational Renewal: Better Teachers, Better Schools*, San Francisco, Jossey-Bass, 1994.

Grace, G. : *School Leadership: Beyond Educational Management*, London, Falmer, 1995.

Hirsch, Bette: *Languages of Thought: Thinking, Reading, and Foreign Languages,* New York, The College Board, 1989.

Jeffs, T. and Smith, M. : *Using Informal Education*, Milton Keynes, Open University Press, 1990.

Johnson, R.K.: *The Second Language Curriculum,* New York, Cambridge University Press, 1989.

Kakar, Sudhir : *The Inner World: A Psychoanalytic Study of Childhood and Society in India*, New Delhi, Oxford University Press, 1978.

Kennedy, K.J. : *Citizenship Education and the Modern State*, Washington, D.C: Falmer Press, 1997.

Kirkwood, G. and Kirkwood, C. : *Living Adult Education, Freire in Scotland*, Milton Keynes, Open University Press, 1989.

Lovett, T. : *Adult Education, Community Development and the Working Class*, London, Ward Lock, 1975.

McConnell, C. : *Community Education: The Making of an Empowering Profession*, Edinburgh, Scottish Community Education Council, 1996.

McGivney, V. : *Informal Learning in the Community, A Trigger for Change and Development*, Leicester, NIACE, 1999.

Nadler, L.: *Designing Training Programs: The Critical Events Model*, Reading, PA: Addison-Wesley, 1982.

Nelson, Bryce E.: *Good Schools: The Seattle Public School System, 1901-1930.* U. of Washington Press, 1988.

Nuna, S.C. : *Child Education and Development*, NIEPA, New Delhi, 1987.

Nurullah, S. and J.P. Naik : *A Students History of Education in India,* New Delhi, Macmillan, 1974.

O'Brien, Thomas V. *The Politics of Race and Schooling: Public Education in Georgia, 1900-1961.* Lexington Books, 1999.

Okech, J.G.; Asiachi, A.J. : *Curriculum Development for Schools*, Nairobi, Educational Research Publications, 1992.

Poster, C. and Kruger, A. : *Community Education in the Western World*, London, Routledge, 1990.

Potter D. : *Information Technology and Higher Education: A Twenty Year View*, Unpublished Paper, 1996.

Premi, M.K. : *Educational Planning in India*, New Delhi, Sterling, 1972.

Reimer, E. : *School is Dead, An Essay on Alternatives in Education*, Harmondsworth, Penguin, 1971.

Scott, C. : *Social Education*, Boston, Ginn and Co., 1908.

Simkins, T. : *Non-formal Education and Development*, Manchester, Manchester University, 1977.

Smith, M.K. : *Local Education, Community, Conversation, Action*, Buckingham, Open University Press, 1994.

Stark, J. S., & Lattuca, L. R.: *Shaping the College Curriculum: Academic Plans in Action*, Boston, Allyn and Bacon, 1997.

Starratt, R.J. : *Centering Educational Administration: Cultivating Meaning, Community and Responsibility*, Mahwah, Lawrence Earlbaum, 2003.

Stenhouse, L. : *Authority, Education and Emancipation*, London, Heinemann, 1983.

Stoner, W.S. : *Natural Education*, Indianapolis, Bobbs Merrill, 1914.

Taylor, C. : *Multiculturalism: Examining the Politics of Recognition*, Princeton, Princeton University Press, 1994.

Thomas, A. : *Educating Children at Home,* London, Cassell, 1998.

Tiongson, E. R.: *Education Policy Reforms,* Washington, DC: The World Bank, 2004.

Wiggins, Grant : *Educative Assessment: Designing Assessments to inform and Improve Student Performance*, San Francisco, Jossey-Bass, 1998.

Yeaxlee, B. : *Lifelong Education, A Sketch of the Range and Significance of the Adult Education Movement*, London, Cassell and Company, 1929.

Index

□□□